Charles Stuart Parlas.

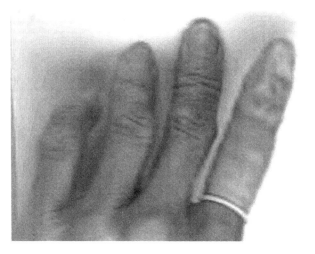

THE COUNT OF MONTE-CRISTO

THE

UNT OF MONTE-CRISTO.

BY

ALEXANDRE DUMAS

*NEARLY FIVE HUNDRED ILLUSTRATIONS FROM DESIGNS BY G. STAAL,
J. A. BEAUCE, AND OTHER EMINENT FRENCH ARTISTS*

IN FIVE VOLUMES

VOL. I

GEORGE ROUTLEDGE AND SONS

LONDON AND NEW-YORK

1888

DANTÈS CAST INTO THE SEA.

TABLE OF CONTENTS

LIST OF ILLUSTRATIONS

"MY NAME IS EDMOND DANTÈS."

THE COUNT OF MONTE-CRISTO

CHAPTER I

ON the 24th of February, 1815, the watch-tower of Notre-Dame de la Garde signaled the three-master, the *Pharaon*, from Smyrna, Trieste, and Naples.

As usual, a pilot put off immediately, and, rounding the Château d'If, got on board the vessel between Cape Morgion and the Isle of Rion. Immediately, and as usual, the platform of Fort Saint Jean was covered with lookers-on; it is always a great event at Marseilles for a ship to come into port, especially when this ship, like the *Pharaon*, had been built, rigged, and laden on the stocks of the old Phocœa, and belonged to an owner of the city.

The ship drew on; she had safely passed the strait which some volcanic shock has made between the Isle of Calasareigne and the Isle of Jaros; had doubled Pomègue, and approached the harbor under topsails, jib, and foresail, but so slowly, and in so cheerless a manner, that the idlers, with that instinct which foresees misfortune, asked one another what accident could have happened on board. However, those experienced in navigation saw plainly that if any accident had occurred, it was not to the vessel herself, for she bore down with all the evidence of being skillfully handled, the anchor ready to be dropped, the bowsprit-shrouds loose, and beside the pilot who was steering the *Pharaon* through the narrow entrance of the port of Marseilles, was a young man, with rapid gestures and vigilant eye, who superintended every motion of the ship, and repeated each order of the pilot.

The vague disquietude which prevailed amongst the spectators had so much affected one of the crowd on the terrace of Saint Jean, that he did not await the arrival of the vessel in harbor, but, jumping into a small skiff, desired to be pulled alongside the *Pharaon*, which he reached as she rounded the creek of La Réserve.

When the young sailor saw this man approach, he left his station by the pilot, and came, hat in hand, to the side of the ship's bulwarks.

He was a fine, tall, slim young fellow, of from eighteen to twenty years, with beautiful black eyes, and hair like ebony; and his whole appearance bespoke that calmness and resolution peculiar to men accustomed from their cradle to contend with danger.

"Ah! is it you, Dantès?" cried the man in the skiff. "What's the matter? and why have you such an air of sadness aboard?"

"A great misfortune, M. Morrel!" replied the young man,—"a great misfortune, for me especially! Off Civita Vecchia we lost our brave Captain Leclere."

"And the cargo?" inquired the owner, eagerly.

"Is all safe, M. Morrel; and I think you will be satisfied on that head. But poor Captain Leclere ——"

"What happened to him?" asked the owner, with an air of considerable relief. "What happened to the worthy captain?"

"He died."

"Fell into the sea?"

"No, sir; he died of the brain-fever, in dreadful agony."

Then, turning to the crew, he said:

"Look out there! all ready to drop anchor!"

All hands obeyed. At the same moment eight or ten seamen sprang some to the main-sheets, others to the braces, others to the halliards, others to the jib-ropes, and others to the topsail-brails.

The young sailor gave a look to see that his orders were promptly and accurately obeyed, and then turned again to the owner.

"And how did this misfortune occur?" inquired he, resuming the conversation suspended for a moment.

"Alas! sir, in the most unexpected manner. After a long conversation with the harbor-master, Captain Leclere left Naples greatly disturbed in his mind. At the end of twenty-four hours he was attacked by a fever, and died three days afterward. We performed the usual burial service, and he is at his rest, sewn up in his hammock with two balls of thirty-six pounds each at his head and feet, off the island of El Giglio. We bring to his widow his sword and cross of honor. It was worth while, truly," added the young man with a melancholy smile, "to make war against the English for ten years, and to die at last, like everybody else, in his bed."

Edmond Dantès.

"Why, you see, Edmond," replied the owner, who appeared more comforted at every moment, "we are all mortal, and the old must make way for the young. If not, why, there would be no promotion; and as you have assured me that the cargo ——"

"Is all safe and sound, M. Morrel, take my word for it; and I advise you not to take 100,000 francs for the profits of the voyage."

Then, as they were just passing the Round Tower, the young man shouted out:

"Ready, there, to lower topsails, foresail, and jib!"

The order was executed as promptly as if on board a man-of-war.

"Let go! and brail all!" At this last word all the sails were lowered, and the bark moved almost imperceptibly onward, advancing only under the impulse already given.

"Now, if you will come on board, M. Morrel," said Dantès, observing the owner's impatience, "here is your supercargo, M. Danglars, coming out of his cabin, who will furnish you with every particular. As for me, I must look after the anchoring, and dress the ship in mourning."

The owner did not wait to be twice invited. He seized a rope which Dantès flung to him, and, with an activity that would have done credit to a sailor, climbed up the side of the ship, whilst the young man, going to his task, left the conversation to the individual whom he had announced under the name of Danglars, who now coming out of the cabin advanced toward the owner. He was a man of twenty-five or twenty-six years of age, of unprepossessing countenance, obsequious to his superiors, insolent to his inferiors; and then, besides his position as responsible agent on board, which is always obnoxious to the sailors, he was as much disliked by the crew as Edmond Dantès was beloved by them.

"Well, M. Morrel," said Danglars, "you have heard of the misfortune that has befallen us?"

"Yes — yes! poor Captain Leclere! He was a brave and an honest man!"

"And a first-rate seaman, above all, grown old between sky and ocean, as should a man charged with the interests of a house so important as that of Morrel and Son," replied Danglars.

"But," replied the owner, following with his look Dantès, who was watching the anchoring of his vessel, "it seems to me that a sailor needs not to be so old as you say, Danglars, to understand his business; for our friend Edmond there does his, it seems to me, like a man who has no need to ask instruction from any one."

"Yes," said Danglars, casting toward Edmond a look in which a feeling of hate was strongly visible. "Yes, he is young, and youth is invariably self-confident. Scarcely was the captain's breath out of his body than he assumed the command without consulting any one, and he caused us to lose a day and a half at the Isle of Elba, instead of making for Marseilles direct."

"As to taking the command of the vessel," replied Morrel, "that was his duty as first mate; as to losing a day and a half off the Isle of Elba, he was wrong, unless the ship wanted some repair."

The Pharaon.

"The ship was as well as I am, and as, I hope, you are, M. Morrel, and this day and a half was lost from pure whim, for the pleasure of going ashore, and nothing else."

"Dantès!" said the shipowner, turning toward the young man, "come this way!"

"In a moment, sir," answered Dantès, "and I'm with you!"

Then, calling to the crew, he said, "Let go!"

The anchor was instantly dropped, and the chain ran rattling through the port-hole. Dantès continued at his post, in spite of the presence of the pilot, until this manœuvre was completed, and then he added:

"Lower the pennant half-mast high; put the ensign in a weft, and slope the yards!"

"You see," said Danglars, "he fancies himself captain already, upon my word."

"And so, in fact, he is," said the owner.

"Except your signature and your partner's, M. Morrel."

"And why should he not have this?" asked the owner; "he is young, it is true, but he seems to me a thorough seaman, and of full experience."

A cloud passed over Danglars's brow.

"Your pardon, M. Morrel," said Dantès approaching; "the ship now rides at anchor, and I am at your service. You called me, I think?"

Danglars retreated a step or two.

"I wished to inquire why you stopped at the Isle of Elba."

"I do not know, sir; it was to fulfill a last instruction of Captain Leclere, who, when dying, gave me a packet for the Maréchal Bertrand."

"Then, did you see him, Edmond?"

"Who?"

"The maréchal."

"Yes."

Morrel looked around him, and then, drawing Dantès on one side, he said suddenly—

"And how is the Emperor?"

"Very well, as far as I could judge from my eyes."

"You saw the Emperor, then?"

"He entered the maréchal's apartment whilst I was there."

"And you spoke to him?"

"Why, it was he who spoke to me, sir," said Dantès, with a smile.

"And what did he say to you?"

"Asked me questions about the ship,—the time she left Marseilles, the course she had taken, and what was her cargo. I believe, if she had been in ballast, and I had been her master, he would have bought her. But I told him I was only mate, and that she belonged to the firm of Morrel and Son. 'Ah! ah!' he said, 'I know them! The Morrels have been shipowners from father to son; and there was a Morrel who served in the same regiment with me when I was in garrison a Valence.'"

"*Pardieu!* and that is true!" cried the owner, greatly delighted. "And that was Policar Morrel, my uncle, who was afterward a captain. Dantès, you must tell my uncle that the Emperor remembered him, and you will see it will bring tears into the old soldier's eyes. Come, come!"

continued he, patting Edmond's shoulder kindly, "you did very right, Dantès, to follow Captain Leclere's instruction, and touch at the Isle of Elba, although if it were known that you had conveyed a packet to the maréchal, and had conversed with the Emperor, it might bring you into trouble."

"How could that bring me into trouble, sir?" asked Dantès; "for I did not even know of what I was the bearer; and the Emperor merely made such inquiries as he would of the first-comer. But, your pardon, here are the officers of health and the customs coming alongside. You will excuse me?"

"Certainly, certainly, my dear Dantès!"

The young man went to the gangway, and, as he departed, Danglars approached, and said—

"Well, it appears that he has given you satisfactory reasons for his landing at Porto-Ferrajo?"

"Yes, most satisfactory, my dear Danglars."

"Well, so much the better," said the supercargo; "for it is always painful to see a comrade who does not do his duty."

"Dantès has done his," replied the owner, "and there is nothing to say about it. It was Captain Leclere who gave orders for this delay."

"Talking of Captain Leclere, has not Dantès given you a letter from him?"

"To me?—no—was there one?"

"I believe that, besides the packet, Captain Leclere had confided a letter to his care."

"Of what packet are you speaking, Danglars?"

"Why, that which Dantès left at Porto-Ferrajo."

"How do you know he had a packet to leave at Porto-Ferrajo?"

Danglars turned very red.

"I was passing close to the door of the captain's cabin, which was half-open, and I saw him give the packet and letter to Dantès."

"He did not speak to me of it," replied the shipowner; "but if there be any letter he will give it to me."

Danglars reflected for a moment.

"Then, M. Morrel, I beg of you," said he, "not to say a word to Dantès on the subject; I may have been mistaken."

At this moment the young man returned, and Danglars retreated.

"Well, my dear Dantès, are you now free?" inquired the owner.

"Yes, sir."

"You have not been long detained."

"No. I gave the custom-house officers a copy of our manifest; and as to the consignment, they sent a man off with the pilot, to whom I gave our papers."

"Then you have nothing more to do here?"

Dantès cast a glance around.

"No; all is arranged now."

"Then you can come and dine with me?"

"Excuse me, M. Morrel, excuse me, if you please; but my first visit is due to my father, though I am not the less grateful for the honor you have done me."

"Right, Dantès, quite right. I always knew you were a good son."

Mercédès.

"And," inquired Dantès, with some hesitation, "he is well, as far as you know? My father is well?"

"Well, I believe, my dear Edmond, though I have not seen him lately."

" Yes, he likes to keep himself shut up in his little room."

" That proves, at least, that he has wanted for nothing during your absence."

Dantès smiled.

" My father is proud, sir; and if he had not a meal left, I doubt if he would have asked anything from any one in the world, except God."

" Well, then, after this first visit has been made we rely on you."

" I must again excuse myself, M. Morrel; for after this first visit has been paid I have another, which I am no less anxious to pay."

" True, Dantès, I forgot that there was at the Catalans some one who expects you no less impatiently than your father—the lovely Mercédès."

Dantès blushed.

" Ah! ah!" said the shipowner, " that does not astonish me, for she has been to me three times, inquiring if there were any news of the *Pharaon*. *Peste!* Edmond, you are a lucky fellow, you have a very handsome mistress!"

" She is not my mistress," replied the young sailor, gravely; " she is my betrothed."

" Sometimes one and the same thing," said Morrel, with a smile.

" Not with us, sir," replied Dantès.

" Well, well, my dear Edmond," continued the owner, " do not let me detain you. You have managed my affairs so well that I ought to allow you all the time you require for your own. Do you want any money?"

" No, sir; I have all my pay to take — nearly three months' wages."

" You are a careful fellow, Edmond."

" Say I have a poor father, sir."

" Yes, yes, I know how good a son you are, so now haste away to see your father. I have a son too, and I should be very wroth with those who detained him from me after a three months' voyage."

" Then I have your leave, sir?" said the young man, with a salute.

" Yes, if you have nothing more to say to me."

" Nothing."

" Captain Leclere did not, before he died, give you a letter for me?"

" He was unable to write, sir. But that reminds me that I must ask your leave of absence for some days."

" To get married?"

" Yes, first, and then to go to Paris."

" Very good; have what time you require, Dantès. It will take quite six weeks to unload the cargo, and we cannot get you ready for sea until three months after that; only be back again in three months, for the *Pharaon*," added the owner, patting the young sailor on the back, " cannot sail without her captain."

" Without her captain ? " cried Dantès, his eyes sparkling with animation ; " pray mind what you say, for you are touching on the most secret
wishes of my heart. Is it really your intention to nominate me captain
of the *Pharaon ?* "

" If I were sole owner I would give you my hand, my dear Dantès,
and say, ' It is settled '; but I have a partner, and you know the Italian
proverb — *Chi ha compagno ha padrone* — ' He who has a partner has
a master.' But the thing is at least half done, as you have one out of
two voices. Rely on me to procure you the other ; I will do my best."

" Ah ! M. Morrel," exclaimed the young seaman, with tears in his
eyes, and grasping the owner's hand, " M. Morrel, I thank you in the
name of my father and of Mercédès."

" Good, good ! Edmond. There's a sweet little cherub that sits up
aloft that keeps a good watch for good fellows ! Go and see your
father ; go and see Mercédès, and come to me afterward."

" Shall I row you on shore ? "

" No, I thank you ; I shall remain and look over the accounts with
Danglars. Have you been satisfied with him this voyage ? "

" That is according to the sense you attach to the question, sir. Do
you mean, he is a good comrade ? No, for I think he never liked me
since the day when I was silly enough, after a little quarrel we had, to
propose to him to stop for ten minutes at the isle of Monte-Cristo to settle the dispute — a proposition which I was wrong to suggest, and he
quite right to refuse. If you mean as supercargo that you ask me the
question, I believe there is nothing to say against him, and that you
will be content with the way in which he has performed his duty."

" But tell me, Dantès, if you had the command of the *Pharaon*, should
you be glad to retain Danglars ? "

" Captain or mate, M. Morrel," replied Dantès, " I shall always have
the greatest respect for those who possess our owners' confidence."

" Good ! good ! Dantès. I see you are a thorough good fellow, and
will detain you no longer. Go, for I see how impatient you are."

" Then I have leave ? "

" Go, I tell you."

" May I have the use of your skiff ? "

" Certainly."

" Then, for the present, M. Morrel, farewell, and a thousand thanks ! "

" I hope soon to see you again, my dear Edmond. Good luck to
you ! "

The young sailor jumped into the skiff, and sat down in the stern,
desiring to be put ashore at the Cannebière. The two rowers bent to
their work, and the little boat glided away as rapidly as possible in the

midst of the thousand vessels which choke up the kind of narrow street which leads between the two rows of ships from the mouth of the harbor to the Quai d'Orléans.

The shipowner, smiling, followed him with his eyes until he saw him spring out on the quay and disappear in the midst of the motley throng, which, from five o'clock in the morning until nine o'clock at night, choke up this famous street of La Cannebière, of which the modern Phocéens are so proud, and say with all the gravity in the world, and with that accent which gives so much character to what is said, "If Paris had La Cannebière, Paris would be a little Marseilles." On turning round, the owner saw Danglars behind him, who apparently attended his orders, but in reality followed, as he did, the young sailor with his eyes.

Only there was a great difference in the expression of the looks of the two who thus watched the movements of the same man.

CHAPTER II

FATHER AND SON

E will leave Danglars struggling with the feelings of hatred, and endeavoring to insinuate in the ear of the shipowner some evil suspicions against his comrade, and follow Dantès, who, after having traversed the Cannebière, took the Rue de Noailles, and entering into a small house situated on the left side of the Allées de Meilhan, rapidly ascended four stories of a dark staircase, holding the baluster in one hand, whilst with the other he repressed the beatings of his heart, and paused before a half-opened door, which revealed all the interior of a small apartment.

This apartment was occupied by Dantès' father.

The news of the arrival of the *Pharaon* had not yet reached the old man, who, mounted on a chair, was amusing himself with staking, with tremulous hand, some nasturtiums which, mingled with clematis, formed a kind of trellis at his window.

Suddenly, he felt an arm thrown round his body, and a well-known voice behind him exclaimed, "Father! dear father!"

The old man uttered a cry, and turned round; then, seeing his son, he fell into his arms, pale and trembling.

"What ails you, my dearest father?" inquired the young man, much alarmed, "Are you ill?"

"No, no, my dear Edmond — my boy — my son! — no; but I did not expect you; and joy, the surprise of seeing you so suddenly —— Ah! I really seem as if I were going to die."

"Come, come, cheer up, my dear father! 'Tis I — really I! They say joy never hurts, and so I come to you without any warning. Come now, look cheerfully at me, instead of gazing as you do with your eyes so wide. Here I am back again, and we will now be happy."

"Yes, yes, my boy, so we will — so we will," replied the old man; " but how shall we be happy? Will you never leave me again? Come, tell me all the good fortune that has befallen you."

"God forgive me," said the young man, "for rejoicing at happiness derived from the grief of others; but, Heaven knows, I did not desire this good fortune: it has happened, and I really cannot affect to lament it. The good Captain Leclere is dead, father, and it is probable that, with the aid of M. Morrel, I shall have his place. Do you understand, father? Only imagine me a captain at twenty, with a hundred louis pay, and a share in the profits! Is this not more than a poor sailor like me could have hoped for?"

"Yes, my dear boy," replied the old man. "It is great good fortune."

"Well, then, with the first money I touch, I mean you to have a small house, with a garden to plant your clematis, your nasturtiums, and your honeysuckles. But what ails you, father? Are not you well?"

"'Tis nothing, nothing; it will soon pass away."

And as he said so the old man's strength failed him, and he fell backward.

"Come, come," said the young man, "a glass of wine, father, will revive you. Where do you keep your wine?"

"No, no; thank ye. You need not look for it; I do not want it," said the old man.

"Yes, yes, father, tell me where it is," and he opened two or three cupboards.

"It is no use," said the old man, "there is no more wine."

"What! no more wine?" said Dantès, turning pale and looking alternately at the hollow and pallid cheeks of the old man and the empty cupboards. "What! no wine? Have you wanted money, father?"

"I want nothing since I see you," said the old man.

"Yet," stammered Dantès, wiping the perspiration from his brow,— " yet I gave you two hundred francs when I left, three months ago."

"Yes, yes, Edmond, that is true, but you forgot at that time a little debt to our neighbor, Caderousse. He reminded me of it, telling me if I did not pay for you, he would go and get paid by M. Morrel; and so, you see, lest he might do you an injury ——"

"Well — "

"Why, I paid him."

"But," cried Dantès, "it was a hundred and forty francs I owed Caderousse."

"Yes," stammered the old man.

"And you paid him out of the two hundred francs I left you?"

The old man made a sign in the affirmative.

"So that you have lived for three months on sixty francs?" muttered the young man.

"You know how little I require," said the old man.

"Heaven pardon me," cried Edmond, going on his knees before the old man.

"What are you doing?"

"You have wounded my very heart."

"Never mind it, for I see you once more," said the old man; "and now all is forgotten—all is well again."

"Yes, here I am," said the young man, "with a happy future and a little money. Here, father! here!" he said, "take this—take it, and send for something immediately."

And he emptied his pockets on the table, whose contents consisted of a dozen pieces of gold, five or six crowns, and some smaller coin.

The countenance of old Dantès brightened.

"Whom does this belong to?" he inquired.

"To me! to you! to us!" Take it; buy some provisions; be happy, and to-morrow we shall have more."

"Gently, gently," said the old man, with a smile; "and by your leave I will use your purse moderately, for they would say, if they saw me buy too many things at a time, that I had been obliged to await your return, in order to be able to purchase them."

"Do as you please; but, first of all, pray have a servant, father. I will not have you left alone so long. I have some smuggled coffee and most capital tobacco, in a small chest in the hold, which you shall have to-morrow. But, hush! here comes somebody."

"'Tis Caderousse, who has heard of your arrival, and no doubt comes to congratulate you on your fortunate return."

"Ah! lips that say one thing, whilst the heart thinks another," murmured Edmond. "But, never mind, he is a neighbor who has done us a service on a time, so he's welcome."

As Edmond finished his sentence in a low voice, there appeared, framed by the door of the landing, the black and bearded head of Caderousse. He was a man of twenty-five or twenty-six years of age, and held in his hand a morsel of cloth, which, in his capacity as a tailor, he was about to turn into the lining of a coat.

"What! is it you, Edmond, returned?" said he, with a broad Marseillaise accent, and a broad grin that displayed his teeth as white as ivory.

"Yes, as you see, neighbor Caderousse; and ready to be agreeable to you in any and every way," replied Dantès, but ill-concealing his coldness under this appearance of civility.

"Thanks — thanks; but, fortunately, I do not want for anything; and it chances that at times there are others who have need of me." Dantès made a gesture. "I do not allude to you, my boy. No! — no! I lent you money, and you returned it; that's like good neighbors, and we are quits."

"We are never quits with those who oblige us," was Dantès' reply; "for when we do not owe them money, we owe them gratitude."

"What's the use of mentioning that? What is done is done. Let us talk of your happy return, my boy. I had gone on the quay to match a piece of mulberry cloth, when I met friend Danglars.

"'What! you at Marseilles?' — 'Yes,' says he.

"'I thought you were at Smyrna.'—'I was; but am now back again.'

"'And where is the dear boy, our little Edmond?'

" 'Why, with his father, no doubt,' replied Danglars. And so I came," added Caderousse, " as fast as I could to have the pleasure of shaking hands with a friend."

" Worthy Caderousse!" said the old man, " he is so much attached to us !"

Caderousse.

" Yes, to be sure I am. I love and esteem you, because honest folks are so rare! But it seems you have come back rich, my boy," continued the tailor, looking askance at the handful of gold and silver which Dantès had thrown on the table.

The young man remarked the greedy glance which shone in the dark eyes of his neighbor.

"Eh!" he said, negligently, "this money is not mine: I was expressing to my father my fears that he had wanted many things in my absence, and to convince me he emptied his purse on the table. Come, father," added Dantès, "put this money back in your box — unless neighbor Caderousse wants anything, and in that case it is at his service."

"No, my boy, no," said Caderousse. " I am not in any want, thank God! the trade keeps me. Keep your money — keep it, I say; — one never has too much; — but, at the same time, my boy, I am as much obliged by your offer as if I took advantage of it."

"It was offered with good-will," said Dantès.

"No doubt, my boy; no doubt. Well, you stand well with M. Morrel, I hear, — you insinuating dog, you!"

"M. Morrel has always been exceedingly kind to me," replied Dantès.

"Then you were wrong to refuse to dine with him."

"What! did you refuse to dine with him?" said old Dantès; "and did he invite you to dine?"

"Yes, my dear father," replied Edmond, smiling at his father's astonishment at the excessive honor paid to his son.

"And why did you refuse, my son?" inquired the old man.

"That I might the sooner be with you again, my dear father," replied the young man. "I was most anxious to see you."

"But it must have vexed M. Morrel, good, worthy man," said Caderousse. "And when you are looking forward to be captain, it was wrong to vex the owner."

"But I explained to him the cause of my refusal," replied Dantes; "and I hope he fully understood it."

"Yes, but to be captain one must give way a little to one's patrons."

"I hope to be captain without that," said Dantès.

"So much the better — so much the better! Nothing will give greater pleasure to all your old friends; and I know one down there behind the citadel of Saint Nicolas who will not be sorry to hear it."

"Mercédès?" said the old man.

"Yes, my dear father, and with your permission, now I have seen you, and know you are well, and have all you require, I will ask your consent to go and pay a visit to the Catalans."

"Go, my dear boy," said old Dantès; "and Heaven bless you in your wife, as it has blessed me in my son!"

"His wife!" said Caderousse; "why, how fast you go on, father Dantès; she is not his wife yet, I fancy."

"No, but according to all probability she soon will be," replied Edmond.

" Yes — yes," said Caderousse; " but you were right to be in a hurry, my boy."

" And why ? "

Dantès' father.

" Because Mercédès is a very fine girl, and fine girls never lack lovers; she, particularly, has them by dozens."

" Really!" answered Edmond, with a smile which had in it traces of slight uneasiness.

"Ah, yes," continued Caderousse, "and capital offers, too; but, you know, you will be captain, and who could refuse you then?"

"Meaning to say," replied Dantès, with a smile which but ill-concealed his trouble, "that if I were not a captain——"

"Eh—eh!" said Caderousse, shaking his head.

"Come, come," said the sailor, "I have a better opinion than you of women in general, and of Mercédès in particular; and I am certain that, captain or not, she will remain ever faithful to me."

"So much the better—so much the better," said Caderousse. "When one is going to be married, there is nothing like implicit confidence; but never mind that, my boy,— but go and announce your arrival, and let her know all your hopes and prospects."

"I will go directly," was Edmond's reply.

Then, embracing his father, and saluting Caderousse, he left the apartment.

Caderousse lingered for a moment; then, taking leave of old Dantès, he went downstairs to rejoin Danglars, who awaited him at the corner of the Rue Senac.

"Well," said Danglars, "did you see him?"

"I have just left him," answered Caderousse.

"Did he allude to his hope of being captain?"

"He spoke of it as a thing already decided."

"Patience!" said Danglars; "he is in too much hurry, it appears to me."

"Why, it seems M. Morrel has promised him the thing."

"So that he is quite elate about it!"

"That is to say, he is actually insolent on the matter — has already offered me his patronage, as if he were a grand personage, and proffered me a loan of money, as though he were a banker."

"Which you refused?"

"Most assuredly; although I might easily have accepted it, for it was I who put into his hands the first silver he ever earned; but now M. Dantès has no longer any occasion for assistance — he is about to become a captain."

"Pooh!" said Danglars; "he is not one yet."

"*Ma foi!* — and it will be as well he never should be," answered Caderousse; "for, if he should be, there will be really no speaking to him."

"If we choose," replied Danglars, "he will remain what he is; and perhaps become even less than he is."

"What do you mean?"

"Nothing — I was speaking to myself. And is he still in love with the fair Catalane?"

"Over head and ears; but, unless I am much mistaken, there will be a storm in that quarter."

"Explain yourself."

"Why should I?"

"It is more important than you think, perhaps. You do not like Dantès?"

"I never like upstarts."

"Then tell me all you know relative to the Catalane."

"I know nothing for certain; only I have seen things which induce me to believe, as I told you, that the future captain will find some annoyance in the environs of the road of the Vieilles Infirmeries."

" What have you seen ?— come, tell me ! "

" Well, every time I have seen Mercédès come into the city, she has been accompanied by a tall, strapping, black-eyed Catalan, with a red complexion, brown skin, and fierce air, whom she calls cousin."

" Really ; and you think this cousin pays her attentions ? "

" I suppose so. What else can a strapping chap of twenty-one mean with a fine lass of seventeen ? "

" And you say Dantès has gone to the Catalans ? "

" He went before I came down."

" Let us go the same way ; we will stop at La Réserve, and we can drink a glass of La Malgue, whilst we wait for news."

" Come along," said Caderousse ; " but mind you pay the shot."

" Certainly," replied Danglars.

The two walked quickly to the spot alluded to ; on their reaching it, they called for a bottle of wine and two glasses.

Père Pamphile had seen Dantès pass not ten minutes before.

Assured that Dantès was at the Catalans, they sat down under the budding foliage of the planes and sycamores, in the branches of which the birds were joyously singing on one of the first fair days in spring.

CHAPTER III

BOUT a hundred paces from the spot where the two friends were, with their looks fixed on the distance, and their ears attentive, whilst they imbibed the sparkling wine of La Malgue, behind a bare wall, torn and worn by sun and storm, was the small village of the Catalans.

One day a mysterious colony quitted Spain and settled on the tongue of land on which it is to this day. It arrived from no one knew where, and spoke an unknown tongue. One of its chiefs, who understood Provençal, begged the commune of Marseilles to give them this bare and barren promontory, on which, like the sailors of the ancient times, they had run their boats ashore. The request was granted; and three months afterward, around the twelve or fifteen small vessels which had brought these gypsies of the sea, a small village sprang up.

This village, constructed in a singular and picturesque manner, half Moorish, half Spanish, is the one we behold at the present day inhabited by the descendants of those men who speak the language of their fathers. For three or four centuries they remained faithful to this small promontory on which they had settled like a flight of sea-birds, without mixing with the Marseillaise population, intermarrying and preserving their original customs and the costume of their mother-country, as they have preserved its language.

Our readers will follow us along the only street of this little village, and enter with us into one of the houses, on the outside of which the sun had stamped that beautiful dead-leaf color peculiar to the buildings of the country, and within, a coat of limewash, of that white tint which forms the only ornament of Spanish posadas. A young and beautiful girl, with hair as black as jet, her eyes as velvety as the gazelle's, was leaning with her back against a partition, rubbing in her slender fingers, molded after the antique, an innocent spray of heath, the flowers of which she was picking off and strewing on the floor; her arms, bare to the elbow, embrowned, but which seemed modeled after those of the Venus at Arles, moved with a kind of restless impatience, and she tapped the earth with her pliant and well-formed foot, so as to display the pure and full shape of her well-turned leg, in its red cotton stocking with gray and blue clocks.

At three paces from her, seated in a chair which he balanced on two legs, leaning his elbow on an old worm-eaten table, was a tall young man of twenty or two-and-twenty, who was looking at her with an air in which vexation and uneasiness were mingled. He questioned her with his eyes, but the firm and steady gaze of the young girl controlled his look.

"You see, Mercédès," said the young man, "here is Easter come round again; it is the time for a wedding; what do you say?"

"I have answered you a hundred times, Fernand; and really you must be your own enemy to ask me again."

"Well, repeat it,—repeat it, I beg of you, that I may at last believe it! Tell me for the hundredth time that you refuse my love, which had your mother's sanction. Make me fully comprehend that you are trifling with my happiness, that my life or death is immaterial to you. Ah! to have dreamed for ten years of being your husband, Mercédès, and to lose that hope, which was the only object of my existence!"

"At least it was not I who ever encouraged you in that hope, Fernand," replied Mercédès; "you cannot reproach me with the slightest coquetry. I have always said to you, 'I love you as a brother; but do not ask from me more than sisterly affection, for my heart is another's.' Is not this true, Fernand?"

"Yes, I know it well, Mercédès," replied the young man. "Yes, you have been cruelly frank with me; but do you forget that it is among the Catalans a sacred law to intermarry?"

"You mistake, Fernand, it is not a law, but merely a custom; and, I pray of you, do not cite this custom in your favor. You are included in the conscription, Fernand, and are only at liberty on sufferance, liable at any moment to be called upon to take up arms. Once a soldier, what would you do with me, a poor orphan, forlorn, without fortune, with nothing but a hut, half in ruins, containing some ragged nets, a miserable inheritance left by my father to my mother, and by my mother to me? She has been dead a year, and you know, Fernand, I have been living almost on public charity. Sometimes you pretend I am useful to you, and that is an excuse to share with me the produce of your fishing, and I accept it, Fernand, because you are the son of my father's brother, because we were brought up together, and still more because it would give you so much pain if I refuse. But I feel very deeply that this fish which I go and sell, and with the produce of which I buy the flax I spin,— I feel very keenly, Fernand, that this is charity."

Fernand and Mercédès.

"And if it were, Mercédès, poor and lone as you are, you suit me as well as the daughter of the first shipowner, or the richest banker of Marseilles! What do such as we desire but a good wife and careful housekeeper, and where can I look for these better than in you?"

"Fernand," answered Mercédès, shaking her head, "a woman becomes a bad manager, and who shall say she will remain an honest woman when she loves another man better than her husband? Rest content with my friendship, for I repeat to you that is all I can promise, and I will promise no more than I can bestow."

"I understand," replied Fernand, "you can endure your own wretchedness patiently, but you are afraid of mine. Well, Mercédès, beloved by you, I would tempt fortune; you would bring me good luck. I might get a place as clerk in a warehouse, and become myself a merchant in time."

"You could do no such thing, Fernand; you are a soldier, and if you remain at the Catalans it is because there is not a war; so remain a fisherman, cherish no dreams that will make the reality still more terrible; be contented with my friendship, as I cannot give you more."

"Well, you are right, Mercédès. I will be a sailor; instead of the costume of our fathers, which you despise, I will wear a varnished hat, a striped shirt, and a blue jacket with an anchor on the buttons. Would not that dress please you?"

"What do you mean?" asked Mercédès, darting at him an imperious glance,—"what do you mean? I do not understand you."

"I mean, Mercédès, that you are thus harsh and cruel with me, because you are expecting some one who is thus attired; but, perhaps, he whom you await is inconstant, or, if he is not, the sea is so to him."

"Fernand!" cried Mercédès, "I believed you were good-hearted, and I was mistaken! Fernand, you are wicked to call to the aid of your jealousy the anger of God! Yes, I will not deny it, I do await, and I do love him to whom you allude; and, if he does not return, instead of accusing him of the inconstancy which you insinuate, I will tell you that he died loving me, and me only."

The young Catalan made a gesture of rage.

"I understand you, Fernand; you would be revenged on him because I do not love you; you would cross your Catalan knife with his dirk. What end would that answer? To lose you my friendship if you were conquered, and see that friendship changed into hate if you were conqueror. Believe me, to seek a quarrel with a man is a bad method of pleasing the woman who loves that man. No, Fernand, you will not thus give way to evil thoughts. Unable to have me for your wife, you will content yourself with having me for your friend and sister; and besides," she added, her eyes troubled and moistened with tears, "wait, wait, Fernand; you said just now that the sea was treacherous, and he has been gone four months, and during these four months I have counted many, many storms."

Fernand made no reply, nor did he attempt to check the tears which flowed down the cheeks of Mercédès, although for each of these tears he would have given a cupful of his heart's blood; but these tears flowed for another. He arose, paced awhile up and down the hut, and then, suddenly stopping before Mercédès, with his eyes stern and his hands clenched,

"Say, Mercédès," he said, "once for all, is this your final determination?"

"I love Edmond Dantès," the young girl calmly replied, "and none but Edmond shall ever be my husband."

"And you will always love him?"

"As long as I live."

Fernand let fall his head like a defeated man, heaved a sigh which resembled a groan, and then suddenly looking her full in the face, with clenched teeth and expanded nostrils, said:

"But if he is dead——?"

"If he is dead, I shall die too."

"If he has forgotten you——?"

"Mercédès!" cried a voice, joyously, outside the house,—"Mercédès!"

"Ah!" exclaimed the young girl, blushing with delight, and springing up with love, "you see he has not forgotten me, for here he is!" And rushing toward the door, she opened it, saying,

"Here, Edmond, here I am!"

Fernand, pale and trembling, receded like a traveler at the sight of a serpent, and fell into a chair beside him.

Edmond and Mercédès were clasped in each other's arms. The burning sun of Marseilles, which penetrated the room by the open door, covered them with a flood of light. At first they saw nothing around them. Their intense happiness isolated them from all the rest of the world, and they only spoke in broken words, which are the tokens of a joy so extreme that they seem rather the expression of sorrow. Suddenly Edmond saw the gloomy countenance of Fernand, as it was defined in the shadow, pale and threatening, and by a movement, for which he could scarcely account to himself, the young Catalan placed his hand on the knife at his belt.

"Ah! your pardon," said Dantès, frowning in his turn; "I did not perceive that there were three of us." Then, turning to Mercédès, he inquired, "Who is this gentleman?"

"One who will be your best friend, Dantès, for he is my friend, my cousin, my brother; it is Fernand—the man whom, after you, Edmond, I love the best in the world. Do you not remember him?"

"Yes!" said Edmond, and without relinquishing Mercédès' hand clasped in one of his own, he extended the other to the Catalan with a cordial air. But Fernand, instead of responding to this amiable gesture, remained mute and motionless as a statue. Edmond then cast his eyes scrutinizingly at Mercédès, agitated and embarrassed, and then again on Fernand, gloomy and menacing. This look told him all, and his brow became suffused and angry.

"I did not know, when I came with such haste to you, that I was to meet an enemy here."

"An enemy!" cried Mercédès, with an angry look at her cousin. "An enemy in my house, do you say, Edmond! If I believed that, I would place my arm under yours and go with you to Marseilles, leaving the house to return to it no more."

Fernand's eye darted lightning. "And should any misfortune occur to you, dear Edmond," she continued, with the same implacable calmness which proved to Fernand that the young girl had read the very innermost depths of his sinister thought, "if misfortune should occur to you, I would ascend the highest point of the Cape de Morgion, and cast myself headlong from it on the rocks below."

Fernand became deadly pale.

"But you are deceived, Edmond," she continued. "You have no enemy here — there is no one but Fernand, my brother, who will grasp your hand as a devoted friend."

And at these words the young girl fixed her imperious look on the Catalan, who, as if fascinated by it, came slowly toward Edmond, and offered him his hand. His hatred, like a powerless though furious wave, was broken against the strong ascendency which Mercédès exercised over him. Scarcely, however, had he touched Edmond's hand than he felt he had done all he could do, and rushed hastily out of the house.

"Oh!" he exclaimed, running furiously and plunging his hands in his hair—"Oh! who will deliver me from this man? Wretched—wretched that I am!"

"Halloo, Catalan! Halloo, Fernand! where are you running to?" exclaimed a voice.

The young man stopped suddenly, looked around him, and perceived Caderousse sitting at table with Danglars under an arbor.

"Well," said Caderousse, "why don't you come? Are you really in such a hurry that you have no time to say 'how do' to your friends?"

"Particularly when they have still a full bottle before them," added Danglars. Fernand looked at them both with a stupefied air, but did not say a word.

"He looks sheepish," said Danglars, pushing Caderousse with his knee. "Are we mistaken, and is Dantès triumphant in spite of all we have believed?"

"Why, we must inquire into that," was Caderousse's reply; and, turning toward the young man, said, "Well, Catalan, can't you make up your mind?"

Fernand wiped away the perspiration steaming from his brow, and slowly entered the arbor, whose shade seemed to restore somewhat of calmness to his senses, and whose coolness somewhat of refreshment to his exhausted body.

"Good-day," said he. "You called me, didn't you?" And he fell, rather than sat down, on one of the seats which surrounded the table.

"I called you because you were running like a madman, and I was afraid you would throw yourself into the sea," said Caderousse, laughing. "Why! when a man has friends, they are not only to offer him a glass of wine, but, moreover, to prevent his swallowing three or four pints of water unnecessarily!"

Fernand gave a groan, which resembled a sob, and dropped his head into his hands, crossed over each other, on the table.

"Well, Fernand, I must say," said Caderousse, beginning the conversation, with that brutality of the common people in which curiosity destroys all diplomacy, "you look uncommonly like a rejected lover"; and he accompained this joke with a hoarse laugh.

"Bah!" said Danglars, "a lad of his make was not born to be unhappy in love. You are laughing at him, Caderousse!"

"No," he replied; "only hark how he sighs! Come, come, Fernand!" said Caderousse, "hold up your head, and answer us. It's not polite not to reply to friends who ask news of your health."

"My health is well enough," said Fernand, clenching his hands without raising his head.

"Ah! you see, Danglars," said Caderousse, winking at his friend, "this is how it is: Fernand, whom you see here, is a good and brave Catalan, one of the best fishermen in Marseilles, and he is in love with a very fine girl, named Mercédès; but it appears, unfortunately, that the fine girl is in love with the second in command on board the *Pharaon;* and, as the *Pharaon* arrived to-day — why, you understand!"

"No, I do not understand," said Danglars.

"Poor Fernand has been dismissed," continued Caderousse.

"Well, and what then?" said Fernand, lifting up his head, and looking at Caderousse like a man who looks for some one on whom to vent his anger; "Mercédès is not accountable to any person, is she? Is she not free to love whomsoever she will?"

"Oh! if you take it in that sense," said Caderousse, "it is another thing! But I thought you were a Catalan, and they told me the Catalans were not men to allow themselves to be supplanted by a rival. It was even told me that Fernand, especially, was terrible in his vengeance."

Fernand smiled piteously. "A lover is never terrible," he said.

"Poor fellow!" remarked Danglars, affecting to pity the young man from the bottom of his heart. "Why, you see, he did not expect to see Dantès return so suddenly! he thought he was dead, perhaps; or perchance faithless! These things always come on us more severely when they come suddenly."

"Ah, *ma foi*, under any circumstances!" said Caderousse, who drank as he spoke, and on whom the fumes of the wine of La Malgue began to take effect,— "under any circumstances Fernand is not the only person put out by the fortunate arrival of Dantès; is he, Danglars?"

"No, you are right — and I should say that would bring him ill-luck."

"Well, never mind," answered Caderousse, pouring out a glass of wine for Fernand, and filling his own for the eighth or ninth time, whilst Danglars had merely sipped his. "Never mind — in the meantime he marries Mercédès — the lovely Mercédès — at least, he returns to do that."

During this time Danglars fixed his piercing glance on the young man, on whose heart Caderousse's words fell like molten lead.

"And when is the wedding to be?" he asked.

"Oh, it is not yet fixed!" murmured Fernand.

"No, but it will be," said Caderousse, "as surely as Dantès will be captain of the *Pharaon* — eh, Danglars?"

Danglars shuddered at this unexpected attack, and turned to Caderousse, whose countenance he scrutinized, to try and detect whether the blow was premeditated; but he read nothing but envy in a countenance already rendered almost stupid by drunkenness.

"Well," said he, filling the glasses, "let us drink to Captain Edmond Dantès, husband of the beautiful Catalane!"

Caderousse raised his glass to his mouth with unsteady hand, and swallowed the contents at a gulp. Fernand dashed his on the ground.

"Eh! eh! eh!" stammered Caderousse. "What do I see down there by the wall, in the direction of the Catalans? Look, Fernand! your eyes are better than mine. I believe I see double. You know wine is a deceiver; but I should say it was two lovers walking side by side, and hand in hand. Heaven forgive me! they do not know that we can see them, and they are actually embracing!"

Danglars did not lose one pang that Fernand endured.

"Do you know them, M. Fernand?" he said.

"Yes," was the reply, in a low voice. "It is M. Edmond and Mademoiselle Mercédès!"

"Ah! see there; now!" said Caderousse; "and I did not recognize them! Halloo, Dantès! halloo, lovely damsel! Come this way, and let us know when the wedding is to be, for M. Fernand here is so obstinate he will not tell us!"

"Hold your tongue, will you?" said Danglars, pretending to restrain Caderousse, who, with the tenacity of drunkards, leaned out of the

Danglars.

arbor. "Try to stand upright, and let the lovers make love without interruption. See, look at M. Fernand, and follow his example; he is well-behaved!"

Fernand, probably excited beyond bearing, pricked by Danglars, as the bull is by the bandilleros, was about to rush out; for he had risen from his seat, and seemed to be collecting himself to dash headlong upon his rival, when Mercédès, smiling and graceful, lifted up her lovely head, and showed her clear and bright eye. At this Fernand recollected her threat of dying if Edmond died, and dropped again despairingly on his seat. Danglars looked at the two men, one after the other, the one brutalized by liquor, the other overwhelmed with love.

" I shall extract nothing from these fools," he muttered; "and I am very much afraid of being here between a drunkard and a coward. Here is a man deservedly crazy, who fuddles himself with wine, while he ought to intoxicate himself with gall; there is a great idiot whose mistress is taken from under his very eyes, and who does nothing but weep and whine like a baby. Yet this Catalan has eyes that glisten, like the Spaniards, Sicilians, and Calabrians, who practice revenge so well; he has fists that would crush the skull of an ox as surely as the butcher's ax. Unquestionably, Edmond's star is in the ascendant, and he will marry the splendid girl — he will be captain, too, and laugh at us all, unless — " a sinister smile passed over Danglars' lips — " unless I mingle in the affair," he added.

" Halloo ! " continued Caderousse, half rising, and with his fist on the table, "halloo, Edmond ! do you not see your friends, or are you too proud to speak to them ? "

"No, my dear fellow ! " replied Dantès, " I am not proud, but I am happy; and happiness blinds, I think, more than pride."

" Ah ! very well, that's an explanation ! " said Caderousse. " Well, good-day, Madame Dantès ! "

Mercédès courtesied gravely, and said —" That is not my name, and in my country it bodes ill-fortune, they say, to call young girls by the name of their betrothed before he becomes their husband. Call me, then, Mercédès, if you please."

" We must excuse our worthy neighbor, Caderousse," said Dantès, " he is so easily mistaken."

" So, then, the wedding is to take place immediately, M. Dantès ? " said Danglars, bowing to the young couple.

" As soon as possible, M. Danglars; to-day all preliminaries will be arranged at my father's, and to-morrow, or next day at latest, the wedding festival here at La Réserve. My friends will be there, I hope; that is to say, you are invited, M. Danglars, and you, Caderousse."

" And Fernand," said Caderousse with a chuckle; " Fernand, too, is invited ! "

" My wife's brother is my brother," said Edmond; " and we, Mercédès and I, should be very sorry if he were absent at such a time."

Fernand opened his mouth to reply, but his voice died on his lips, and he could not utter a word.

"To-day the preliminaries, to-morrow or next day the ceremony! you are in a hurry, captain!"

"Danglars," said Edmond, smiling, "I will say to you as Mercédès said just now to Caderousse, 'Do not give me a title which does not belong to me'; that may bring me bad luck."

"Your pardon," replied Danglars, "I merely said you seemed in a hurry, and we have lots of time; the *Pharaon* cannot be under way again in less than three months."

"We are always in a hurry to be happy, M. Danglars; for when we have suffered a long time, we have great difficulty in believing in good fortune. But it is not selfishness alone that makes me thus in haste; I must go to Paris."

"To Paris! really! and will it be the first time you have ever been there, Dantès?"

"Yes."

"Have you business there?"

"Not of my own; the last commission of poor Captain Leclere; you understand, Danglars,— it is sacred. Besides, I shall only take the time to go and return."

"Yes, yes, I understand," said Danglars, aloud; and then in a low tone he added, "To Paris, no doubt, to deliver the letter which the Grand Marshal gave him. Ah! this letter gives me an idea — a capital idea! Ah! Dantès, my friend, you are not yet registered number one on board the good ship *Pharaon*"; then, turning toward Edmond, who was walking away, "Good journey," he cried.

"Thank ye," said Edmond, with a friendly nod, and the two lovers continued their route, calm and joyous as two blessed souls that ascend to heaven.

CHAPTER IV

CONSPIRACY

ANGLARS followed Edmond and Mercédès with his eyes until the two lovers disappeared behind one of the angles of Fort Saint Nicolas; then, turning round, he perceived Fernand, who had fallen, pale and trembling, into his chair, whilst Caderousse stammered out the words of a drinking-song.

"Well, my dear sir," said Danglars to Fernand, "here is a marriage which does not appear to make everybody happy."

"It drives me to despair," said Fernand.

"Do you, then, love Mercédès?"

"I adore her!"

"Have you loved her long?"

"Ever since I have known her."

"And you sit there, tearing your hair, instead of seeking to remedy your condition; I did not think it was thus the men of your nation acted."

"What would you have me do?" said Fernand.

"How do I know! Is it my affair? I am not the one who is in love with Mademoiselle Mercédès; but you. Seek, says Scripture, and you shall find."

"I have found already."

"What?"

"I would stab the man, but the woman told me that if any misfortune happened to her betrothed, she would kill herself."

"Pooh! women say those things, but never do them."

"You do not know Mercédès; what she threatens she will do."

"Idiot!" muttered Danglars; "whether she kill herself or not, what matter, provided Dantès is not captain?"

"Before Mercédès should die," replied Fernand, with the accents of unshaken resolution, "I would die myself!"

"That's what I call love!" said Caderousse, with a voice more tipsy than ever. "That's love, or I don't know what love is."

"Come," said Danglars, "you appear to me a good sort of fellow, and hang me! but I should like to help you, but——"

"Yes," said Caderousse, "but how?"

"My dear fellow," replied Danglars, "you are three-parts drunk; finish the bottle, and you will be completely so. Drink, then, and do not meddle with what we are doing, for what we are doing requires all one's wits."

"I — drunk!" said Caderousse; "well, that's a good one! I could drink four more such bottles; they are no bigger than Eau-de-Cologne flasks. Père Pamphile, more wine!"

And Caderousse, to add the proof to the proposition, rattled his glass upon the table.

"You were saying, sir——" said Fernand, awaiting with great anxiety the end of the interrupted remark.

"What was I saying? I forget. This drunken Caderousse has made me lose the thread of my thoughts."

"Drunk, if you like; so much the worse for those who fear wine, for it is because they have some bad thoughts which they are afraid the liquor will extract from their hearts."

And Caderousse began to sing the last two lines of a song very popular at the time:

> "' Les méchants sont beuveurs d'eau;
> Bien prouvé par le déluge.'"*

"You said, sir, resumed Fernand, "you would like to help me, but——"

"Yes; but I added, to help you it would be sufficient that Dantès did not marry her you love; and the marriage may easily be thwarted, methinks, and yet Dantès need not die."

"Death alone can separate them," remarked Fernand.

"You talk like a noodle, my friend," said Caderousse; "and here is Danglars, who is a wide-awake, clever, deep fellow, who will prove to you that you are wrong. Prove it, Danglars. I have answered for you. Say there is no need why Dantès should die: it would, indeed, be a pity he should. Dantès is a good fellow; I like Dantès! Dantès, your health."

Fernand rose impatiently.

"Let him run on," said Danglars, restraining the young man; "drunk

---

* All the bad are water-drinkers;
Noah's deluge is a proof.

as he is, he is not much out in what he says. Absence severs as well **as**
death, and if the walls of a prison were between Edmond and Mercédès
they would be as effectually separated as if he lay under a tombstone."

"Yes; only people get out of prison," said Caderousse, who, with **what**

sense was left him, listened eagerly to the conversation, "and when they
get out, and their names are Edmond Dantès, they revenge ——"

"What matters that ?" muttered Fernand.

"And why, I should like to know," persisted Caderousse, "should they
put Dantès in prison ? he has neither robbed, nor killed, nor murdered."

"Hold your tongue !" said Danglars.

"I won't hold my tongue!" replied Caderousse; "I say I want to know why they should put Dantès in prison; I like Dantès; Dantès, your health!"

And he swallowed another glass of wine.

Danglars saw in the muddled look of the tailor the progress of his intoxication, and, turning toward Fernand, said:

"Well, you understand there is no need to kill him."

"Certainly not, if, as you said just now, you have the means of having Dantès arrested. Have you that means?"

"It is to be found for the searching. But why should I," he continued, "meddle in the matter? it is no affair of mine."

"I know not why you meddle," said Fernand, seizing his arm; "but this I know, you have some motive of personal hatred against Dantès, for he who himself hates is never mistaken in the sentiments of others."

"I! motives of hatred against Dantès? None, on my word! I saw you were unhappy, and your unhappiness interested me; that's all; but the moment you believe I act for my own account, adieu, my dear friend, get out of the affair as best you may."

Danglars made a pretense of rising.

"No, no," said Fernand, restraining him, "stay! It is of very little consequence to me, after all, whether you have any angry feeling or not against Dantès. I hate him! I confess it openly. Do you find the means, I will execute it, provided it is not to kill the man, for Mercédès has declared she will kill herself if Dantès is killed."

Caderousse, who had let his head drop on the table, now raised it, and, looking at Fernand with his dull and fishy eyes, he said:

"Kill Dantès! who talks of killing Dantès? I won't have him killed — I won't! He's my friend, and this morning offered to share his money with me, as I shared mine with him. I won't have Dantès killed — I won't!"

"And who has said a word about killing him, muddlehead?" replied Danglars. "We were merely joking: drink to his health," he added, filling Caderousse's glass, "and do not interfere with us."

"Yes, yes, Dantes' good health!" said Caderousse, emptying his glass, "here's to his health! his health! — hurrah!"

"But the means — the means?" said Fernand.

"Have you not hit upon any?"

"No! — you undertook to do so."

"True," replied Danglars; "the French have this superiority over the Spaniards, that the Spaniards ruminate, whilst the French invent."

"Invent, then!" said Fernand, impatiently.

"Waiter," said Danglars, "pen, ink, and paper."

"Pen, ink, and paper?" muttered Fernand.

"Yes; I am a supercargo; pen, ink, and paper are my tools, and without my tools I am fit for nothing."

"Pen, ink, and paper!" called Fernand, in his turn.

"All you require is on that table," said the waiter, pointing to the writing materials.

"Bring them here." The waiter took the pen, ink, and paper, and placed them on the table where they were drinking.

"When one thinks," said Caderousse, letting his hand drop on the paper, "there is here wherewithal to kill a man more surely than if we

waited at the corner of a wood to assassinate him! I have always had more dread of a pen, a bottle of ink, and a sheet of paper, than of a sword or pistol."

"The fellow is not so drunk as he appears to be," said Danglars. "Give him some more wine, Fernand."

Fernand filled Caderousse's glass, who, toper as he was, lifted his hand from the paper and seized the glass.

The Catalan watched him until Caderousse, almost overcome by this fresh assault on his senses, rested, or rather allowed his glass to fall upon the table.

"Well!" resumed the Catalan, as he saw the final glimmer of Caderousse's reason vanishing before the last glass of wine.

"Well, then, I should say, for instance," resumed Danglars, "that if after a voyage such as Dantès has just made, and in which he touched at Naples and the isle of Elba, some one were to denounce him to the king's procureur as a Bonapartist agent ——"

"I will denounce him!" exclaimed the young man, hastily.

"Yes, but they will make you then sign your declaration, and confront you with him you have denounced; I will supply you with the means of supporting your accusation, I am quite sure. But Dantès cannot remain forever in prison, and one day or other he will leave it, and the day when he comes out, woe betide him who was the cause of his incarceration!"

"Oh, I should wish nothing better than that he would come and seek a quarrel with me."

"Yes, and Mercédès! Mercédès, who will detest you if you have only the misfortune to scratch the skin of her dearly beloved Edmond!"

"True!" said Fernand.

"No! no!" continued Danglars; "if we resolve on such a step, it would be much better to take, as I now do, this pen, dip it into this ink, and simply write with the left hand (that the writing may not be recognized) a little denunciation like this."

And Danglars, uniting practice with theory, wrote with his left hand, and in a back-hand that had no analogy to his usual writing, the following lines, which he handed to Fernand, and which Fernand read on in undertone:

"The Procureur du Roi is informed by a friend of the throne and religion that one Edmond Dantès, mate of the ship *Pharaon*, arrived this morning from Smyrna, after having touched at Naples and Porto-Ferrajo, has been intrusted by Murat with a letter for the usurper, and by the usurper with a letter for the Bonapartist Committee, in Paris.

"Proof of this crime will be found on arresting him, for the letter will be found upon him, or at his father's, or in his cabin on board the *Pharaon*."

"Very good," resumed Danglars; "now your revenge looks like common sense, for in no way can it revert to yourself, and the matter will thus work its own way; there is nothing to do now but fold the letter as I am doing, and write upon it, 'To M. le Procureur Royal,' and all would be settled."

And Danglars wrote the address as he spoke.

"Yes, all would be settled!" exclaimed Caderousse, who, by a last effort of intellect, had followed the reading of the letter, and instinctively comprehended all the misery which such a denunciation must entail. "Yes, and all that would be settled: only it will be an infamous deed"; and he stretched out his hand to reach the letter.

"Moreover," said Danglars, taking it from beyond his reach, "and as what I say and do is merely in jest, and as I, amongst the first and foremost, should be sorry if anything happened to Dantès — the worthy Dantès — look here!" And taking the letter, he squeezed it up in his hands and threw it into a corner of the arbor.

"All right!" said Caderousse. "Dantès is my friend, and I won't have him ill-used."

"And who thinks of using him ill? Certainly neither I nor Fernand!" said Danglars, rising and looking at the young man, who still remained seated, but whose sidelong looks were fixed on the denunciatory sheet of paper flung into the corner.

"In this case," replied Caderousse, "let's have some more wine. I wish to drink to the health of Edmond and the lovely Mercédès."

"You have had too much already, drunkard," said Danglars; "and if you continue, you will be compelled to sleep here, because unable to stand on your legs."

"I ?" said Caderousse, rising with all the fatuous dignity of a drunken man, "I can't keep on my legs! Why, I'll bet a wager I go up into the belfry of the Accoules, and without staggering, too!"

"Well, done!" said Danglars, "I'll take your bet; but to-morrow — to-day it is time to return. Give me your arm, and let us go."

"Very well, let us go," said Caderousse; "but I don't want your arm at all. Come, Fernand, won't you return to Marseilles with us?"

"No," said Fernand; "I shall return to the Catalans."

"You're wrong. Come with us to Marseilles — come along."

"I have nothing to do at Marseilles, I don't want to go there."

"What do you mean? you will not? Well, just as you like, my prince; there's liberty for all the world. Come along, Danglars, and let the young gentleman return to the Catalans if he chooses."

Danglars took advantage of Caderousse's temper at the moment, to take him off toward Marseilles, only to give Fernand a shorter and easier road. In place of returning by the quay of the Réve Neuve, he returned by the Porte Saint Victor.

Caderousse followed, staggering, and holding on by his arm.

When they had advanced about twenty yards, Danglars looked back and saw Fernand stoop, pick up the crumpled paper, and, putting it into his pocket, then rush out of the arbor toward Pillon.

"Well," said Caderousse, "why, what a lie he told! He said he was going to the Catalans, and he is going to the city. Halloo, Fernand! You are coming, my boy!"

"Oh, it is you who see wrong," said Danglars; "he's gone right by the road to the Vieilles Infirmeries."

"Well," said Caderousse, "I should have sworn that he turned to the right — how treacherous wine is!"

"Come, come," said Danglars to himself, "now the thing is well started, and there is nothing to be done but let it go on by itself."

CHAPTER V

THE next day was a beautiful one. The morning sun rose clear and resplendent, and his first rays of red and purple studded with their rubies the foamy crest of the waves.

The plenteous feast had been prepared on the first floor of La Réserve, with whose arbor the reader is already familiar. The apartment destined for the purpose was spacious, and lighted by five or six windows, over each of which was written in golden letters—explain the phenomenon if you can—the name of one of the principal cities of France; beneath these windows a wooden balcony extended the entire length of the house.

And although the entertainment was fixed for twelve o'clock at noon, an hour previous to that time the balcony was filled with impatient and expectant guests, consisting of the favored part of the crew of the *Pharaon*, and some soldier friends of Dantès, the whole of whom had arrayed themselves in their choicest costumes, in order to do greater honor to the day.

Various rumors were afloat among the guests to the effect that the owners of the *Pharaon* had promised to attend the nuptial feast of its mate, but all seemed unanimous in doubting that an act of such rare and exceeding condescension could possibly be intended.

Danglars, however, who now made his appearance, accompanied by Caderousse, effectually confirmed the report, stating that he had recently conversed with M. Morrel, who had himself assured him he intended joining the festive party at La Réserve.

A moment afterward an enthusiastic burst of applause from the crew of the *Pharaon* announced the presence of M. Morrel. The visit of the shipowner was to them as a sure indication that the man whose wedding-feast he thus delighted to honor would ere long be first in command of the *Pharaon;* and as Dantès was universally beloved on board his vessel, the sailors put no restraint on the tumultuous joy at finding the opinion and choice of the owner so exactly coincide with their own.

This noisy though hearty welcome over, Danglars and Caderousse were dispatched to the residence of the bridegroom to convey to him the intelligence of the arrival of the important personage who had caused such a sensation, and to desire he would hasten.

Danglars and Caderousse started off upon their errand at full speed; but ere they had gone many steps they perceived at the powder magazine the little troop advancing toward them. This little troop was composed of a party of young girls in attendance on the bride, who leaned on the arm of Dantès. By her side walked Dantès' father; last, came Fernand, with his evil smile.

Neither Mercédès nor Edmond observed this evil smile. Happy in their innocent love, they saw only themselves and the clear, pure sky that blessed them.

Having acquitted themselves of their errand, and exchanged a hearty shake of the hand with Edmond, Danglars and Caderousse took their places beside Fernand and old Dantès,— the latter of whom attracted universal notice.

The old man was attired in a suit of black, trimmed with steel buttons beautifully cut and polished. His thin but still powerful legs were arrayed in a pair of richly embroidered clocked stockings, evidently of English manufacture, and smuggled, while from his three-cornered hat depended a long streaming knot of white and blue ribbons. Thus he came along, supporting himself on a stick, twisted its whole length like the ancient *pedum.* He might have been one of those *mascadins* who, in 1796, promenaded in the newly reopened gardens of the Luxemborg and Tuileries.

Beside him crept Caderousse, whose desire to partake of the good things provided for the wedding party had induced him to become reconciled to the Dantès, father and son, although there still lingered in his mind a faint and imperfect recollection of the events of the preceding night; just as the brain retains on waking the dim and misty outline of the dream that has "murdered sleep."

As Danglars approached the disappointed lover, he cast on him a look of deep meaning, while Fernand, as he slowly paced behind the happy pair, completely forgotten by the bride, who, with the juvenile and charming egotism of love, had eyes only for her Edmond, was pale, with occasional deep flushes that disappeared only to give place to her ever-increasing pallor. From time to time he looked toward Marseilles,

BY HER SIDE WALKED DANTÈS' FATHER.

and then a nervous, involuntary trembling made him quiver. Fernand seemed to expect, or at least anticipate, some great event.

Dantès himself was simply, though becomingly, clad in the dress peculiar to the merchant service — a costume somewhat between a uniform and a civil garb; and his fine countenance, radiant with joy and happiness, was in keeping with this garb.

Lovely as the Greeks of Cyprus or Ceos, Mercédès boasted the same eyes of jet and coral lips, while she walked with that free, frank step that distinguishes the women of Arles and Andalusia. One more practiced in the arts of great cities would have hid her joy beneath a veil, or, at least, beneath her thickly-fringed lashes; but Mercédès, on the contrary, smiled and looked at those around her. Her look and her smile said, as plainly as words could have done, "If you are my friends, rejoice with me, for, in truth, I am very happy."

As soon as the bridal *cortége* came in sight of La Réserve, M. Morrel came forth to meet it, followed by the soldiers and sailors there assembled, to whom he had repeated the promise already given, that Dantès should be the successor to the late Captain Leclere. Edmond, at the approach of his patron, respectfully placed the arm of his affianced bride within that of M. Morrel, who, forthwith conducting her up the flight of wooden steps leading to the chamber in which the feast was prepared, was gayly followed by the guests, beneath whose thronging numbers the slight structure creaked and groaned as though alarmed at the unusual pressure.

"Father," said Mercédès, stopping when she had reached the center of the table, "sit, I pray you, on my right hand; on my left I will place him who has ever been as a brother to me," pointing with a sweetness that struck Fernand to his inmost heart like the blow of a dagger. His lips became ghastly pale, and even beneath the dark hue of his complexion the blood might be seen retreating as though driven back to the heart.

During this time, Dantès, at the opposite side of the table, had been occupied in similarly placing his most honored guests. M. Morrel was seated at his right hand, Danglars at his left; while, at a sign from Edmond, the rest of the company ranged themselves as they found it most agreeable.

Already there passed round the table sausages of Arles, with their brown meat and piquant flavor; lobsters in their dazzling red cuirasses; prawns of brilliant color, the sea-urchins looking like chestnut-burrs, with their prickly outside; the clams, esteemed by the epicures of the south as more than rivaling the exquisite flavor of the oyster, north. All these, in conjunction with the numerous delicacies cast up by the wash of waters on the sandy beach, and styled by the grateful fishermen "sea fruits," served to furnish forth this marriage table.

"A pretty silence, truly!" said the old father of the bridegroom, as he carried to his lips a glass of wine of the hue of the topaz, and which had just been placed before Mercédès by Father Pamphile himself. "Now, would anybody think that this room contained thirty people who desire nothing better than to laugh?"

"Ah!" sighed Caderousse, "a man cannot always feel happy because he is about to be married."

"The truth is," replied Dantès, "that I am too happy for noisy mirth; if that is what you meant by your observation, my worthy friend, you are right; joy takes a strange effect at times: it oppresses like sorrow."

Danglars looked toward Edmond, whose impressionable nature received and betrayed each fresh emotion.

"Why, what ails you?" said he. "Do you fear any approaching evil? I should say that you were the happiest man alive at this instant."

"And that is the very thing that alarms me," returned Dantès. "Man does not appear to me to be intended to enjoy felicity so unmixed; happiness is like the palaces of the enchanted isles, where dragons guard the doors. We must fight to win it. I do not know how I have deserved the honor of being the husband of Mercédès."

"Husband, husband," cried Caderousse, laughing, "not yet, captain. Just try to play the husband, and see how you are received."

The bride blushed. Fernand, restless and uneasy, started at every sound, occasionally wiping away the large drops of perspiration that gathered on his brow like the first rain-drops of a storm.

"Well, never mind that, neighbor Caderousse," said Dantès; "it is not worth while to contradict me for such a trifle as that. 'Tis true that Mercédès is not actually my wife; but," added he, drawing out his watch, "in an hour and a half from this she will be."

A general exclamation of surprise ran round the table, with the exception of the elder Dantès, whose laugh displayed the still perfect beauty of his large white teeth. Mercédès looked pleased without a blush, while Fernand grasped the handle of his knife with a convulsive clutch.

"In an hour?" inquired Danglars, turning pale. "How is that, my friend?"

"Why, thus it is," replied Dantès. "Thanks to the influence of M. Morrel, to whom, next to my father, I owe every blessing I enjoy, every difficulty has been removed. We have got the license, and at half-past two o'clock the Mayor of Marseilles will be waiting at the Hôtel de Ville. Now, as a quarter-past one has already struck, I do not consider

I have asserted too much in saying, that in another hour and thirty minutes Mercédès will be called Madame Dantès."

Fernand closed his eyes, a cloud of flame scorched his eyelids, and he leaned on the table to prevent his falling; but, in spite of all his

efforts, he could not refrain from uttering a deep groan, which, however, was lost amid the noisy felicitations of the company.

"Upon my word," cried the old man, "you make short work of this kind of affairs. Arrived here only yesterday morning, and married to-day at three o'clock! Commend me to a sailor for going the quick way to work!"

"But," asked Danglars, in a timid tone, "how did you manage about the other formalities — the contract — the settlement?"

"Oh, bless you," answered Dantès, laughingly, "our papers were soon drawn up. Mercédès has nothing, nor have I. We settle our property in common. So, you see, our papers were quickly written out, and certainly do not come very expensive."

This joke elicited a fresh burst of applause.

" So that what we presumed to be merely the betrothal feast turns out to be the actual wedding dinner!" said Danglars.

"No, no!" answered Dantès; "you'll lose nothing. Take it easy. To-morrow morning I start for Paris: four days to go, and four days to return, with one day to discharge the commission intrusted to me, and I shall be back here by the first of March; the next day I give my real marriage feast."

This prospect of fresh festivity redoubled the hilarity of the guests to such a degree, that the elder Dantès, who, at the commencement of the repast, complained of the silence that prevailed, now made vain efforts, amid the general din of voices, to drink to the health and prosperity of the bride and bridegroom.

Dantès, perceiving the wish of his father, responded by a look of grateful pleasure; while Mercédès began to look at the clock, and made a slight gesture to Edmond.

Around the festive board reigned that noisy hilarity and mirthful freedom which is usually found at the termination of social meetings among those of inferior station. Such as had not been able to seat themselves according to their inclination, rose and sought other neighbors. All spoke at the same time, and yet none cared to reply to what his interlocutor said, but merely to his own thoughts.

The paleness of Fernand appeared to have communicated itself to Danglars. As for Fernand himself, he seemed one of the damned in the burning lake; he was among the first to quit the table, and, as though seeking to close his ears to the roar of songs and the clink of glasses, he continued to pace backward and forward.

Caderousse approached him just as Danglars, whom Fernand seemed most anxious to avoid, had joined him in a corner of the room.

" Upon my word," said Caderousse, from whose mind the friendly treatment of Dantès, united with the effect of the excellent wine of Father Pamphile, had effaced every feeling of envy at Dantès' good fortune,— "upon my word, Dantès is a downright good fellow, and when I see him sitting there beside his pretty wife that is so soon to be, I cannot help thinking it would have been a great pity to have served him that trick you were planning yesterday."

"Well," said Danglars, "you saw that it ended in nothing. Poor Fernand was so upset that I was sorry for him at first; but, as he has gone so far as to be his rival's best man, there is nothing more to say."

Caderousse looked full at Fernand — he was ghastly pale.

"Certainly," continued Danglars, "the sacrifice was no trifling one when the beauty of the bride is concerned. Upon my soul, that future captain of mine is a lucky dog! Gad! I only wish he would let me take his place."

"Shall we not set forth?" asked the sweet, silvery voice of Mercédès; "two o'clock has just struck, and you know we are expected at the Hôtel de Ville in a quarter of an hour."

"Yes! yes!" cried Dantès, eagerly quitting the table; "let us go"

"Let us go," said the whole party in chorus.

At this moment Danglars, who had been incessantly observing Fernand, perceived him open his haggard eyes, rise with an almost convulsive spasm, and fall back against a seat placed near one of the open windows. At the same instant the ear caught an indistinct sound on the stairs, a measured tread, a confused murmur of voices, mixed with the clanking of arms, deadening even the mirth of the party, and attracting general curiosity, which displayed itself almost instantaneously by a restless stillness.

Nearer and nearer came the sounds.   Three knocks, against the door, resounded.   Each looked inquiringly in the countenance of his neighbor.

" In the name of the law! " said a harsh voice, to which no voice replied.

The door was opened, and a magistrate, wearing his official scarf, presented himself, followed by four soldiers and a corporal.

Uneasiness now yielded to dread.

" May I venture to inquire the reason of this unexpected visit ? " said M. Morrel, addressing the magistrate, whom he knew ; " there is doubtless some mistake."

" If it be so," replied the magistrate, " rely upon every reparation being made ; meanwhile, I am the bearer of an order of arrest, and although I most reluctantly perform the task assigned me, it must, nevertheless, be fulfilled.   Who among the persons here assembled answers to the name of Edmond Dantès ? "

Every eye was turned toward the individual so described, who, spite of agitation, advanced with dignity, and said :

" I am he ; what is your pleasure with me ? "

" Edmond Dantès," replied the magistrate, " I arrest you in the name of the law ! "

" Me ! " repeated Edmond, slightly changing color, " and wherefore, I pray ? "

" I cannot inform you, but you will be duly acquainted with the reasons that have rendered such a step necessary at your first examination."

M. Morrel felt that further resistance was useless.   An officer, girt with his scarf, is no longer a man ; he is the statue of law, cold, deaf, and dumb.

Old Dantès, on the other hand, rushed toward the officer. There are things which the heart of a father or mother can never comprehend. He prayed and supplicated, but tears and prayers were useless.   Still his despair was so deep that the officer was touched.   " My worthy friend," said he, " let me beg of you to calm yourself.   Your son has probably neglected some prescribed form in registering his cargo, and it is more than probable he will be set at liberty directly he has given the information required."

"What is the meaning of all this?" inquired Caderousse, frowningly, of Danglars, who had assumed an air of utter surprise.

"How can I tell you?" replied he; "I am, like yourself, utterly bewildered at all that is going on, not a word of which do I understand."

Caderousse then looked around for Fernand, but he had disappeared.

The scene of the previous night now came back to his mind with startling accuracy. The painful catastrophe appeared to have rent away the veil which the intoxication of the evening before had raised between himself and his memory.

"So! so!" said he, in a hoarse voice, to Danglars, "this, then, I suppose, is a part of the trick you were concerting yesterday? All I can say is, that if it be so, woe to him who has done it, for it is a foul one!"

"Nonsense!" returned Danglars. "You know very well that I tore the paper to pieces."

"No, you did not!" answered Caderousse, "you threw it in a corner. There's the whole matter."

"Hold your tongue, you fool!—what should you know about it?—why, you were drunk!"

"Where is Fernand?" inquired Caderousse.

"How do I know?" replied Danglars; "after his own affairs, most likely. Never mind where he is; let us try and help our poor friends in this their affliction."

During this conversation, Dantès, after having exchanged a shake of the hand with all his friends, had surrendered himself, merely saying, with a smile, "Make yourselves quite easy, there is some little mistake to clear up, and very likely I may not have to go so far as the prison."

"Oh, to be sure!" responded Danglars, who had now approached the group, "nothing more than a mistake."

Dantès descended the staircase, preceded by the principal officer of police, and followed by the soldiers. A carriage awaited him at the door; he got in, followed by two soldiers and the officer; the door was shut, and the vehicle drove off toward Marseilles.

"Adieu! adieu! dearest Edmond!" cried Mercédès, leaning forward from the balcony.

The prisoner heard her cry, as it were a sob from the lacerated heart of his beloved, thrust his head out of the carriage window and cried, "Good-bye—we shall soon meet again!" and disappeared round one of the turnings of Fort Saint Nicolas.

"Wait for me here!" cried M. Morrel; I will take the first conveyance I find, and hurry to Marseilles, whence I will bring you word how all is going on."

"Go!" exclaimed a multitude of voices; "go, and return as quickly as you can!"

This second departure was followed by a long and fearful state of terrified silence on the part of those who were left behind.

The old father and Mercédès remained for some time apart, each

THE ARREST OF EDMOND DANTÈS.

absorbed in their separate griefs; but at length the two poor victims of the same blow raised their eyes, and with a simultaneous burst of feeling rushed into each other's arms.

Meanwhile Fernand made his reappearance, poured out for himself a glass of water, which he drank, and went to sit down on a chair.

This was, by mere chance, placed next to the seat on which poor Mercédès had fallen when released from the embrace of old Dantès.

Instinctively, Fernand drew back his chair.

"He has done it," whispered Caderousse, who had never taken his eyes off Fernand, to Danglars.

"I do not think so," answered the other; "he is too stupid. In any case, let the mischief fall upon the head of whoever wrought it."

"You don't mention him who advised it," said Caderousse.

"Pooh!" replied Danglars; "who can be responsible for every random word?"

"But if the random word hits the mark?"

Meantime the subject of the arrest was being canvassed in every different form.

"What think you, Danglars," said one of the party, "of the affair?"

"Why," replied he, "I think he may have brought in some smuggled goods."

"But how could he have done so without your knowledge, Danglars, who were the ship's supercargo?"

"Why, as for that, I could only know what I was told respecting the merchandise. I know she was loaded with cotton, and that she took in her freight at Alexandria from the magazine of M. Pastret, and at Smyrna from M. Pascal's. Don't ask me anything more."

"Now I recollect!" said the afflicted old father; "my poor boy told me yesterday he had got a small case of coffee, and another of tobacco for me!"

"There, you see!" exclaimed Danglars. The custom-house people have been to the ship in our absence, and discovered poor Dantès' hidden treasures."

Mercédès, however, did not believe a word of this. Her grief, hitherto restrained, now burst out in sobs.

"Come, come — hope!" said the old man, hardly knowing what he said.

"Hope!" repeated Danglars.

"Hope!" faintly murmured Fernand; but the word choked him, his lips quivered, and no sound escaped them.

"Good news!" shouted forth one of the party stationed in the balcony on the look-out. "Here comes M. Morrel back. No doubt, now, he brings us good news."

Mercédès and the old man rushed to meet him at the door. He was deadly pale.

"What news?" exclaimed a general burst of voices.

"Alas! my friends," replied M. Morrel, with a shake of his head, "the thing has assumed a more serious aspect than I expected."

"Oh! indeed—indeed, sir, he is innocent!" sobbed forth Mercédès.

"That I believe!" answered M. Morrel; "but still he is charged——"

"With what?" inquired the elder Dantès.

"With being a Bonapartist agent!" Many of my readers may be able to recollect how formidable such an accusation became in the period at which our story is dated.

A cry escaped the lips of Mercédès, while the old father fell into a chair.

"Ah, Danglars!" whispered Caderousse, "you have deceived me— the trick has been played; but I cannot suffer a poor old man or an innocent girl to die of grief. I will tell them all."

"Be silent, you simpleton!" cried Danglars, grasping him by the arm, "or I will not answer even for your own safety. Who can tell whether Dantès be innocent or guilty? The vessel did touch at Elba, where he quitted it, and passed a whole day at Porto-Ferrajo. Now, should any letters of a compromising character be found upon him, will it not be taken for granted that all who uphold him are his accomplices?"

With the rapid instinct of selfishness, Caderousse readily perceived the solidity of this mode of reasoning; he gazed with eyes of grief and terror on Danglars, and then for every step forward he had taken, he took two back.

"Let us, then, wait!" said he.

"To be sure!" answered Danglars. "Let us wait, by all means. If he be innocent, of course he will be set at liberty; if guilty, why, it is no use involving ourselves in his conspiracy."

"Then let us go hence. I cannot stay longer here."

"With all my heart!" replied Danglars, but too pleased to find a partner in his retreat. "Come, let us leave them to get out of it as they best can."

After their departure, Fernand, who had now again become the support of Mercédès, led the girl back to the Catalans, while some friends of Dantès conducted his father, nearly lifeless, to the Allées de Meilhan.

The rumor of Edmond's arrest as a Bonapartist agent was not slow in circulating throughout the city.

"Could you ever have credited such a thing, my dear Danglars?" asked M. Morrel, as he overtook his supercargo and Caderousse, on his return to the port for the purpose of gleaning fresh tidings of Dantès from the deputy Procureur du Roi, M. de Villefort, whom he knew slightly. "Could you have believed such a thing possible?"

"Why, you know I told you," replied Danglars, "that I considered

the circumstance of his having anchored in the isle of Elba as a very suspicious circumstance."

"And did you mention these suspicions to any person beside myself?"

"Certainly not!" returned Danglars; then added, in a low whisper,

"You understand that, on account of your uncle M. Policar Morrel, who served under the *other*, and who does not conceal what he thinks, you are suspected of regretting Napoleon. I should have feared to injure both Edmond and yourself, had I divulged my own apprehensions to a soul. There are things which a subordinate is bound to acquaint the shipowner with, and to conceal from all else."

"Yes! yes! Danglars," replied M. Morrel. "You are a worthy fellow; and I had already thought of you in the event of poor Edmond having become captain of the *Pharaon*."

"How so?"

"Yes, indeed; I previously inquired of Dantès what was his opinion of you, and if he should have any reluctance to continue you in your post, for somehow I had perceived a sort of coolness between you two."

"And what was his reply?"

"That he certainly did think he had given you offense in an affair which he did not speak about, but that whoever possessed the confidence of the ship's owners would have his also."

"The hypocrite!" murmured Danglars between his teeth.

"Poor Dantès!" said Caderousse. "No one can deny his being a noble-hearted young fellow!"

"But, meanwhile," continued M. Morrel, "the *Pharaon* has no captain."

"Oh!" replied Danglars, "since we cannot leave this port for the next three months, let us hope that by that period Dantès will be set at liberty."

"No doubt; but in the mean time what are we to do?"

"I am entirely at your service, M. Morrel," answered Danglars. "You know that I am as capable of managing a ship as the most experienced captain in the service; and it will be so far advantageous to you to accept my services, that upon Edmond's release from prison there will be no one to dismiss. Dantès and myself each will resume our respective posts."

"Thanks, Danglars — that will smooth all difficulties. Assume the command of the *Pharaon*, and look carefully to the unloading. Private misfortunes must never induce us to neglect business."

"All right, M. Morrel; but when shall we be allowed to see him, at least, poor Edmond."

"I will let you know that directly I have seen M. de Villefort, whom I shall endeavor to interest in Edmond's favor. I am aware he is a furious royalist; but, in spite of that, and of his being the king's procureur, he is a man, and I fancy not a bad one!"

"Perhaps not," replied Danglars; "but he is said to be ambitious, and that is much the same."

"Well, well!" returned M. Morrel, "we shall see! But now hasten on board; I will join you there ere long."

So saying, the shipowner quitted the two allies, and proceeded in the direction of the Palais de Justice.

"You see," said Danglars, addressing Caderousse, "the turn things have taken. Do you still feel any desire to stand up in his defense?"

"Not the slightest, but yet it is a shocking thing a joke should lead to such consequences."

"But who perpetrated that joke? let me ask; neither you nor myself, but Fernand: you know very well that I threw the paper into a corner of the room,—indeed, I fancied I had destroyed it."

"Oh, no!" replied Caderousse, "that I can answer for, you did not. I only wish I could see it now as plainly as I saw it lying all crushed and crumpled in a corner of the arbor."

"Well, then, if you did, depend upon it, Fernand picked it up, and either copied it or caused it to be copied; perhaps, even, he did not take the trouble of recopying it. And now I think of it, by Heavens! he may have sent the letter itself! Fortunately, for me, the handwriting was disguised."

"Then you were aware of Dantès being engaged in a conspiracy?"

"Not a bit in the world! As I before said, I thought the whole thing was a joke, nothing more. It seems, however, that, like Harlequin, I have unconsciously stumbled upon the truth."

"All the same," argued Caderousse, "I would give a great deal if nothing of the kind had happened; or, at least, that I had had no hand in it. You will see, Danglars, that it will turn out an unlucky job for both."

"Nonsense! If any harm comes of it, it should fall on the guilty person; and that, you know, is Fernand. How can harm come to us? All we have got to do is, to keep quiet, not breathing a word to any living soul; and you will see that the storm will pass away without the thunder-bolt striking."

"Amen!" responded Caderousse, waving adieu to Danglars, and bending his steps toward the Allées de Meilhan, moving his head to and fro, and muttering as he went, after the manner of one thoroughly preoccupied.

"So far, then," said Danglars, "all has gone as I would have it. I am, temporarily, commander of the *Pharaon*, with the certainty of being permanently so, if that fool of a Caderousse can be persuaded to hold his tongue. My only fear is the chance of Dantès being released. But, bah!" added he, with a smile, "Justice is justice; I'll leave it to her."

So saying, he leaped into a boat, desiring to be rowed on board the *Pharaon*, where M. Morrel, it will be remembered, had appointed to meet him.

CHAPTER VI

N one of those old aristocratical mansions, built by Puget, situated in the Rue du Grand Cours opposite the fountain of Medusa, a second marriage feast was being celebrated, on the same day and at the same hour; only, while the actors in one scene were plain people, sailors and soldiers, in the other they belonged to the heads of Marseillaise society,—magistrates who had resigned their office during the usurper's reign ; officers who had deserted our ranks to join the army of Condé; youths who had been brought up by their family, hardly yet assured of their existence, in spite of the substitutes they had paid for, to hate and execrate the man whom five years of exile ought to have converted into a martyr, and fifteen of restoration elevated to a demi-god.

The guests were at table, and the conversation was animated and heated with all the passions of the epoch — passions more terrible, active, and bitter in the south, because for five years religious hatreds had reënforced political hatreds.

The emperor, now king of the petty isle of Elba, after having held sovereign sway over one half of the world, counting us, his subjects, a population of five or six thousand,— after having been accustomed to hear the *Vive Napoléons* of one hundred and twenty millions uttered in ten different languages,—was looked upon as a man ruined forever for France and the throne.

The magistrates talked of political blunders; the military talked of Moscow and Leipsic, and the women of his divorce from Josephine. It seemed to this royalist world, joyous and triumphant, less at the fall of the man than at the annihilation of the principles he represented, as if life were again beginning after a peaceful dream.

An old man, decorated with the cross of Saint Louis, now rose and proposed the health of King Louis XVIII. He was the Marquis de Saint-Méran. This toast, recalling at once the patient exile of Hartwell and the king and pacificator of France, excited great applause; glasses were elevated in the air *à l'Anglaise*, and the ladies, detaching their bouquets, strewed the table with them. In a word, poetical enthusiasm prevailed.

"Ah! they would own, were they here," said the Marquise de Saint-Méran, a woman with a hard eye, thin lips, and aristocratic mien, though still elegant-looking, despite her fifty years—"ah! these revolutionists, who drove us out, and whom we leave now in our turn to conspire at their ease in the old chateaux which they purchased for a mere trifle during the Reign of Terror, would be compelled to own, were they here, that all true devotion was on our side, since we attached ourselves to a falling monarch, while they, on the contrary, worshiped the rising sun, and made their fortunes while we lost ours. Yes, yes, they could not help admitting that the king, our king, was in truth 'Louis the well-beloved,' while their emperor was never anything but 'Napoleon the accursed.' Am I not right, Villefort?"

"I beg your pardon, madame, but—in truth—I was not attending to the conversation."

"Marquise, marquise!" interposed the same elderly personage who had proposed the toast, "let the young people alone; on their wedding day they naturally have to speak of something else than politics."

"Pardon me, dearest mother," said a young and lovely girl, with a profusion of light brown hair, and eyes that seemed to float in liquid crystal, "I yield to you M. de Villefort, whom I had seized for a moment. M. Villefort, my mother speaks to you."

"If Madame la Marquise will deign to repeat the words I but imperfectly caught, I shall be delighted to answer," said M. de Villefort.

"Never mind, Renée," replied the marquise, with such a look of tenderness as all were astonished to see on her harsh features; for a woman's heart is so constituted that, however withered it be by the blasts of prejudice and etiquette, there is always one spot fertile and smiling, the spot consecrated by God to maternal love. "I forgive you. What I was saying, Villefort, was, that the Bonapartists had neither our sincerity, enthusiasm, nor devotion."

"They had, however, what supplied the place of those fine qualities," replied the young man, "and that was fanaticism. Napoleon is the Mahomet of the West, and is worshiped by his commonplace but ambitious followers, not only as a leader and lawgiver, but also as a type, as the personification of equality."

"Of equality!" cried the marquise, "Napoleon the type of equality!

For mercy's sake, then, what would you call M. de Robespierre? It seems to me that you rob him of his place and give it to the Corsican."

"Nay, madame; I would place each on his right pedestal—that of Robespierre on his scaffold in the Place Louis; that of Napoleon on

M. de Villefort.

the column of the Place Vendôme; only the one made the equality that elevates, the other the equality that depresses; the one brings a king to the level of the guillotine, the other the people to a level with the throne. Observe," said Villefort, smiling, "I do not mean to deny that both were revolutionary scoundrels, and that the 9th Thermidor and the 4th of April, 1814, were lucky days for France, worthy of being equally remembered by every friend to monarchy and order; and that explains how, fallen as I trust he is forever, Napoleon has still preserved a train of fanatical adherents. Still, marquise, it has been so with other usurpers: Cromwell, who was not half of a Napoleon, had his."

"Do you know, Villefort, that you are talking in a revolutionary strain? But I excuse it; it is impossible to be the son of a Girondin and be free from a spice of the old leaven."

A deep crimson suffused the countenance of Villefort.

"'Tis true, madame," answered he, "that my father was a Girondin, but he did not vote for the king's death; he was an equal sufferer with yourself during the Reign of Terror, and had well-nigh lost his head on the same scaffold as your own father."

"True," replied the marquise, without the tragical remembrance producing the slightest change in her features; "only our respective parents underwent proscription from diametrically opposite principles; in proof of which I may remark, that while my family remained adherents of the exiled princes, your father lost no time in joining the new government; and that after the Citizen Noirtier had been a Girondin, the Count Noirtier became a senator."

"Dear mother," interposed Renée, "you know very well it was agreed that all these disagreeable reminiscences should be spoken of no more."

"Suffer me, also, madame," rejoined Villefort, "to add my earnest request that you will kindly forget the past. What avails recrimination touching circumstances before which even the will of God himself is powerless? God can change the future; he cannot modify the past. What we human beings can do is not to deny, but to cast a veil over it. For my own part, I have laid aside the name of my father, as well as his principles. He was — nay, probably may still be — a Bonapartist, and is called Noirtier; I, on the contrary, am a royalist, and style myself de Villefort. Let what may remain of revolutionary sap die away with the old trunk, and only regard the young shoot which has started up from this trunk, without having the power, any more than the wish, to separate itself entirely."

"Bravo, Villefort!" cried the marquis; "excellently well said! I, too, have always preached to the marquise oblivion of the past without ever obtaining it. You, I hope, will be more fortunate."

"With all my heart," replied the marquise; "let the past be forever forgotten! I ask no more. All I ask is, that Villefort will be inflexible for the future. Remember, also, Villefort, that we have pledged ourselves to his majesty for you, and that at our recommendation the king consented to forget it" (and here she extended to him her hand), "as I now do at your entreaty. Only, if there fall in your way some conspirator, remember that there are so many more eyes on you, as it is known you belong to a family which, perhaps, is in sympathy with these conspirators."

The Marquise de Saint-Méran.

"Alas! madame," returned Villefort, "my profession, as well as the times in which we live, compel me to be severe. I shall be so. I have already successfully conducted several public prosecutions, and proved my faith. But we have not done with the thing yet."

" Do you, indeed, think so ?" inquired the marquise.

" I am, at least, fearful of it. Napoleon, in the island of Elba, is too near France, and his presence, almost in sight of our coasts, keeps up the hopes of his partisans. Marseilles is filled with half-pay officers, who are daily, under one frivolous pretext or other, getting up quarrels with the royalists; hence duels among the higher classes, and assassinations in the lower."

" You have heard, perhaps," said the Count de Salvieux, one of M. de Saint-Méran's oldest friends, and chamberlain to the Count d'Artois, " that the Holy Alliance purpose removing him from thence ?"

" Ah !" they were talking about it when we left Paris," said M. de Saint-Méran; " and where is it decided to transfer him ?"

" To Saint Helena."

" Saint Helena! where is that ?" asked the marquise.

" An island situated on the other side of the equator, at least two thousand leagues from hence," replied the count.

" So much the better! As Villefort observes, it is a great act of folly to have left such a man between Corsica, where he was born, Naples, of which his brother-in-law is king, and Italy, the sovereignty of which he coveted for his son."

" Unfortunately," said Villefort, " there are the treaties of 1814, and without violating them Napoleon cannot be touched."

" They will be violated," said the Count de Salvieux. " Did he regard treaty-clauses when he shot the hapless Duc d'Enghien ?"

" Well," said the marquise, " the Holy Alliance will free Europe of Napoleon, and, M. de Villefort, Marseilles of his partisans. The king either reigns or does not. If he reigns, his government must be strong, and his agents inflexible. This is the way to prevent mischief."

" Unfortunately, madame," answered Villefort, a deputy Procureur du Roi only appears when the mischief is done."

" Then all he has got to do is to endeavor to repair it."

" Nay, madame, we cannot repair it; we can only avenge the wrong done."

" Oh! M. de Villefort," cried a beautiful young creature, daughter to Count Salvieux, and the cherished friend of Mademoiselle de Saint-Méran, " do try and get up some famous trial while we are at Marseilles. I never was in a law-court; I am told it is so very amusing !"

" Amusing, certainly," replied Villefort, " for, in place of a fictitious tragedy, you have a real drama; in place of theatrical woes, real woes; the man whom you see there, instead of going home when the curtain falls, and supping with his family, and sleeping peacefully to begin again another day, goes back to prison, where he finds the executioner.

You will see that for nervous persons who seek emotions no spectacle can be more attractive. Be assured, mademoiselle, if the circumstance presents itself, I will give you an opportunity."

" He makes us shudder — and he smiles!" said Renée, becoming quite pale.

" Why, it is a duel. I have already recorded sentence of death, five or six times, against political criminals, and who can say how many daggers may be now sharpening or already directed against me ? "

" Gracious heavens! M. de Villefort," said Renée, becoming more and more terrified; " you surely are not in earnest!"

" Indeed I am," replied the young magistrate with a smile; " and in the interesting trial that young lady desires, to satisfy her curiosity, and I to satisfy my ambition, the case would only be still more aggravated. All these soldiers of Napoleon, accustomed to charge the enemy blindly, what did they think about burning a cartridge or rushing on a bayonet? Will they think a bit more about killing a man whom they believe their personal enemy, than about killing a Russian, Austrian, or Hungarian whom they have never seen ? It is this — it is this which justifies our profession ! I, myself, when I see the eye of the accused gleaming with the flash of rage, I feel myself encouraged and elevated. It is no longer a trial, it is a combat; I thrust at him, he lunges back; I thrust again, and all is ended, as in all combats, by a victory or a defeat! This is what I call pleading ! This is the power of eloquence ! A prisoner who smiled at me after my reply would make me believe that I had spoken badly — that my address was colorless, feeble, insufficient. Think, then, of the sensation of pride which is felt by a prosecutor, convinced of the guilt of the accused, when he sees the prisoner blanch and crouch beneath the weight of his proofs and the thunders of his eloquence! That head drops; that head will fall!"

Renée uttered a low cry.

" Bravo!" cried one of the guests; " that is what I call talking."

" Just the person we require at a time like the present," said a second.

" What a splendid business that last cause of yours was, my dear Villefort!" remarked a third; " I mean the trial of the man for murdering his father. Upon my word, you killed him ere the executioner had laid his hand upon him."

" Oh! as for parricides," interposed Renée, " it matters very little what is done to them; but, as regards poor political criminals ——"

" But it is still worse, Renée, as the king is father of his people, to wish to overthrow or kill the father of thirty-two millions of souls."

" I don't know anything about that," replied Renée; " but, M. de Villefort, you promise to show mercy to those I plead for ? "

" Make yourself quite easy on that point," answered Villefort, with one of his sweetest smiles; " you and I will always consult upon our verdicts."

" My love," said the marquise, "attend to your humming-birds, your lap-dogs, and embroidery; let your husband mind his business. Nowadays the military profession has rest; the long robe is in credit. There is a Latin proverb about it, very profound."

Cedant arma togæ, said Villefort, with a bow.

" I would not dare to speak Latin," replied the marquise.

" Well," said Renée, " I cannot help regretting you were not a physician. Do you know I always felt a shudder at the idea of even a *destroying* angel, angel though he be ?"

" Dear, good, Renée !" whispered Villefort, as he gazed with tenderness on the speaker.

" Let us hope, my child," cried the marquis, " that M. de Villefort may prove the moral and political physician of this province; if so, he will have achieved a noble work."

" And one which will go far to efface the recollection of his father's conduct," added the incorrigible marquise.

" Madame," replied Villefort, with a mournful smile, "I have already had the honor to observe that my father has — at least I hope so — abjured his past errors, and that he is, at the present moment, a firm and zealous friend to religion and order — a better royalist, possibly, than his son; for he is one, with repentance; I, only with passion."

Having made this well-turned speech, Villefort looked carefully round to mark the effect of his oratory, much as he would have done in the court after a like phrase.

" Do you know, my dear Villefort," cried the Count de Salvieux, " that is as nearly as possible what I myself said the other day at the Tuileries, when questioned by his majesty's principal chamberlain touching the singularity of an alliance between the son of a Girondin and the daughter of an officer of the Duke de Condé. He understood it thoroughly. This system of fusion is that of Louis XVIII. Then the king, who, without our suspecting it, had overheard our conversation, interrupted us by saying, ' Villefort,' — observe that the king did not pronounce the word Noirtier, but, on the contrary, placed considerable emphasis on that of Villefort — ' Villefort,' said his majesty, ' is a young man of discretion, who will make a figure; I like him much, and it gave me great pleasure to hear that he was about to become the son-in-law of M. le Marquis and Madame la Marquise de Saint-Méran. I should myself have recommended the match, had not the noble marquis anticipated my wishes by requesting my consent to it.' "

" The king said that, Count ?" asked the enraptured Villefort.

"I give you his very words; and if the marquis chooses to be candid, he will confess that they perfectly agree with what his majesty said to him, when he went, six months ago, to consult him upon the subject of your espousing his daughter."

Renée de Saint-Méran.

" Certainly," answered the marquis.

" How much do I owe this gracious prince! What would I not do to evince my gratitude!"

" That is right," cried the marquise. " I love to see you thus. Now, then, were a conspirator to fall into your hands, he would be most welcome."

" For my part, dear mother," interposed Renée, "I hope God will not hear you, and that Providence will only permit petty offenders, poor debtors, and miserable cheats to fall into M. de Villefort's hands; then I shall be contented."

"Just the same as though," said Villefort, laughing, "you prayed that a physician might only be called upon to prescribe for headaches, measles, and the stings of wasps, or any other slight affection of the epidermis. If you wish to see me the king's procureur, you must desire for me some of those violent and dangerous diseases from the cure of which so much honor redounds to the physician."

At this moment, and as though the utterance of Villefort's wish had sufficed to effect its accomplishment, a servant entered the room and whispered a few words in his ear. Villefort immediately rose from table and quitted the room upon the plea of urgent business: he soon, however, returned, his whole face beaming with delight.

Renée regarded him with fond affection; for, with his blue eyes, olive complexion, and the black whiskers which framed his face, he was truly a handsome, elegant young man, and the whole soul of the young girl seemed hanging on his lips till he explained the cause of his sudden departure.

"You were wishing just now," said Villefort, addressing her, "that I were a doctor instead of a lawyer. Well, I at least resemble the disciples of Esculapius in one thing [people spoke in this style in 1815], that of not being able to call a day my own, not even that of my betrothal."

"And wherefore were you called away just now?" asked Mademoiselle de Saint-Méran, with an air of interest.

" For a patient who is, according to the report given me, near his end. A serious case, likely to end in the scaffold."

"How dreadful!" exclaimed Renée.

"Is it possible?" burst simultaneously from all.

"Why, if my information prove correct, a sort of Bonapartist conspiracy has just been discovered."

"Can I believe my ears?" cried the marquise.

"I will read you the letter containing the accusation, at least," said Villefort:

"'The procureur du roi is informed by a friend to the throne and the religious institutions of his country, that an individual, named Edmond Dantès, second in command on board the *Pharaon*, this day arrived from Smyrna, after having touched at Naples and Porto-Ferrajo, has been the bearer of a letter from Murat to the usurper, and from the usurper to the Bonapartist Club in Paris. Proof may be obtained by arresting him, for the letter is in the possession either of him or his father, or on board the *Pharaon* in his cabin.'"

"But," said Renée, "this letter, which, after all, is but an anonymous scrawl, is not even addressed to you, but to the procureur du roi."

"True; but that gentleman being absent, his secretary, by his orders, opened his letters: thinking this one of importance, he sent for me, but,

not finding me, took upon himself to give the necessary orders for arresting the accused party."

"Then the guilty person is in custody?" said the marquise.

"Say the accused person," cried Renée.

"He is in custody," answered Villefort; "and if the letter alluded to is found, as I just said to Mademoiselle Renée, the patient is very sick."

"And where is the unfortunate being?" asked Renée.

"He is at my house."

"Come, my friend," interrupted the marquise, "do not neglect your duty to linger with us. You are the king's servant, and must go whithersoever that service calls you."

"Oh, M. de Villefort!" cried Renée, clasping her hands, "be merciful on this the day of our betrothal."

The young man passed round to the side of the table where the fair pleader sat, and, leaning over her chair, said tenderly:

"To give you pleasure," he whispered, "I promise, dear Renée, to show all the lenity in my power; but if the charges are correct, the accusation proved, we must cut short this rank growth of Bonapartism."

Renée shuddered at the word cut, for the growth in question had a head.

"Never mind that foolish girl, Villefort," said the marquise; "she will soon get over these things."

So saying, Madame de Saint-Méran extended her dry hand to Villefort, who, while kissing it, looked at Renée, saying with his eyes, "It is your hand I kiss, or would fain be kissing, at least."

"Sad auspices!" sighed Renée.

"Upon my word, child!" exclaimed the angry marquise, "your folly exceeds all bounds. I should be glad to know what connection there can possibly be between your sickly sentimentality and the affairs of the state!"

"Oh, mother!" murmured Renée.

"Pardon, marquise," said Villefort; "for this bad royalist, I promise to act conscientiously, that is, to be horribly severe."

But while he addressed these words to the old marquise, he cast a glance at his betrothed which said, "Have no fear, Renée; your love will make me merciful." Renée replied to the look by a smile, and Villefort departed with paradise in his heart.

CHAPTER VII

THE EXAMINATION

O sooner had Villefort left the saloon than he dropped the mask of gayety and assumed the grave air of a man who holds the balance of life and death in his hands. But, in spite of the mobility of his features, a mobility which he had more than once studied, as a clever actor does, before his mirror, it was on this occasion a labor for him to contract his brows and make his countenance stern and judicial. Except the recollection of the line of politics his father had adopted, and which might interfere, unless he acted with the greatest prudence, with his own career, Villefort was as happy as a man could be. Already rich, he held a high official situation, though only twenty-seven. He was about to marry a young and charming woman, whom he loved, not passionately, but discreetly, as a magistrate ought to love; and besides her personal attractions, which were very great, Mademoiselle de Saint-Méran's family possessed considerable political influence, which her parents, having no other child, would, of course, exert in his favor. The dowry of his wife amounted to thirty thousand dollars, besides the prospect of inheriting one hundred thousand more at her father's death.

At the door he met the commissary of police, who was waiting for him. The sight of this officer recalled Villefort from the third heaven to earth; he composed his face as we have before described, and said:

"I have read the letter, monsieur, and you have acted rightly in arresting this man; now inform me what you have discovered concerning him and the conspiracy."

"We know nothing as yet of the conspiracy, monsieur; all the papers found have been sealed up and placed on your bureau. The prisoner himself is named Edmond Dantès, mate on board the three-master, the

Pharaon, trading in cotton with Alexandria and Smyrna, and belonging to Morrel and Son, of Marseilles."

" Before he entered the merchant service, had he ever served in the navy ? "

" Oh, no, monsieur; he is very young."

" How old ? "

" Nineteen or twenty at the most."

At this moment, and as Villefort, following the Grand Rue, had arrived at the corner of the Rue des Conseils, a man, who seemed to have been waiting for him, approached: it was M. Morrel.

" Ah ! M. de Villefort," cried he, " I am delighted to see you. Some of your people have committed the strangest, most unheard-of mistake — they have just arrested Edmond Dantès, the mate of my ship."

" I know it, monsieur," replied Villefort, " and I am now going to examine him."

" Oh," said Morrel, carried away by his friendship, " you do not know him, and I do. He is the most estimable, the most trustworthy man, and, I will venture to say, the man who knows his business best in all the merchant service. Oh, M. de Villefort, I beseech your indulgence for him."

Villefort, as we have seen, belonged to the aristocratic party at Marseilles; Morrel to the plebeian. The first was an ultra royalist; the other suspected of Bonapartism. Villefort looked disdainfully at Morrel, and replied coldly :

" You are aware, monsieur, that a man may be estimable and trustworthy in private life and his commercial relations, and the best seaman in the merchant service, and yet be, politically speaking, a great criminal. Is it not true ? "

The magistrate laid emphasis on these words, as if he wished to apply them to the owner himself, whilst his eyes seemed to plunge into the heart of him who, whilst he interceded for another, had himself need of indulgence.

Morrel reddened, for his own conscience was not quite clear on politics; besides, what Dantès had told him of his interview with the grand-marshal, and what the emperor had said to him, embarrassed him. He replied, however, in a tone of deep interest :

" I entreat you, M. de Villefort, be just, as is your duty, and, as you always are, kind, and give him back to us soon."

This *give us* sounded revolutionary in the sub-prefect's ears.

" Ah, ah !" murmured he, " is Dantès then a member of some Carbonari society, that his protector thus employs the collective form ? He was, if I recollect, arrested in a cabaret, in company with a great many others." Then he added aloud:

" Monsieur, you may rest assured I shall perform my duty impartially, and that if he be innocent you shall not have appealed to me in vain ; should he, however, be guilty, in this present epoch, impunity would furnish a dangerous example, and I must do my duty."

As he had now arrived at the door of his own house, which adjoined the Palais de Justice, he entered with an air of majesty, after having saluted with freezing politeness the shipowner, who stood, as if petrified, on the spot where Villefort had left him.

The antechamber was full of agents of police and gendarmes, in the midst of whom, carefully watched, but calm and smiling, stood the prisoner.

Villefort traversed the antechamber, cast a side glance at Dantès, and, taking a packet which a gendarme offered him, disappeared, saying:

"Bring in the prisoner."

Rapid as had been Villefort's glance, it had served to give him an idea of the man he was about to interrogate. He had recognized intelligence in the high forehead, courage in the dark eye and bent brow, and frankness in the thick lips that showed a set of pearly teeth.

Villefort's first impression was favorable; but he had been so often warned to mistrust first impulses, especially if they were good, that he applied the maxim to the impression, forgetting the difference between the two words. He stifled, therefore, the better instincts that were rising, composed his features before the glass into a grave and menacing aspect, and sat down at his bureau.

An instant after, Dantès entered. He was pale, but calm and smiling, and, saluting his judge with easy politeness, looked round for a seat, as if he had been in the saloon of M. Morrel. It was then that he encountered, for the first time, Villefort's look,—that look peculiar to lawyers who do not wish their thoughts to be read. This look told him he was in presence of the stern figure of justice.

"Who and what are you?" demanded Villefort, turning over a pile of papers, containing information relative to the prisoner, that an agent of police had given to him on his entry, and which within an hour had become voluminous, so rapidly does the unhappy man, styled the accused, become the object of detective corruption.

"My name is·Edmond Dantès," replied the young man calmly; "I am mate of the *Pharaon*, belonging to Messrs. Morrel and Son."

"Your age?" continued Villefort.

"Nineteen," returned Dantès.

"What were you doing at the moment you were arrested?"

"I was at the festival of my marriage, monsieur," said the young man, his voice slightly tremulous, so great was the contrast between that happy moment and the painful ceremony he was now undergoing; so great was the contrast between the somber aspect of M. de Villefort and the radiant face of Mercédès.

"You were at the festival of your marriage?" said the deputy, shuddering in spite of himself.

"Yes, monsieur, I am on the point of marrying a young girl I have been attached to for three years."

Villefort, impassive as he usually was, was struck with this coincidence; and the tremulous voice of Dantès, surprised in the midst of his happiness, struck a sympathetic chord in his own bosom;—he also was on the point of being married, and he was summoned from his own happiness to destroy that of a man who, like himself, had happiness at his grasp.

"This philosophic reflection," thought he, "will make a great sensation at M. de Saint-Méran's." And he arranged mentally, whilst Dantès awaited further questions, the antithesis by which orators often create those phrases which sometimes pass for real eloquence. When this speech was arranged, Villefort turned to Dantès.

" Continue, sir," said he.

" What would you have me continue ? "

" To give all the information in your power."

" Tell me on which point you desire information, and I will tell all I know ; only," added he, with a smile, " I warn you I know very little."

" Have you served under the usurper ? "

" I was about to be incorporated in the naval forces when he fell."

" It is reported your political opinions are extreme," said Villefort, who had never heard anything of the kind, but was not sorry to make this inquiry, as if it were an accusation.

" My political opinions ! " replied Dantès. " Alas ! sir, I never had, I am almost ashamed to say, any opinions. I am hardly nineteen; I know nothing; I have no part to play. What I am and what I shall be, if I obtain the situation I desire, I shall owe to M. Morrel. Thus all my opinions — I will not say public, but private — are confined to these three sentiments : I love my father, I respect M. Morrel, and I adore Mercédès. This, sir, is all I can tell you, and you see how uninteresting it is."

As Dantès spoke, Villefort gazed at his ingenuous and open countenance, and recollected the words of Renée, who, without knowing who the culprit was, had besought his indulgence for him. With the deputy's knowledge of crime and criminals, every word the young man uttered convinced him more and more of his innocence. This lad, — for he was scarcely a man, — simple, natural, eloquent with that eloquence of the heart never found when sought for ; full of affection for everybody, because he was happy, and because happiness renders even the wicked good, extended, even to his judge, the affability which overflowed his heart. Edmond, in his looks, his tones, and his gestures, severe and harsh as Villefort had been, displayed only gentleness and respect.

" *Pardieu !* " said Villefort to himself, " he is a noble fellow ! I hope I shall gain Renée's favor easily by obeying the first command she ever imposed on me. I shall have at least a pressure of the hand in public, and a sweet kiss in private."

Full of this idea, Villefort's face became so joyous, that when he turned to Dantès, the latter, who had watched the change on his physiognomy, was smiling also.

" Sir," said Villefort, " have you any enemies, at least that you know ? "

" I have enemies ? " replied Dantès ; " my position is not sufficiently elevated for that. As for my character, that is, perhaps, somewhat too hasty ; but I have striven to repress it toward my subordinates. I have had ten or twelve sailors under me ; and if you question them, they will tell you that they love and respect me, not as a father, for I am too young, but as an elder brother."

"But, instead of enemies, you may have excited jealousy. You are about to become captain at nineteen — an elevated post in your profession; you are about to marry a pretty girl, who loves you, a happiness rare in any position; and these two pieces of good fortune may have excited the envy of some one."

"You are right; you know men better than I do, and what you say may possibly be the case, I confess; but if they are among my friends I prefer not knowing them, because then I should be forced to hate them."

"You are wrong; you should always strive to see clearly around you. You seem a worthy young man; I will depart from the strict line of my duty to aid you in throwing light on the matter, by communicating to you the information which has brought you here. Here is the paper; do you know the writing?"

As he spoke, Villefort drew the letter from his pocket, and presented it to Dantès. Dantès read it. A cloud passed over his brow as he said:

"No, monsieur, I do not know the writing. It is disguised, and yet it is tolerably plain. Whoever did it writes well. I am very fortunate," added he, looking gratefully at Villefort, "to be examined by such a man as you; for this envious person is a real enemy."

And by the rapid glance that the young man's eyes shot forth, Villefort saw how much energy lay hid beneath this mildness.

"Now," said the deputy, "answer me frankly, not as a prisoner to a judge, but as one man in a false position to another who takes an interest in him, what truth is there in the accusation contained in this anonymous letter?"

And Villefort threw disdainfully on his bureau the letter Dantès had just given back to him.

"None at all. I will tell you the real facts. I swear by my honor as a sailor, by my love for Mercédès, by the life of my father ——"

"Speak, monsieur," said Villefort. Then, internally, "If Renée could see me, I hope she would be satisfied, and would no longer call me a decapitator."

"Well, when we quitted Naples, Captain Leclere was attacked with a brain-fever. As we had no doctor on board, and he was so anxious to arrive at Elba that he would not touch at any other port, his disorder rose to such a height that at the end of the third day, feeling he was dying, he called me to him. 'My dear Dantès,' said he, 'swear to perform what I am going to tell you, for it is a matter of the deepest importance.'

"'I swear, captain,' replied I.

"'Well, as after my death the command devolves on you as mate, assume the command, and bear up for the isle of Elba, disembark at Porto-Ferrajo, ask for the grand-marshal, give him this letter; — perhaps he will give you another letter, and charge you with a commission. You will accomplish the mission that I was to have done, and derive all the honor from it.'

"'I will do it, captain; but, perhaps, I shall not be admitted to the grand-marshal's presence as easily as you expect?'

"'Here is a ring that will obtain audience of him, and remove every difficulty,' said the captain. At these words he gave me a ring. It was time; — two hours after he was delirious; the next day he died."

"And what did you do then?"

"What I ought to have done, and what every one would have done in my place. Everywhere the last requests of a dying man are sacred; but with a sailor the last requests of his superior are commands. I sailed for the isle of Elba, where I arrived the next day; I ordered everybody to remain on board, and went on shore alone. As I had expected, I found some difficulty in obtaining access to the grand-marshal; but I sent the ring I had received as my credentials, and was instantly admitted. He questioned me concerning Captain Leclere's death; and, as the latter had told me, gave me a letter to carry in person to Paris. I undertook it because it was what my captain had bade me do. I landed here, regulated the affairs of the vessel, and hastened to visit my affianced bride, whom I found more lovely than ever. Thanks to M. Morrel, all the forms were got over; in a word, I was, as I told you, at my marriage feast; and I should have been married in an hour, and to-morrow I intended to start for Paris, when, on this accusation which you now seem to despise as much as I do, I was arrested."

"Ah!" said Villefort, "this seems to me the truth. If you have been culpable, it was imprudence, and this imprudence was legitimized by the orders of your captain. Give up this letter you have brought from Elba, and pass your word you will appear should you be required, and go and rejoin your friends."

"I am free, then, sir?" cried Dantès, joyfully.

"Yes; but first give me this letter."

"You have it already; for it was taken from me with some others which I see in that packet."

"Stop a moment," said the deputy, as Dantès took his hat and gloves. "To whom is it addressed?"

"*To Monsieur Noirtier, Rue Coq-Héron, Paris.*"

Had a thunder-bolt fallen into the room, Villefort could not have been more stupefied. He sank into his seat, and, hastily turning over the packet, drew forth the fatal letter, at which he glanced with an expression of terror.

"M. Noirtier, Rue Coq-Héron, No. 13," murmured he, growing still paler.

"Yes," said Dantès ; "do you then know him ?"

"No," replied Villefort ; "a faithful servant of the king does not know conspirators."

"It is a conspiracy, then ?" asked Dantès, who, after believing him-

self free, now began to feel a tenfold alarm. "I have already told you,
however, sir, I was ignorant of the contents of the letter."

"Yes, but you knew the name of the person to whom it was addressed,"
said Villefort.

"I was forced to read the address to know to whom to give it."

"Have you shown this letter to any one?" asked Villefort, becoming
still more pale.

"To no one, on my honor."

"Everybody is ignorant that you are the bearer of a letter from the
isle of Elba, and addressed to M. Noirtier?"

"Everybody, except the person who gave it to me."

"This is too much," murmured Villefort. Villefort's brow darkened
more and more, his white lips and clenched teeth filled Dantès with
apprehension. After reading the letter, Villefort covered his face with
his hands, and remained for an instant overpowered.

"Oh!" said Dantès, timidly, "what is the matter?"

Villefort made no answer, but raised his head at the expiration of a
few seconds, and again perused the letter.

"You give me your honor that you are ignorant of the contents of
this letter?"

"I give you my honor, sir," said Dantès; "but what is the matter!
You are ill; — shall I ring for assistance? — shall I call?"

"No," said Villefort, rising hastily; "stay where you are. Don't say
a word! It is for me to give orders here, and not you."

"Monsieur," replied Dantès, proudly, "it was only to summon assistance for you."

"I want none; it was a temporary indisposition. Attend to yourself;
answer me."

Dantès waited, expecting a question, but in vain. Villefort fell back
on his chair, passed his hand over his brow, moist with perspiration,
and, for the third time, read the letter.

"Oh! if he knows the contents of this!" murmured he, "and that
Noirtier is the father of Villefort, I am lost!" And he fixed his eyes
upon Edmond as if he would have penetrated his thoughts.

"Oh! it is impossible to doubt it," cried he suddenly.

"In heaven's name!" cried the unhappy young man, "if you doubt
me, question me; I will answer you."

Villefort made a violent effort, and in a tone he strove to render
firm:

"Sir," said he, "your examination has resulted in very grave charges
against you. I am no longer able, as I had hoped, to restore you immediately to liberty; before doing so, I must consult the judge of instruction; but you see how I behave toward you."

"Oh! monsieur, and I thank you," cried Dantès; "you have been rather a friend than a judge."

"Well, I must detain you some time longer, but I will strive to make it as short as possible. The principal charge against you is this letter, and you see ——— "

Villefort approached the fire, cast it in, and waited until it was entirely consumed.

"You see, I destroy it !"

"Oh!" exclaimed Dantès, "you are goodness itself."

"Listen," continued Villefort; "you can now have confidence in me after what I have done."

"Oh! order me, and I will obey."

" Listen! this is not an order, but a counsel, I give you."

" Speak, and I will follow your advice."

" I shall detain you until this evening in the Palais de Justice. Should any one else interrogate you, tell him all you have told me, only do not breathe a word of this letter."

" I promise."

It was Villefort who seemed to entreat, and the prisoner who re-assured him.

" You see," continued he, looking at the ashes which still retained the shape of the paper and were dancing above the flames, " the letter is destroyed; you and I alone know of its existence; should you, therefore, be questioned, deny all knowledge of it."

" Fear nothing; I will deny it."

" Good," said Villefort, laying his hand on the bell-rope, and then checking himself.

" It was the only letter you had ? "

" It was."

" Swear it."

" I swear it."

Villefort rang. An agent of police entered. Villefort whispered some words in his ear, to which the officer replied by a motion of his head.

" Follow him," said Villefort to Dantès. Dantès saluted Villefort and retired. Hardly had the door closed, than Villefort threw himself into a chair, nearly fainting.

" Alas! alas!" murmured he, "on what chances life and fortune depend! if the procureur de roi had been at Marseilles! if the judge of instruction had been called instead of me, I should have been ruined. This paper, this accursed letter, would have destroyed all my hopes. Oh! my father, will you always be an obstacle to my happiness, and have I forever to struggle against your past? "

Suddenly a light seemed to pass over his spirit and illuminate his face; a smile played round his mouth, and his lips became unclenched, and his haggard eyes seemed to pause on some new thought.

" This will do," said he, " and from this letter, which might have ruined me, I will make my fortune."

And after having assured himself the prisoner was gone, the deputy procureur hastened to the house of his bride.

. THE CHÂTEAU D'IF.

CHAPTER VIII

HE commissary of police, as he traversed the antechamber, made a sign to two gendarmes, who placed themselves one on Dantès' right and the other on his left. A door that communicated with the Palais de Justice was opened, and they traversed a long range of gloomy corridors, whose appearance might have made even the boldest shudder. The Palais de Justice communicated with the prison,— a somber edifice, that from its gaping windows looks on the clock-tower of the Accoules rising before it. After numberless windings, Dantès saw an iron door and wicket. The commissary knocked thrice, every blow seeming to Dantès as if struck on his heart. The door opened, the two gendarmes gently pushed him forward, and the door closed with a loud sound behind him. The air he inhaled was no longer pure, but thick and mephitic,— he was in prison.

He was conducted to a tolerably neat chamber, but grated and barred, and its appearance, therefore, did not greatly alarm him; besides, the words of Villefort, who seemed to interest himself so much, resounded still in his ears like a promise of hope. It was four o'clock when Dantès was placed in this chamber. It was, as we have said, the 1st of March, and the prisoner was soon buried in darkness. The obscurity augmented the acuteness of his hearing: at the slightest sound he rose and hastened to the door, convinced they were about to liberate him; but the sound died away, and Dantès sank again into his seat. At last, about ten o'clock, and just as Dantès began to despair, sounds were again heard and seemed to approach his chamber; steps echoed in the corridor and stopped at his door, a key turned in the lock, the bolts creaked, the massy oaken door flew open, and a flood of light from two torches pervaded the apartment.

By the torchlight Dantès saw the glittering sabers and carbines of four gendarmes. He had advanced at first, but stopped at sight of this fresh accession of force.

" Are you come to fetch me ? " asked he.

" Yes," replied a gendarme.

" By the orders of the deputy of the king's procureur ? "

" I believe so."

" Well," said Dantès, " I am ready to follow you."

The conviction that they came from M. de Villefort relieved all Dantès' apprehensions; he advanced calmly, and placed himself in the center of the escort. A carriage waited at the street door, the coachman was on the box, and an exempt seated behind him.

" Is this carriage for me ? " said Dantès.

" It is for you," replied a gendarme.

Dantès was about to speak, but feeling himself urged forward, and having neither the power nor the intention to resist, he mounted the steps, and was in an instant seated inside between two gendarmes; the two others took their places opposite, and the carriage rolled heavily over the stones.

The prisoner glanced at the windows — they were grated; he had changed his prison for another that was conveying him he knew not whither. Through the close-barred grating, however, Dantès saw they were passing through the Rue Caisserie, and by the Quay Saint-Laurent and the Rue Taramis, to the quay. Soon he saw, through the grating of the coach and the railing of the edifice, the gleam of the lights of La Consigne.

The carriage stopped, the exempt descended, approached the guard-house, a dozen soldiers came out and formed themselves in order; Dantès saw the reflection of their muskets by the light of the lamps on the quay.

" Can all this military force be summoned on my account ? " thought he.

The exempt opened the door, which was locked, and, without speaking a word, answered Dantès' question; for he saw between the ranks of the soldiers a passage formed from the carriage to the port. The two gendarmes who were opposite to him descended first, then he was ordered to alight, and the gendarmes on each side of him followed his example. They advanced toward a boat, which a custom-house officer held near the quay by a chain.

The soldiers looked at Dantès with an air of stupid curiosity. In an instant he was placed in the stern-sheets of the boat, between the gendarmes, whilst the exempt stationed himself at the bow; a shove sent the boat adrift, and four sturdy oarsmen impelled it rapidly toward the Pilon. At a shout from the boat, the chain that closes the mouth of the port was lowered, and in a second they were outside the harbor.

The prisoner's first feeling was joy at again breathing the pure air — for air is freedom, and he eagerly inhaled the fresh breeze that brings

on its wings all the unknown scents of the night and the sea. But he soon sighed, for he passed before La Réserve, where he had that morning been so happy, and now through the open windows came the laughter and revelry of a ball. Dantès folded his hands, raised his eyes to heaven, and prayed fervently.

The boat continued her voyage. They had passed the Tête de More, were now in front of the light-house, and about to double the battery. This manœuvre was incomprehensible to Dantès.

" Whither are you taking me ?" asked he.

" You will soon know."

" But, still —— "

" We are forbidden to give you any explanation." Dantès was half a soldier and knew that nothing would be more absurd than to question subordinates, who were forbidden to reply, and remained silent.

The most vague and wild thoughts passed through his mind. The boat they were in could not make a long voyage; there was no vessel at anchor outside the harbor; he thought perhaps they were going to leave him on some distant point and tell him he was free. He was not bound, nor had they made any attempt to handcuff him; this seemed a good augury. Besides, had not the deputy, who had been so kind to him, told him that, provided he did not pronounce the dreaded name of Noirtier, he had nothing to apprehend ? Had not Villefort in his presence destroyed the fatal letter, the only proof against him ? He waited silently, striving to pierce through the obscurity of the night with his sailor's eye, accustomed to darkness and distance.

They had left the Ile Ratonneau, where the light-house stood, on the right, and were now opposite the Point des Catalans. His eyesight redoubled its vigor, and it seemed to the prisoner that he could distinguish a female form on the beach, for it was there Mercédès dwelt. How was it that a presentiment did not warn Mercédès her lover was near her ?

One light alone was visible; and Dantès recognized it as coming from the chamber of Mercédès. She was the only being awake in the little colony. A loud cry could be heard by her. He did not utter it. A false shame restrained him. What would his guards think if they heard him shout like a madman ?

He remained silent, his eyes fixed upon the light; the boat went on, but the prisoner only thought of Mercédès. A rising ground hid the light. Dantès turned and perceived that they had got out to sea. Whilst he had been absorbed in thought, they had hoisted the sail, and the bark was borne onward by the wind.

In spite of his repugnance to address the guards, Dantès turned to the nearest gendarme, and, taking his hand,

" Comrade," said he, " I adjure you, as a Christian and a soldier, to tell me where we are going. I am Captain Dantès, a loyal Frenchman, though accused of I know not what treason; tell me where you are conducting me, and I promise you, on my honor, I will submit to my fate."

DANTÈS IN THE DUNGEON.

The gendarme scratched his ear and looked irresolutely at his companion, who returned for answer a sign that said, " I see no great harm in telling him now," and the gendarme replied:

" You are a native of Marseilles, and a sailor, and yet you do not know where you are going ? "

" On my honor, I have no idea."

" And you cannot guess ? "

" I cannot."

" That is impossible."

" I swear to you it is true. Tell me, I entreat."

" But my orders."

" Your orders do not forbid your telling me what I must know in ten minutes, in half an hour, or an hour. You will merely spare me ages of uncertainty. I ask you as if you were my friend. You see I cannot escape, even if I intended."

" Unless you are blind, or have never been outside the harbor, you must know."

" I do not."

" Look round you then."

Dantès rose and looked forward, when he saw rise within a hundred yards of him the black and frowning rock on which stands the Château d'If.

This strange mass, this prison around which such deep terror reigns, this fortress that for three hundred years has filled Marseilles with its gloomy traditions, appearing thus suddenly to Dantès, who was not thinking about it, seemed to him what the scaffold seems to the condemned prisoner.

" The Château d'If ? " cried he, " what are we going there for ? "

The gendarme smiled.

" I am not going there to be imprisoned," said Dantès ; " it is only used for political prisoners. I have committed no crime. Are there any magistrates or judges at the Château d'If ? "

" There are only," said the gendarme, " a governor, a garrison, turnkeys, and good thick walls. Come, come, do not look so astonished, or you will make me think you are laughing at me in return for my good nature."

Dantès pressed the gendarme's hand as though he would crush it.

" You think, then," said he, " that I am conducted to the château to be imprisoned there ? "

" It is probable; but there is no occasion to squeeze so hard."

" Without any further formality ? "

" All the formalities have been gone through."

" In spite of M. de Villefort's promises ? "

" I do not know what M. de Villefort promised you," said the gendarme, " but I know we are taking you to the Château d'If. But what are you doing ? — Help ! comrades, help ! "

By a rapid movement, which the gendarme's practiced eye had perceived, Dantès sprang forward to precipitate himself into the sea; but four vigorous arms seized him as his feet quitted the flooring of the boat. He fell back, foaming with rage.

" Good ! " said the gendarme, placing his knee on his chest; " this is the way you keep your word as a sailor ! Believe soft-spoken gentlemen again ! Hark ye, my friend, I have disobeyed my first order, but I will not disobey the second; and if you move, I lodge a bullet in your brain."

And he leveled his carbine at Dantès, who felt the muzzle touch his head.

For a moment the idea of struggling crossed his mind, and of thus ending the unexpected evil that had overtaken him. But just because it was unexpected, he believed it would not last long, and he bethought him of Villefort's promise; and, besides, death in a boat from the hand of a gendarme seemed too repulsive. He remained motionless, but gnashing his teeth with fury.

At this moment a violent shock made the bark tremble. One of the sailors leaped on the rock which the bow had just touched, a cord creaked as it ran through a pulley, and Dantès guessed they were at the end of the voyage and mooring the boat.

His guardians, taking hold of his arms and collar, forced him to rise and land, and dragged him toward the steps that lead to the gate of the fortress, whilst the exempt followed, armed with a carbine and bayonet.

Dantès made no resistance; he was dazed and tottering like a drunken man; he saw soldiers who stationed themselves on the sides; he felt himself forced up fresh stairs; he perceived he passed through a door, and the door closed behind him; but all this as mechanically as through a mist, nothing distinctly. He did not even see the sea, that terror of prisoners who regard its expanse with the awful feeling that they cannot cross it.

They halted for a minute, during which he strove to collect his thoughts. He looked around: he was in a square court surrounded by four high walls; he heard the measured tread of sentinels, and as they passed before the light reflected on the walls from two or three lamps in the interior of the fortress, he saw the barrels of their muskets shine.

They waited upward of ten minutes. Certain Dantès could not

escape, the gendarmes released him. They seemed awaiting orders. The orders arrived.

"Where is the prisoner?" said a voice.

"Here," replied the gendarmes.

"Let him follow me; I am going to conduct him to his room."

"Go!" said the gendarmes, pushing Dantès.

The prisoner followed his conductor, who led him into a room almost under ground, whose bare and reeking walls seemed as though impregnated with tears. A lamp placed on a stool, its wick floating in stinking fat, illumined the apartment faintly, and showed Dantès the features of his conductor, an under-jailer, ill-clothed, and of sullen appearance.

"Here is your chamber for to-night," said he. "It is late, and Monsieur le Gouverneur is asleep. To-morrow perhaps, when he awakes and has examined the orders concerning you, he may change you. In the mean time there are bread, water, and fresh straw; and that is all a prisoner can wish for. Good-night."

And before Dantès could open his mouth, before he had noticed where the jailer placed his bread, or where the water was, before he had glanced toward the corner where the straw was, the jailer disappeared, taking with him the lamp, whose dull rays showed him the dripping walls of his prison.

Dantès was alone in darkness and in silence, mute as the vault above him, and cold as the shadows that fell on his burning forehead. With the first dawn of day the jailer returned, with orders to leave Dantès where he was. He found the prisoner in the same position, as if fixed there by an iron hand, his eyes swollen with weeping. He had passed the night standing, and without sleep. The jailer advanced; Dantès appeared not to perceive him. He touched him on the shoulder; Edmond started.

"Have you not slept?" said the jailer.

"I do not know," replied Dantès.

The jailer stared.

"Are you hungry?" continued he.

"I do not know."

"Do you wish for anything?"

"I wish to see the governor."

The jailer shrugged his shoulders and left the chamber.

Dantès followed him with his eyes, and stretched forth his hands toward the open door; but the door closed. All his emotion then burst forth, tears streamed from his swollen lids in rivulets; he cast himself on the ground, praying, recalling all his past life, and asking himself what crime he had committed that he, still so young, was thus punished.

The day passed thus; he scarcely tasted food; at times he sat rapt in thought, at times he walked round and round the cell like a wild beast in its cage. One thought in particular tormented him,—namely, that during his journey hither he had sat so still, whereas he might, a dozen times, have plunged into the sea, and, thanks to his powers of diving, for which he was famous, have disappeared beneath the water, eluded his keepers, have gained the shore, concealed himself until the arrival of a Genoese or Spanish vessel, and escaped to Spain or Italy, where Mercédès could have joined him. He had no fears as to how he should live — good seamen are welcome everywhere. He spoke Italian like a Tuscan, and Spanish like a Castilian; he would then have been free and happy with Mercédès and his father, for his father must come too, whereas he was now confined in the Château d'If, ignorant of the future destiny of his father and Mercédès; and all this because he had trusted to Villefort's promise. The thought was maddening, and Dantès threw himself furiously down on his straw. The next morning the jailer made his appearance.

" Well," said the jailer, " are you more reasonable to-day ? "

Dantès made no reply.

" Come, take courage; do you want anything in my power to do for you ? "

" I wish to see the governor."

" I have already told you it was impossible."

" Why so ? "

" Because it is not allowed by the rules."

" What is allowed then ? "

" Better fare, if you pay for it, books, and leave to walk about."

" I do not want books, I am satisfied with my food, and I do not care to walk about; but I wish to see the governor."

" If you worry me by repeating the same thing, I will not bring you any more to eat."

" Well, then," said Edmond, " if you do not, I shall die of famine — that is all."

The jailer saw by his tone he would be happy to die; and as every prisoner is worth sixpence a day to his jailer, the man, after reflecting on the loss his death would cause him, replied in a more subdued tone:

" What you ask is impossible. Do not ask it again. The governor never comes to a prisoner's cell; but if you are very well behaved, you will be allowed to walk about, and some day you will meet the governor. You can ask him, and if he chooses to reply, that is his affair."

" But," asked Dantès, " how long shall I have to wait ? "

" Ah ! a month — six months — a year."

" It is too long a time. I wish to see him at once."

" Ah," said the jailer, " do not always brood over what is impossible, or you will be mad in a fortnight."

"You think so ? "

" Yes; they all begin in this way. We have an instance here: it was by always offering a million of francs to the governor for his liberty that the abbé who was in this chamber before you became mad."

"How long has he left it?"

"Two years."

"Was he liberated then?"

"No; he was put in a dungeon."

"Listen!" said Dantès. "I am not an abbé, I am not mad; perhaps

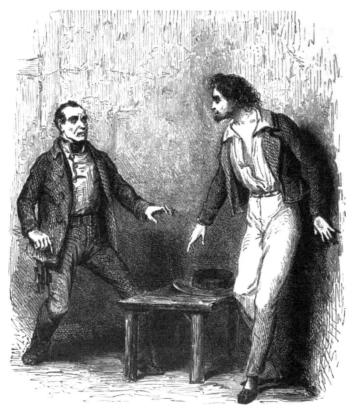

I shall be, but at present, unfortunately, I am not. I will make you
another offer."

"What is that?"

"I do not offer you a million, because I have it not; but I will give
you a hundred crowns if, the first time you go to Marseilles, you will

seek out a young girl named Mercédès, at the Catalans, and give her a letter—no, not even a letter; just two lines from me."

" If I took them, and were detected, I should lose my place, which is worth two thousand francs a year; so that I should be a great fool to run such a risk for three hundred."

" Well," said Dantès, "mark this: If you refuse to tell the governor that I wish to speak with him; if you refuse at least to tell Mercédès I am here, I will some day hide myself behind the door, and when you enter I will dash out your brains with this stool."

" Threats!" cried the jailer, retreating and putting himself on the defensive; "you are certainly going mad. The abbé began like you, and in three days you will want a strait-waistcoat; but, fortunately, there are dungeons here."

Dantès whirled the stool round his head.

" Oh!" said the jailer, "you shall see the governor at once."

" That is right," returned Dantès, dropping the stool and sitting on it as if he were in reality mad.

The jailer went out, and returned in an instant with a corporal and four soldiers.

" By the governor's orders," said he, "conduct the prisoner to the story beneath."

" To the dungeon, then," said the corporal.

" Yes; we must put the madman with the madmen."

The soldiers seized Dantès, who followed passively. He descended fifteen steps, and the door of a dungeon was opened, and he entered, murmuring, "He is right; the madman with the madmen!" The door closed, and Dantès advanced with outstretched hands until he touched the wall; he then sat down in the corner until his eyes became accustomed to the darkness. The jailer was right; Dantès wanted but little of being utterly mad.

CHAPTER IX

THE EVENING OF THE BETROTHAL

ILLEFORT had, as we have said, hastened back to the Place du Grand Cours, and on entering the house found all the guests in the salon at coffee. Renée was, with all the rest of the company, anxiously awaiting him, and his entrance was followed by a general exclamation.

"Well, Decapitator, Guardian of the State, royalist Brutus, what is the matter?" said one.

"Are we threatened with a fresh Reign of Terror?" asked another.

"Has the Corsican ogre broke loose?" cried the third.

"Madame la Marquise," said Villefort, approaching his future mother-in-law, "I request your pardon for thus leaving you. M. le Marquis, honor me by a few moments' private conversation!"

"Ah! this affair is really serious, then?" asked the marquis, remarking the cloud on Villefort's brow.

"So serious, that I must take leave of you for a few days; so," added he, turning to Renée, "judge for yourself if it be not important."

"You are going to leave us?" cried Renée, unable to hide the emotion caused by this unexpected intelligence.

"Alas!" returned Villefort, "I must!"

"Where, then, are you going?" asked the marquise.

"That, madame, is the secret of justice; but if you have any commissions for Paris, a friend of mine is going there to-night, and will gladly fulfill them."

The guests looked at each other.

"You wish to speak to me alone?" said the marquis.

"Yes; let us go into your cabinet."

The marquis took his arm and left the salon.

"Well!" asked he, as soon as they were in his closet, "tell me, what is it?"

"An affair of the greatest importance, that demands my immediate presence in Paris. Now, excuse the indiscretion, marquis, but have you any funded property?"

"All my fortune is in the funds;—six or seven hundred thousand francs."

"Then sell out—sell out, marquis, as soon as you can."

"Eh! how can I sell out here?"

"You have a broker, have you not?"

"Yes."

"Then give me a letter to him, and tell him to sell out without an instant's delay; perhaps, even now I shall arrive too late."

"What say you?" said the marquis, "let us lose no time, then!"

And, sitting down, he wrote a letter to his broker, ordering him to sell out at any loss.

CHAPTER IX

THE EVENING OF THE BETROTHAL

VILLEFORT had, as we have said, hastened back to the Place du Grand Cours, and on entering the house found all the guests in the salon at coffee. Renée was, with all the rest of the company, anxiously awaiting him, and his entrance was followed by a general exclamation.

"Well, decapitator, guardian of the state, royalist Brutus, what is the matter?" said one.

"Are we threatened with a fresh Reign of Terror?" asked another.

"Has the Corsican ogre broken loose?" cried the third.

"Madame la Marquise," said Villefort, approaching his future mother-in-law, "I request your pardon for thus leaving you. M. le Marquis, honor me by a few moments' private conversation."

"Ah! the affair is really serious, then?" asked the marquis, remarking the cloud on Villefort's brow.

"So serious that I must take leave of you for a few days; so," added he, turning to Renée, "judge for yourself if it be not important."

"You are going to leave us?" cried Renée, unable to hide the emotion caused by this unexpected intelligence.

"Alas!" returned Villefort, "I must!"

"Where, then, are you going?" asked the marquise.

"That, madame, is the secret of justice; but if you have any commissions for Paris, a friend of mine is going there to-night, and will gladly undertake them."

The guests looked at each other.

"You wish to speak to me alone?" said the marquis.

"Yes, let us go into your cabinet."

The marquis took his arm and left the salon.

"Well," asked he, as soon as they were in his closet, "tell me what it is."

"An affair of the greatest importance, that demands my immediate presence in Paris. Now, excuse the indiscretion, marquis, but have you any funded property?"

"All my fortune is in the funds—six or seven hundred thousand francs."

"Then sell out—sell out, marquis, as soon as you can."

"Eh! how can I sell out here?"

"You have a broker, have you not?"

"Yes."

"Then give me a letter to him, and tell him to sell out without an instant's delay, perhaps even I shall arrive too late."

"Well, then, let us lose no time, then?"

And he wrote to his broker, ordering him to sell.

"Now, then," said Villefort, placing the letter in his pocket-book, "write another."

"To whom?"

"To the king."

"I dare not write to his majesty."

"I do not ask you to write to his majesty, but ask M. de Salvieux to do so. I want a letter that will enable me to reach the king's presence without all the formalities of demanding an audience; that would occasion a loss of time."

"But address yourself to the keeper of the seals; he has the right of entry, and can procure you audience with the king, day or night."

"Doubtless; but there is no occasion to divide the merit of my discovery with him. The keeper would leave me in the background, and take all the honor to himself. I tell you, marquis, my fortune is made if I only reach the Tuileries the first, for the king will not forget the service I do him."

"In that case make your preparations, and I will call Salvieux and get him to write the letter of introduction."

"Be as quick as possible; I must be *en route* in a quarter of an hour."

"Make your carriage stop at the door."

"You will present my excuses to the marquise and Mademoiselle Renée, whom I leave on such a day with great regret."

"They are both in my room; you can say all this for yourself."

"A thousand thanks — busy yourself with the letter."

The marquis rang, a servant entered.

"Inform the Count de Salvieux I am waiting for him."

"Now, then, go!" said the marquis to Villefort.

"I only go for a few moments."

Villefort hastily quitted the apartment, but reflecting that the sight of the deputy procureur running through the streets would be enough to throw the whole city into confusion, he resumed his ordinary dignified pace. At his door he perceived in the shade, as it were, a white phantom, erect and motionless, that seemed to wait for him. It was Mercédès, who, hearing no news of her lover, had come herself at nightfall from the Pharos to inquire after him.

As Villefort drew near, she advanced and stood before him. Dantès had spoken of his bride, and Villefort instantly recognized her. Her beauty and high bearing surprised him, and when she inquired what had become of her lover, it seemed to him that she was the judge, and he the accused.

"The young man you speak of," said Villefort abruptly, "is a great criminal, and I can do nothing for him, mademoiselle."

Mercédès burst into tears, and, as Villefort strove to pass her, again addressed him.

" But, at least, tell me where he is, that I may learn if he is alive or dead," said she.

" I do not know; he is no longer in my hands," replied Villefort.

And, desirous of putting an end to the interview, he pushed by her, and closed the door, as if to exclude the pain he felt. But remorse is not thus banished; like the wounded hero of Virgil, the arrow remained in the wound, and when he arrived at the salon his limbs failed him.

Villefort, in his turn, uttered a sigh that resembled a sob, and sank into a chair.

At the bottom of his diseased heart, the first roots of a mortal ulcer were forming. The man he sacrificed to his ambition, that innocent victim he made pay the penalty of his father's faults, appeared to him pale and threatening, leading his affianced bride by the hand, and bringing with him remorse, not such as the ancients figured, furious and terrible, but that slow and consuming agony which, at times, strikes the heart and lacerates it with recollections of past deeds,—a laceration whose poignant pangs increase and deepen the evil till death comes. Then he had a moment's hesitation. He had frequently called, without any other emotion than that of the struggle between the prosecution and defense, for capital punishment on criminals, and owing to his irresistible eloquence they had been condemned, and yet the slightest shadow of remorse had never clouded Villefort's brow, because they were guilty, or, at least, he believed so; but here the case was different. He was about to send into perpetual imprisonment an innocent man, an innocent man with a happy future before him, and was destroying not only his liberty, but his happiness. In this case he was not the judge, but the executioner.

As he thus reflected, he felt the sensation we have described, and which had hitherto been unknown to him, arise in his bosom and fill him with vague apprehensions. It is thus that a wounded man trembles instinctively at the approach of the finger to his wound until it be healed, but Villefort's was one of those that never close, or, if they do, only close to re-open more agonizing than ever. If at this moment the sweet voice of Renée had sounded in his ears pleading for mercy, or the fair Mercédès had entered and said, "In the name of God, I conjure you to restore me my affianced husband," his cold and trembling hands would have signed his release at any risk; but no voice broke the stillness of the chamber, and the door was opened only by Villefort's valet, who came to tell him the traveling-carriage was in readiness.

Villefort rose, or rather sprang, from his chair, hastily opened one of the drawers of his *secrétaire*, emptied all the gold it contained into his pocket, stood motionless an instant, his hand pressed to his head, muttered a few inarticulate sounds, and then, perceiving his servant had placed his cloak on his shoulders, he sprang into the carriage, ordering the postilions to go, Rue du Grand Cours, to the house of M. de Saint-Méran.

The wretched Dantès was condemned.

As the marquis had promised, Villefort found the marquise and Renée in the parlor. He started when he saw Renée, for he fancied she was again about to plead for Dantès. Alas ! she was thinking only of Villefort's departure.

She loved Villefort, and he left her at the moment he was about to become her husband. Villefort knew not when he should return,

and Renée, far from pleading for Dantès, hated the man whose crime separated her from her lover.

What had Mercédès to say ?

Mercédès had met Fernand at the corner of the Rue de la Loge ;

she had returned to the Catalans, and had despairingly cast herself on her couch. Fernand, kneeling by her side, took her hand and covered it with kisses that Mercédès did not even feel. She passed the night thus; the lamp died out for want of oil, she saw neither light nor dark, and the day returned without her noticing it. Grief had made her blind to all but one object — that was Edmond.

"Ah! you are there," said she, at length.

"I have not quitted you since yesterday," returned Fernand sorrowfully.

M. Morrel had learned that Dantès had been conducted to prison, and he had gone to all his friends and the influential persons of the city, but the report was already in circulation that Dantès was arrested as a Bonapartist agent; and as the most sanguine looked upon any attempt of Napoleon to remount the throne as impossible, he met with nothing but coldness, alarm, and refusal, and had returned home in despair, confessing that Dantès was in a dangerous position, beyond his aid.

Caderousse was equally restless and uneasy, but, instead of seeking to aid Dantès, he had shut himself up with two bottles of wine, in the hope of drowning reflection. But he did not succeed, and became too intoxicated to fetch any more wine, and yet not so intoxicated as to forget what had happened, and as he leaned on his shaky table, opposite his two empty bottles, he saw in the flare of his dull candle all the specters of Hoffmann's punch-inspired tales.

Danglars alone was content and joyous — he had got rid of an enemy and preserved his situation on board the *Pharaon.* Danglars was one of those men born with a pen behind the ear and an inkstand in place of a heart. Everything with him was multiplication or subtraction, and he estimated the life of a man as less precious than a figure, when that figure could increase, and that life would diminish, the total of the amount.

Villefort, after having received M. de Salvieux's letter, embraced Renée, kissed the marquise's hand, and shaken hands with the marquis, started for Paris.

Old Dantès was dying with anxiety, and, as regards Edmond, we know what had become of him.

CHAPTER X

WE will leave Villefort on the road to Paris, traveling with all speed, and, penetrating the two or three apartments which precede it, enter the small cabinet of the Tuileries with the arched window, so well known as having been the favorite cabinet of Napoleon and Louis XVIII., as also that of Louis Philippe.

There, in this closet, seated before a walnut-tree table he had brought with him from Hartwell, and to which, from one of those fancies not uncommon to great people, he was particularly attached, the king, Louis XVIII., was carelessly listening to a man of fifty or fifty-two years of age, with gray hairs, aristocratic bearing, and exceedingly gentlemanly attire, whilst he was making a note in a volume of Horace, Gryphius's edition,— a bad one, but precious,— which was much indebted to the sagacious observations of the philosophical monarch.

"You say, sir, —— " said the king.

"That I am exceedingly disquieted, sire."

"Really, have you had a visit of the seven fat kine and seven lean kine ?"

"No, sire, for that would only betoken for us seven years of plenty and seven years of scarcity ; and with a king as full of foresight as your majesty, scarcity is not a thing to be feared."

"Then of what other scourge are you afraid, my dear Blacas ? "

"Sire, I have every reason to believe that a storm is brewing in the south."

"Well, my dear duke," replied Louis XVIII., "I think you are wrongly informed, and know positively that, on the contrary, it is very fine weather in that direction."

Man of ability as he was, Louis XVIII. liked a pleasant jest.

"Sire," continued M. de Blacas, "if it only be to re-assure a faithful servant, will your majesty send into Languedoc, Provence, and Dauphiné trusty men who will bring you back a faithful report as to the feeling in these three provinces ? "

Canimus surdis, replied the king, continuing the annotations in his Horace.

" Sire," replied the courtier, laughing, in order that he might seem to comprehend the quotation, "your majesty may be perfectly right in relying on the good feeling of France, but I fear I am not altogether wrong in dreading some desperate attempt."

" By whom ? "

" By Bonaparte, or, at least, his party."

" My dear Blacas," said the king, " you with your alarms prevent me from working."

" And you, sire, prevent me from sleeping with your security."

" Wait, my dear sir, wait a moment ; for I have such a delightful note on the *Pastor quum traheret* — wait, and I will listen to you afterward."

There was a brief pause, during which Louis XVIII. wrote, in a hand as small as possible, another note on the margin of his Horace, and then, looking at the duke with the air of a man who thinks he has an idea of his own, whilst he is but commenting upon the idea of another, he said:

" Go on, my dear duke, go on — I listen."

" Sire," said Blacas, who had for a moment the hope of sacrificing Villefort to his own profit, "I am compelled to tell you that these are not mere rumors destitute of foundation which thus disquiet me ; but a reflective man, deserving all my confidence, and charged by me to watch over the south" (the duke hesitated as he pronounced these words), "has arrived post to tell me a great peril threatens the king, and then I hastened to you, sire."

Mala ducis avi domum, continued Louis XVIII., still annotating.

" Does your majesty wish me to cease as to this subject ? "

" By no means, dear duke ; but just stretch out your hand."

" Which ? "

" Whichever you please — there to the left."

" Here, sire ? "

" I tell you to the left, and you seek the right; I mean on my right — yes, there. You will find the report of the minister of police of yesterday. But here is M. Dandré himself." And M. Dandré, announced by the chamberlain-in-waiting, entered.

" Did you not say M. Dandré ? " said the king to the servant who announced the minister of police.

" Yes, sire, the Baron Dandré," the man replied.

" Of course, the Baron," said Louis XVIII., with an imperceptible smile, "come in, baron, and tell the duke all you know — the latest news of M. de Bonaparte; do not conceal anything, however serious,— let us see, the island of Elba is a volcano, and we may expect to have issuing thence flaming and bristling war — *bella, horrida bella.*"

M. Dandré leaned very respectfully on the back of a chair with his two hands, and said:

"Has your majesty perused yesterday's report?"

"Yes, yes; but tell the count himself, who cannot find anything, what the report contains — give him the particulars of what the usurper is doing in his islet."

"Monsieur," said the baron to the count, "all the servants of his majesty must approve of the latest intelligence which we have from the island of Elba. Bonaparte —— "

M. Dandré looked at Louis XVIII., who, employed in writing a note, did not even raise his head. "Bonaparte," continued the baron, "is mortally wearied, and passes whole days in watching his miners at work at Porto Longone."

"And scratches himself for amusement," added the king.

"Scratches himself?" inquired the count; "what does your majesty mean?"

"Yes, indeed, my dear count. Did you forget that this great man, this hero, this demi-god, is attacked with a malady of the skin which worries him to death, *prurigo?*"

"And, moreover, M. le Comte," continued the minister of police, "we are almost assured that, in a very short time, the usurper will be insane."

"Insane?"

"Insane to a degree; his head becomes weaker. Sometimes he weeps bitterly, sometimes laughs boisterously; at other times he passes hours on the sea-shore, flinging stones in the water, and when the flint makes 'duck-and-drake' five or six times, he appears as delighted as if he had gained another Marengo or Austerlitz. Now, you must agree these are indubitable symptoms of weakness?"

"Or of wisdom, M. le Baron — or of wisdom," said Louis XVIII., laughing; "the greatest captains of antiquity recreated themselves with casting pebbles into the ocean — see Plutarch's life of Scipio Africanus."

M. de Blacas pondered deeply on this blind repose of monarch and minister. Villefort, who did not choose to reveal the whole secret, lest another should reap all the benefit of the disclosure, had yet communicated enough to cause him the greatest uneasiness.

"Well, well, Dandré," said Louis XVIII., "Blacas is not yet convinced; let us proceed, therefore, to the usurper's conversion."

The minister of police bowed.

" The usurper's conversion!" murmured the count, looking at the king and Dandré, who spoke alternately, like Virgil's shepherds. "The usurper converted!"

" Decidedly, my dear count."

" In what way converted?"

" To good principles. Explain all about it, baron."

" Why, this it is, M. le Comte," said the minister, with the gravest air in the world: " Napoleon lately had a review, and as two or three of his old grumblers, as he calls them, testified a desire to return to France, he gave them their dismissal, and exhorted them to 'serve their good king.' These were his own words, M. le Comte; I am certain of that."

" Well, Blacas, what think you of this?" inquired the king triumphantly, and pausing for a moment from the voluminous scholiast before him.

" I say, sire, that M. the minister of police or I am greatly deceived; and as it is impossible it can be the minister of police, as he has the guardianship of the safety and honor of your majesty, it is probable I am in error. However, sire, if I might advise, your majesty will interrogate the person of whom I spoke to you, and I will even urge your majesty to do him this honor."

" Most willingly, count; under your auspices I will receive any person you please, but with arms in hand. M. le Ministre, have you any report more recent than this, dated the 20th February, and this is the 3d of March?"

" No, sire, but I am hourly expecting one; it may have arrived since I left my office."

" Go thither, and if there be none—well, well," continued Louis XVIII., laughing, "make one; that is the usual way, is it not?"

" Oh, sire," replied the minister, " we have no occasion to invent any: every day our desks are loaded with most circumstantial denunciations, coming from crowds of individuals who hope for some return for services which they seek to render, but cannot; they trust to fortune, and rely that some unexpected event will give a kind of reality to their predictions."

" Well, sir, go," said Louis XVIII., " and remember that I am waiting for you."

" I will but go and return, sire; I shall be back in ten minutes."

" And I, sire," said M. de Blacas, " will go and find my messenger."

" Wait, sir, wait," said Louis XVIII. " Really, M. de Blacas, I must change your armorial bearings; I will give you an eagle with outstretched wings, holding in its claws a prey which tries in vain to escape, and bearing this device — *Tenax.*"

" Sire, I listen," said de Blacas, biting his nails with impatience.

" I wish to consult you on this passage, *Molli fugis anhelitu;* you know it refers to a stag flying from a wolf. Are you not a sportsman and a great wolf-hunter? Well, then, what do you think of the *molli anhelitu?*"

Baron Dandré.

" Admirable, sire; but my messenger is like the stag you refer to, for he has posted two hundred and twenty leagues in little more than three days."

" Which is undergoing great fatigue and anxiety, my dear count, when we have a telegraph which corresponds in three or four hours, and that without putting it the least in the world out of breath."

"Ah, sire, you recompense but badly this poor young man, who has come so far, and with so much ardor, to give your majesty useful information. If only for the sake of M. de Salvieux, who recommends him to me, I entreat your majesty to receive him graciously."

"M. de Salvieux, my brother's chamberlain?"

"Yes, sire."

"He is at Marseilles."

"And writes me thence."

"Does he speak to you of this conspiracy?"

"No, but strongly recommends M. de Villefort, and begs me to present him to your majesty."

"M. de Villefort!" cried the king; "is the messenger's name M. de Villefort?"

"Yes, sire."

"And he comes from Marseilles?"

"In person."

"Why did you not mention his name at once?" replied the king, betraying some uneasiness.

"Sire, I thought his name was unknown to your majesty."

"No, no, Blacas; he is a man of strong and elevated understanding, ambitious too, and, *pardieu!* you know his father's name!"

"His father?"

"Yes, Noirtier."

"Noirtier the Girondin? — Noirtier the senator?"

"He himself."

"And your majesty has employed the son of such a man?"

"Blacas, my friend, you have but limited comprehension. I told you Villefort was ambitious, and to attain this ambition Villefort would sacrifice everything, even his father."

"Then, sire, may I present him?"

"This instant, count! Where is he?"

"Waiting below, in my carriage."

"Seek him at once."

"I hasten to do so."

The count left the royal presence with the speed of a young man: his really sincere royalism made him youthful again. Louis XVIII. remained alone, and, turning his eyes on his half-opened Horace, muttered:

Justum et tenacem propositi virum.

M. de Blacas returned with the same rapidity he had descended, but in the antechamber he was forced to appeal to the king's authority. Villefort's dusty garb, his costume, which was not of courtly cut, excited the susceptibility of M. de Brézé, who was all astonishment at finding that this young man had the pretension to enter before the king in such attire. The count, however, superseded all difficulties with a word — " His majesty's order," and, in spite of the observations which the master of the ceremonies made for the honor of his office and principles, Villefort was introduced.

The king was seated in the same place where the count had left him. On opening the door, Villefort found himself facing him, and the young magistrate's first impulse was to pause.

" Come in, M. de Villefort," said the king, " come in."

Villefort bowed, and, advancing a few steps, waited until the king should interrogate him.

" M. de Villefort," said Louis XVIII., " the Count de Blacas assures me you have some interesting information to communicate."

" Sire, the count is right, and I believe your majesty will think it equally important."

" In the first place, and before everything else, sir, is the bad news as great in your opinion as it is wished to make me believe ? "

" Sire, I believe it to be most urgent, but I hope, by the speed I have used, that it is not irreparable."

" Speak as fully as you please, sir," said the king, who began to give way to the emotion which had changed the face of M. de Blacas and affected Villefort's voice. " Speak, sir, and pray begin at the beginning; I like order in everything."

" Sire," said Villefort, " I will render a faithful report to your majesty, but I must entreat your forgiveness if my anxiety creates some obscurity in my language."

A glance at the king after this discreet and subtle exordium assured Villefort of the benignity of his august auditor, and he continued:

" Sire, I have come as rapidly to Paris as possible, to inform your majesty that I have discovered, in the exercise of my duties, not a commonplace and insignificant plot, such as is every day got up in the lower ranks of the people and in the army, but an actual conspiracy — a storm which menaces no less than the throne of your majesty. Sire, the usurper is arming three ships; he meditates some project, which, however mad, is yet, perhaps, terrible. At this moment he will have left Elba, to go whither I know not, but assuredly to attempt a landing either at Naples or on the coast of Tuscany, or perhaps on the shore of France. Your majesty is well aware that the sovereign of the isle of Elba has maintained his relations with Italy and France ? "

"I am, sir," said the king, much agitated; "and recently we have had information that the Bonapartist clubs have had meetings in the Rue Saint-Jacques. But proceed, I beg of you. How did you obtain these details ? "

"Sire, they are the results of an examination which I have made of a man of Marseilles, whom I have watched for some time, and arrested on the day of my departure. This person, a sailor, of turbulent character, and whom I suspected of Bonapartism, has been secretly to the isle of Elba. There he saw the grand-marshal, who charged him with a verbal mission to a Bonapartist in Paris, whose name I could not extract from him; but this mission was to prepare men's minds for a return (it is the man who says this, sire) — a return which will soon occur."

"And where is this man ? "

"In prison, sire."

"And the matter seems serious to you ? "

"So serious, sire, that when the circumstance surprised me in the midst of a family festival, on the very day of my betrothal, I left my bride and friends, postponing everything, that I might hasten to lay at your majesty's feet the fears that impressed me, and the assurance of my devotion."

"True," said Louis XVIII., "was there not a marriage engagement between you and Mademoiselle de Saint-Méran ? "

"Daughter of one of your majesty's most faithful servants."

"Yes, yes; but let us talk of this plot, M. de Villefort."

"Sire, I fear it is more than a plot; I fear it is a conspiracy."

"A conspiracy in these times," said Louis XVIII., smiling, "is a thing very easy to meditate, but more difficult to conduct to an end; inasmuch as, reëstablished so recently on the throne of our ancestors, we have our eyes open at once upon the past, the present, and the future. For the last ten months my ministers have redoubled their vigilance, in order to watch the shore of the Mediterranean. If Bonaparte landed at Naples, the whole coalition would be on foot before he could even reach Piombino; if he land in Tuscany, he will be in an unfriendly territory; if he land in France, it must be with a handful of men, and the result of that is easily foretold, execrated as he is by the population. Take courage, sir; but at the same time rely on our royal gratitude."

"Ah, here is M. Dandré ? " cried de Blacas.

At this instant the minister of police appeared at the door, pale, trembling, and as if ready to faint.

Villefort was about to retire, but M. de Blacas, taking his hand, restrained him.

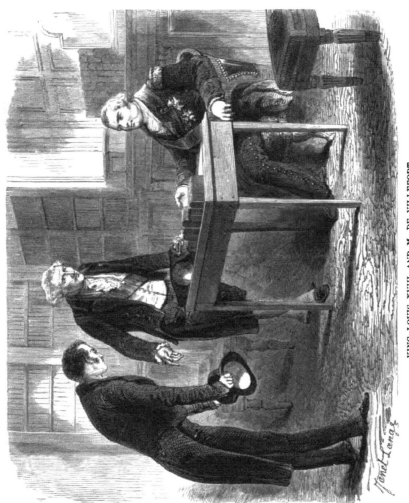

KING LOUIS XVIII. AND M. DE VILLEFORT.

CHAPTER XI

AT the sight of this agitation Louis XVIII. pushed from him violently the table at which he was writing.

"What ails you, M. le Baron?" he exclaimed. "You appear quite aghast. This trouble — this hesitation — have they anything to do with what M. de Blacas has told me, and M. de Villefort has just confirmed?"

M. de Blacas moved suddenly toward the baron, but the fright of the courtier precluded the triumph of the statesman; and besides, as matters were, it was much more to his advantage that the prefect of police should triumph over him than that he should humiliate the prefect.

"Sire, ——" stammered the baron.

"Well, what is it?" asked Louis XVIII.

The minister of police, giving way to an impulse of despair, was about to throw himself at the feet of Louis XVIII., who retreated a step and frowned.

"Will you speak?" he said.

"Oh! sire, what a dreadful misfortune! I am, indeed, to be pitied. I can never forgive myself!"

"Monsieur," said Louis XVIII., "I command you to speak."

"Well, sire, the usurper left Elba on the 26th of February, and landed on the 1st of March."

"And where? In Italy?" asked the king eagerly.

"In France, sire,— at a small port, near Antibes, in the Gulf of Juan."

"The usurper landed in France, near Antibes, in the Gulf of Juan, two hundred and fifty leagues from Paris, on the 1st of March, and you only acquired this information to-day, the 3d of March! Well, sir, what you tell me is impossible. You must have received a false report, or you have gone mad."

"Alas! sire, it is but too true!"

Louis made a gesture of indescribable anger and alarm, and then drew himself up as if this sudden blow had struck him at the same moment in heart and countenance.

"In France!" he cried, "the usurper in France! Then they did not watch over this man. Who knows? they were, perhaps, in league with him."

"Oh, sire!" exclaimed the Comte de Blacas, "M. Dandré is not a man to be accused of treason! Sire, we have all been blind, and the minister of police has shared the general blindness; that is all."

"But ——" said Villefort, and then, suddenly checking himself, he was silent; then he continued. "Your pardon, sire," he said, bowing, "my zeal carried me away. Will your majesty deign to excuse me?"

"Speak, sir, speak boldly," replied Louis. "You alone forewarned us of the evil; now try and aid us with the remedy!"

"Sire," said Villefort, "the usurper is detested in the south; and it seems to me that if he ventured into the south, it would be easy to raise Languedoc and Provence against him."

"Yes, assuredly," replied the minister; "but he is advancing by Gap and Sisteron."

"Advancing! he is advancing!" said Louis XVIII. "Is he then advancing on Paris?" The minister of police kept a silence which was equivalent to a complete avowal.

"And Dauphiné, sir?" inquired the king of Villefort. "Do you think it possible to rouse that as well as Provence?"

"Sire, I am sorry to tell your majesty a cruel fact; but the feeling in Dauphiné is far from resembling that of Provence or Languedoc. The mountaineers are Bonapartists, sire."

"Then," murmured Louis, "he was well informed. And how many men had he with him?"

"I do not know, sire," answered the minister of police.

"What! you do not know? Have you neglected to obtain information of this circumstance? It is true this is of small importance," he added, with a withering smile.

"Sire, it was impossible to learn; the dispatch simply stated the fact of the landing and the route taken by the usurper."

"And how did this dispatch reach you?" inquired the king.

The minister bowed his head, and whilst a deep color overspread his cheeks, he stammered out:

" By the telegraph, sire." Louis XVIII. advanced a step, and folded his arms over his chest as Napoleon would have done.

" So then !" he exclaimed, turning pale with anger, " seven conjoined and allied armies overthrew that man. A miracle of Heaven replaced me

M. de Blacas.

on the throne of my fathers after five-and-twenty years of exile. I have, during those five-and-twenty years, studied, sounded, analyzed the men and things of that France which was promised to me ; and when I have attained the end of all my wishes, the power I hold in my hands bursts and shatters me to atoms !"

" Sire, it is fatality!" murmured the minister, feeling that such a pressure, however light for destiny, was sufficient to overwhelm a man.

" What our enemies say of us is then true. We have learned nothing, forgotten nothing! If I were betrayed as he was, I would console myself; but to be in the midst of persons elevated by myself to dignities, who ought to watch over me more preciously than over themselves; for my fortune is theirs! — before me they were nothing — after me they will be nothing, and perish miserably from incapacity — ineptitude! Oh, yes, sir! you are right — it is fatality!"

The minister was bowed beneath this crushing sarcasm. M. de Blacas wiped the moisture from his brow. Villefort smiled within himself, for he felt his increased importance.

" To fall!" continued King Louis, who at the first glance had sounded the abyss on which the monarchy hung suspended,—" to fall, and learn that fall by the telegraph! Oh! I would rather mount the scaffold of my brother, Louis XVI., than thus descend the staircase of the Tuileries driven away by ridicule. Ridicule, sir — why, you know not its power in France, and yet you ought to know it!"

" Sire, sire," murmured the minister, " for pity's ——"

" Approach, M. de Villefort," resumed the king, addressing the young man, who, motionless and breathless, was listening to a conversation on which depended the destiny of a kingdom. "Approach, and tell monsieur that it is possible to know beforehand all that he has not known."

" Sire, it was really impossible to learn secrets which that man concealed from all the world."

" Really impossible! Yes — that is a great word, sir. Unfortunately, there are great words, as there are great men; I have measured them. Really impossible for a minister who has an office, agents, spies, and fifteen hundred thousand francs for secret service money, to know what is going on at sixty leagues from the coast of France! Well, then, see, here is a gentleman who had none of these resources at his disposal — a gentleman, only a simple magistrate, who learned more than you with all your police, and who would have saved my crown, if, like you, he had the power of directing a telegraph."

The look of the minister of police was turned with concentrated spite on Villefort, who bent his head with the modesty of triumph.

" I do not mean that for you, Blacas," continued Louis XVIII.; "for if you have discovered nothing, at least you have had the good sense to persevere in your suspicions. Any other than yourself would have considered the disclosure of M. de Villefort as insignificant, or else dictated by a venal ambition."

These words were meant to allude to those which the minister of police had uttered with so much confidence an hour before.

Villefort understood the drift of the king. Any other person would, perhaps, have been too much overcome by the intoxication of praise; but he feared to make for himself a mortal enemy of the police minister, although he perceived Dandré was irrevocably lost. In fact, the minister, who, in the plenitude of his power, had been unable to penetrate Napoleon's secret, might in the convulsions of his dying throes penetrate his, Villefort's, secret, for which end he had but to interrogate Dantès. He therefore came to the rescue of the crest-fallen minister, instead of aiding to crush him.

"Sire," said Villefort, "the rapidity of the event must prove to your majesty that God alone can prevent it, by raising a tempest; what your majesty is pleased to attribute to me as profound perspicacity is simply owing to chance; and I have profited by that chance, like a good and devoted servant—that's all. Do not attribute to me more than I deserve, sire, that your majesty may never have occasion to recall the first opinion you have been pleased to form of me."

The minister of police thanked the young man by an eloquent look, and Villefort understood that he had succeeded in his design; that is to say, that without forfeiting the gratitude of the king he had made a friend of one on whom, in case of necessity, he might rely.

"'Tis well!" resumed the king. "And now, gentlemen," he continued, turning toward M. de Blacas and the minister of police, "I have no further occasion for you, and you may retire; what now remains to do is in the department of the minister of war."

"Fortunately, sire," said M. de Blacas, "we can rely on the army; your majesty knows how every report confirms their loyalty and attachment."

"Do not mention reports, sir, to me! for I know now what confidence to place in them. Yet, apropos of reports, M. le Baron, what intelligence have you as to our affair in the Rue Saint-Jacques?"

"The affair in the Rue Saint-Jacques!" exclaimed Villefort, unable to repress an exclamation.

Then, suddenly pausing, he added, "Your pardon, sire, but my devotion to your majesty has made me forget, not the respect I have, for that is too deeply engraven in my heart, but the rules of etiquette."

"Say and act, sir!" replied the king; "you have acquired the right to inquire."

"Sire," replied the minister of police, "I came this moment to give your majesty fresh information which I had obtained on this head, when your majesty's attention was attracted by this terrible affair of the Gulf, and now these facts will cease to interest your majesty."

"On the contrary, sir,— on the contrary," said Louis XVIII., "this affair seems to me to have a decided connection with that which occupies our attention; and the death of General Quesnel will, perhaps, put us on the direct track of a great internal conspiracy."

At the name of General Quesnel, Villefort trembled.

"All combines, sir," said the minister of police, "to insure the probability that this death is not the result of a suicide, as we at first believed, but of an assassination. General Quesnel had quitted, as it appears, a Bonapartist club when he disappeared. An unknown person had been with him that morning, and made an appointment with him in the Rue Saint-Jacques; unfortunately, the general's valet-de-chambre, who was dressing his hair at the moment when the stranger entered, heard the street mentioned, but did not catch the number."

As the police minister related this to the king, Villefort, who seemed as if his very existence hung on his lips, turned alternately red and pale. The king looked toward him.

"Do you not think with me, M. de Villefort, that General Quesnel, whom they believed attached to the usurper, but who was really entirely devoted to me, has perished the victim of a Bonapartist ambush?"

"It is probable, sire," replied Villefort. "But is this all that is known?"

"They are on the traces of the man who appointed the meeting with him."

"On his traces?" said Villefort.

"Yes, the servant has given his description. He is a man of from fifty to fifty-two years of age, brown, with black eyes covered with shaggy eyebrows, and a thick mustache. He was dressed in a blue frock-coat, buttoned up to the chin, and wore at his button-hole the rosette of an officer of the Legion of Honor. Yesterday an individual was followed exactly corresponding with this description, but he was lost sight of at the corner of the Rue de la Jussienne and the Rue Coq-Héron."

Villefort leaned on the back of an arm-chair; for, in proportion as the minister of police spoke, he felt his legs bend under him; but when he learned that the unknown had escaped the vigilance of the agent who followed him, he breathed again.

"Continue to seek for this man, sir," said the king to the minister of police; "for if, as all conspires to convince me, General Quesnel, who would have been so useful to us at this moment, has been murdered, his assassins, Bonapartists or not, shall be cruelly punished."

It required all Villefort's *sang-froid* not to betray the terror with which this declaration of the king inspired him.

" How strange!" continued the king, with some asperity; "the police thinks all is said when it says, 'A murder has been committed,' and particularly when it adds, 'And we are on the track of the guilty persons.'"

" Sire, your majesty will, I trust, be amply satisfied on this point at least."

" We shall see; I will no longer detain you, baron. M. de Villefort, you must be fatigued after so long a journey; go and repose yourself. Of course you stopped at your father's ? "

A faintness came over Villefort.

"No, sire," he replied; "I alighted at the Hotel de Madrid, in the Rue de Tournon."

"But you have seen him ?"

"Sire, I went straight to M. le Comte de Blacas."

"But you will see him, then ?"

"I think not, sire."

"Ah, I forgot," said Louis, smiling in a manner which proved that all these questions were not made without a motive; "I forgot you and M. Noirtier are not on the best terms possible, and that is another sacrifice made to the royal cause, and for which you should be recompensed."

"Sire, the kindness your majesty deigns to evince toward me is a recompense which so far surpasses my utmost ambition that I have nothing more to request."

"Never mind, sir, we will not forget you; make your mind easy. In the mean while" (the king here detached the cross of the Legion of Honor he usually wore over his blue coat, near the cross of St. Louis, above the order of Notre-du-Mont-Carmel and St. Lazare, and gave it to Villefort) — "in the mean while, take this cross."

"Sire," said Villefort, "your majesty mistakes; this cross is that of an officer."

"*Ma foi!*" said Louis XVIII., "take it, such as it is, for I have not the time to procure you another. Blacas, let it be your care to see that the brevet is made out and sent to M. de Villefort."

Villefort's eyes were filled with tears of joy and pride; he took the cross and kissed it.

"And now," he said, "may I inquire what are the orders with which your majesty deigns to honor me ?"

"Take what rest you require, and remember that, unable to serve me here in Paris, you may be of the greatest service to me at Marseilles."

"Sire," replied Villefort, bowing, "in an hour I shall have quitted Paris."

"Go, sir," said the king; "and should I forget you (kings' memories are short), do not be afraid to bring yourself to my recollection. M. le Baron, send for the minister of war. Blacas, remain."

"Ah, sir," said the minister of police to Villefort, as they left the Tuileries, "you enter by the right door — your fortune is made."

"Will it be long first ?" muttered Villefort, saluting the minister, whose career was ended, and looking about him for a hackney-coach. One passed at the moment, which he hailed: he gave his address to the driver, and, springing in, threw himself on the seat and gave loose to dreams of ambition.

Ten minutes afterward Villefort reached his hotel, ordered his horses in two hours, and desired to have his breakfast brought to him. He was about to commence his repast when the sound of a bell, rung by a free and firm hand, was heard. The valet opened the door, and Villefort heard his name pronounced.

"Who could know that I was here already?" said the young man.

The valet entered.

"Well," said Villefort, "what is it?—Who rang?—Who asked for me?"

" A stranger who will not send in his name."

" A stranger who will not send in his name! What can he **want** with me ? "

" He wishes to speak to you."

" To me ? "

" Yes."

" Did he mention my name ? "

" Yes."

" What sort of a person is he ? "

" Why, sir, a man of about fifty."

" Short or tall ? "

" About your own height, sir."

" Dark or fair ? "

" Dark,— very dark : with black eyes, black hair, black eyebrows."

" And how dressed ? " asked Villefort, quickly.

" In a blue frock-coat, buttoned up close, decorated with the Legion of Honor."

" It is he ! " said Villefort, turning pale.

" Eh, *pardieu !* " said the individual, whose description we have twice given, entering the door, "what a great deal of ceremony ! Is it the custom in Marseilles for sons to keep their fathers waiting in their anterooms."

" Father ! " cried Villefort. " Then I was not deceived ; I felt sure it must be you."

" Well, then, if you felt so sure," replied the new-comer, putting his cane in a corner and his hat on a chair, " allow me to say, my dear Gérard, that it was not very filial of you to keep me waiting at the door."

" Leave us, Germain," said Villefort.

The servant quitted the apartment with evident signs of astonishment.

CHAPTER XII

FATHER AND SON

NOIRTIER — for it was indeed he who entered — followed with his eyes the servant until he had closed the door, and then, fearing, no doubt, that he might be overheard in the antechamber, he opened the door again; nor was the precaution useless, as appeared from the rapid retreat of Germain, who proved that he was not exempt from the sin which ruined our first parents. M. Noirtier then took the trouble to close carefully the door of the antechamber, then that of the bedchamber, and then extended his hand to Villefort, who had followed all his motions with surprise which he could not conceal.

"Well, now, my dear Gérard," said he to the young man, with a very significant look, "do you know you seem as if you were not very glad to see me?"

"My dear father," said Villefort, "I am, on the contrary, delighted; but I so little expected your visit that it has somewhat overcome me."

"But, my dear fellow," replied M. Noirtier, seating himself, "I might say the same thing to you, when you announce to me your wedding for the 28th of February, and on the 4th of March here you are in Paris."

"And if I have come, my dear father," said Gérard, drawing closer to M. Noirtier, "do not complain, for it is for you that I came, and my journey will save you."

"Ah, indeed!" said M. Noirtier, stretching himself out at his ease in the chair. "Really, pray tell me all about it, M. le Magistrat, for it must be interesting."

"Father, you have heard speak of a certain club of Bonapartists held in the Rue Saint-Jacques?"

"No. 53; yes, I am vice-president."

"Father, your coolness makes me shudder."

" Why, my dear boy, when a man has been proscribed by the Mountain, has escaped from Paris in a hay-cart, been hunted in the *landes* of Bordeaux by M. Robespierre's blood-hounds, he becomes accustomed to

Noirtier.

most things. But, go on; what about the club in the Rue Saint-Jacques ? "

" Why, they induced General Quesnel to go there, and General Quesnel, who quitted his own house at nine o'clock in the evening, was found the next day in the Seine."

" And who told you this fine story ? "

" The king himself."

" Well, then, in return for your story," continued Noirtier, " I will tell you one."

" My dear father, I think I already know what you are about to tell me."

" Ah, you have heard of the landing of the emperor ? "

" Not so loud, father, I entreat of you — for your own sake as well as mine. Yes, I heard this news, and knew it even before you could; for three days ago I posted from Marseilles to Paris with all possible speed, and half desperate because I could not send with a wish two hundred leagues ahead of me the thought which was agitating my brain."

" Three days ago ! You are crazy. Why, three days ago the emperor had not landed."

" No matter; I was aware of his project."

" How did you learn it ? "

" By a letter addressed to you from the isle of Elba."

" To me ? "

" To you; and which I discovered in the pocket-book of the messenger. Had that letter fallen into the hands of another, you, my dear father, would probably ere this have been shot."

Villefort's father laughed.

" Come, come," said he, " it appears that the Restoration has learned from the Empire the mode of settling affairs speedily. Shot, my dear boy ! you go ahead with a vengeance. Where is this letter you talk about ? I know you too well to suppose you would allow such a thing to pass you."

" I burned it, for fear that even a fragment should remain ; for that letter must have effected your condemnation."

" And the destruction of your future prospects," replied Noirtier; " yes, I can easily comprehend that. But I have nothing to fear whilst I have you to protect me."

" I do better than that, sir — I save you."

" You do ? why, really, the thing becomes more and more dramatic — explain yourself."

" I must refer again to the club in the Rue Saint-Jacques."

" It appears that this club is rather a bore to the police. Why didn't they search more vigilantly ? they would have found —— "

" They have not found ; but they are on the track."

" Yes, that's the usual phrase ; I know it well. When the police is at fault, it declares that it is on the track ; and the government patiently awaits the day when it comes to say, with a sneaking air, that the track is lost."

" Yes, but they have found a corpse; the general has been killed, and in all countries they call that a murder."

" A murder, do you call it? why, there is nothing to prove that the general was murdered. People are found every day in the Seine, having thrown themselves in, or have been drowned from not knowing how to swim."

" Father, you know very well that the general was not a man to drown himself in despair; and people do not bathe in the Seine in the month of January. No, no, do not mistake; this death was a murder in every sense of the word."

" And who thus designated it ? "

" The king himself."

" The king! I thought he was philosopher enough to allow that there was no murder in politics. In politics, my dear fellow, you know as well as I do, there are no men, but ideas — no feelings, but interests; in politics we do not kill a man, we only remove an obstacle — that is all. Would you like to know how matters have progressed? Well, I will tell you. It was thought reliance might be placed in General Quesnel; he was recommended to us from the isle of Elba. One of us went to him, and invited him to the Rue Saint-Jacques, where he would find some friends. He came there, and the plan was unfolded to him of leaving Elba, the projected landing, etc. When he had heard and comprehended all to the fullest extent, he replied that he was a royalist. Then all looked at each other,— he was made to take an oath, and did so, but with such an ill grace that it was really tempting Providence to swear thus; and yet, in spite of that, the general was allowed to depart free— perfectly free. Yet he did not return home. What could that mean? why, my dear fellow, that on leaving us he lost his way — that's all. A murder! really, Villefort, you surprise me. You, a deputy procureur, to found such an accusation on such bad premises! Did I ever say to you, when you were fulfilling your character as a royalist, and cut off the head of one of my party, 'My son, you have committed a murder'? No, I said, 'Very well, sir, you have gained the victory; to-morrow, perchance, it will be our turn.'"

" But, father, take care when our turn comes; our revenge will be sweeping."

" I do not understand you."

" You rely on the usurper's return ? "

" We do."

" You are mistaken ; he will not advance two leagues into the interior of France without being followed, tracked, and caught like a wild beast."

" My dear fellow, the emperor is at this moment on the way to

Grenoble; on the 10th or 12th he will be at Lyons, and on the 20th or 25th at Paris."

" The population will rise."

" Yes, to go and meet him."

" He has but a handful of men with him; and armies will be dispatched against him."

" Yes, to escort him into the capital. Really, my dear Gérard, you are but a child; you think yourself well informed because a telegraph has told you three days after the landing, ' The usurper has landed at Cannes with several men. He is pursued.' But where is he? what is he doing? You do not know well; and in this way they will pursue him to Paris, without drawing a trigger."

" Grenoble and Lyons are faithful cities, and will oppose to him an impassable barrier."

" Grenoble will open her gates to him with enthusiasm; all Lyons will hasten to welcome him. Believe me, we are as well informed as you; and our police is as good as your own. Would you like a proof of it? Well, you wished to conceal your journey from me, and yet I knew of your arrival half an hour after you had passed the barrier. You gave your direction to no one but your postilion, yet I have your address, and in proof I am here the very instant you are going to sit at table. Ring, then, if you please, for a second knife, fork, and plate, and we will dine together."

" Indeed!" replied Villefort, looking at his father with astonishment, " you really do seem very well informed."

" Eh? the thing is simple enough. You who are in power have only the means that money produces; we who are in expectation have those which devotion prompts."

" Devotion!" said Villefort with a sneer.

" Yes, devotion; for that is, I believe, the phrase for hopeful ambition."

And Villefort's father extended his hand to the bell-rope, to summon the servant whom his son had not called. Villefort arrested his arm.

" Wait, my dear father," said the young man; " one other word."

" Say it."

" However ill-conducted is the royalist police, they yet know one terrible thing."

" What is that?"

" The description of the man who, on the morning of the day when General Quesnel disappeared, presented himself at his house."

" Oh, the admirable police have found that out, have they? And what may be that description?"

" Brown complexion; hair, eyebrows, and whiskers black; blue frock-

coat, buttoned up to the chin; rosette of an officer of the Legion of
Honor in his button-hole; a hat with wide brim, and a cane."

"Ah! ah! that is it, is it ?" said Noirtier; "and why, then, have they
not laid hands on the individual ?"

"Because yesterday, or the day before, they lost sight of him at the
corner of the Rue Coq-Héron."

"Didn't I say your police was good for nothing ?"

"Yes; but still it may lay hands on him."

"True," said Noirtier, looking carelessly around him, "true, if this individual were not warned as he is." And he added, with a smile, "He will constantly change looks and costume."

At these words he rose and put off his frock-coat and cravat, went toward a table on which lay all the requisites of the toilette for his son, lathered his face, took a razor, and, with a firm hand, cut off the whiskers that might have compromised him and gave the police so decided a trace. Villefort watched him with alarm, not divested of admiration.

His whiskers cut off, Noirtier gave another turn to his hair; took, instead of his black cravat, a colored neckerchief which lay at the top of an open portmanteau; put on, in lieu of his blue and high-buttoned frock-coat, a coat of Villefort's, of dark brown, and cut away in front; tried on before the glass a narrow-brimmed hat of his son's, which appeared to fit him perfectly, and, leaving his cane in the corner where he had deposited it, he made to whistle in his powerful hand a small bamboo switch, which the dandy deputy used when he walked, and which aided in giving him that easy swagger which was one of his principal characteristics.

"Well," he said, turning toward his wondering son, when this disguise was completed, "well, do you think your police will recognize me now?"

"No, father," stammered Villefort; "at least, I hope not."

"And now, my dear boy," continued Noirtier, "I rely on your prudence to remove all the things which I leave in your care."

"Oh, rely on me," said Villefort.

"Yes, yes! and now I believe you are right, and that you have really saved my life; but be assured I will return the obligation to you hereafter."

Villefort shook his head.

"You are not convinced yet?"

"I hope, at least, that you may be mistaken."

"Shall you see the king again?"

"Perhaps."

"Would you pass in his eyes for a prophet?"

"Prophets of evil are not in favor at the court, father."

"True, but some day they do them justice; and, supposing a second restoration, you would then pass for a great man."

"Well, what should I say to the king?"

"Say this to him: 'Sire, you are deceived as to the feeling in France, as to the opinions of the towns, and the prejudices of the army; he whom in Paris you call the ogre of Corsica, who at Nevers is styled the usurper, is already saluted as Bonaparte at Lyons and emperor at Grenoble. You think he is tracked, pursued, captured; he is advancing as rapidly as his own eagles. The soldiers you believe dying with hunger, worn out with fatigue, ready to desert, increase like atoms of snow about the rolling ball which hastens onward. Sire, go, leave France to its real master, to him who did not buy, but acquired it; go, sire, not that you incur any risk, for your adversary is powerful enough to show you mercy, but because it would be humiliating for a grandson of Saint Louis to owe his life to the man of Arcola, Marengo, Austerlitz.' Tell him this, Gérard; or, rather, tell him nothing. Keep your journey a secret; do not boast of what you have come to Paris to do, or have done. You have made haste to come here, return with all speed; enter Marseilles at night, and your house by the back door, and there remain, quiet, submissive, secret, and, above all, inoffensive; for this time, I swear to you, we shall act like powerful men who know their enemies. Go, my son — go, my dear Gérard, and by your obedience to my paternal orders, or, if you prefer it, friendly counsels, we will keep you in your place. This will be," added Noirtier, with a smile, " one means by which you may a second time save me, if the political balance should one day place you high and me low. Adieu, my dear Gérard, and at your next journey alight at my door."

Noirtier left the room when he had finished, with the same calmness that had characterized him during the whole of this remarkable and trying conversation. Villefort, pale and agitated, ran to the window, put aside the curtain, and saw him pass, cool and collected, by two or three ill-looking men at the corner of the street, who were there, perhaps, to arrest a man with black whiskers, and a blue frock-coat, and hat with broad brim.

Villefort stood watching, breathless, until his father had disappeared at the Rue Bussy. Then he turned to the various articles he had left behind him, put at the bottom of his portmanteau his black cravat and blue frock-coat, threw the hat into a dark closet, broke the cane into small bits and flung it in the fire, put on his traveling-cap, and, calling his valet, checked with a look the thousand questions he was ready to ask, paid his bill, sprang into his carriage, which was ready, learned at Lyons that Bonaparte had entered Grenoble, and in the midst of the tumult which prevailed along the road, at length reached Marseilles, a prey to all the hopes and fears which enter the heart of man with ambition and its first successes.

CHAPTER XIII

NOIRTIER was a true prophet, and things progressed rapidly, as he had predicted. Every one knows the history of the famous return from Elba, a return which, without example in the past, will probably remain without imitation in the future.

Louis XVIII. made but a faint attempt to parry this unexpected blow; his lack of confidence in men deprived him of his confidence in events; the royalty, or rather the monarchy, he had scarcely reconstructed tottered on its precarious foundation, and it needed but a sign of the emperor to hurl to the ground all this edifice composed of ancient prejudices and new ideas. Villefort, therefore, gained nothing save the king's gratitude, which was rather likely to injure him at the present time, and the Cross of the Legion of Honor, which he had the prudence not to wear, although M. de Blacas had duly forwarded the brevet.

Napoleon would, doubtless, have deprived Villefort of his office had it not been for Noirtier, who was all-powerful at the court of the Hundred Days, by the dangers he had faced and the services he had rendered, and thus the Girondin of '93 and the senator of 1806 protected him who so lately had been his protector. All Villefort's influence barely enabled him to stifle the secret Dantès had so nearly divulged. During this re-appearance of the empire, whose second fall could be easily foreseen, the king's procureur alone was deprived of his office, being suspected of royalism.

However, scarcely was the imperial power established — that is, scarcely had the emperor reëntered the Tuileries and issued his numerous orders from that little cabinet into which we have introduced our readers, and on the table of which he found Louis XVIII.'s snuff-box, half full — than Marseilles began to rekindle the flames of civil war, always unextinguished in the south, and it required but little to excite the populace to acts of far greater violence than the shouts and insults with which they assailed the royalists whenever they ventured abroad.

Owing to this natural change, the worthy shipowner became at that moment— we will not say all-powerful, because Morrel was a prudent and rather a timid man, like all who have made a slow success in business; so much so, that many of the most zealous partisans of Bonaparte accused him of *moderation* — but sufficiently influential to make a demand; and this demand, as may be divined, was in favor of Dantès.

Villefort retained his place in spite of the fall of his superior, but his marriage was put off until a more favorable opportunity. If the emperor remained on the throne, Gérard required a different alliance to aid his career, and his father undertook to find it; if Louis XVIII. returned, the influence of M. Saint-Méran and himself became double, and the marriage must be still more suitable. The deputy procureur was, therefore, the first magistrate of Marseilles, when one morning his door opened, and M. Morrel was announced.

Any one else would have hastened to receive him and revealed his weakness; but Villefort was a man of ability, who, if he had not the experience, had the instinct for everything. He made Morrel wait in the antechamber, although he had no one with him, for the simple reason that the king's procureur always makes every one wait; and after a quarter of an hour had passed in reading the papers, he ordered Morrel to be admitted.

Morrel expected Villefort would be dejected; he found him, as he had found him six weeks before, calm, firm, and full of that glacial politeness, that most insurmountable barrier, which separates the well-bred and the vulgar man.

He had penetrated into Villefort's cabinet, convinced the magistrate would tremble at the sight of him; on the contrary, he felt a cold shudder all over him when he beheld Villefort seated, his elbow on his desk, and his head leaning on his hand. He stopped at the door; Villefort gazed at him as if he had some difficulty in recognizing him; then, after a brief interval, during which the honest shipowner turned and turned his hat in his hands,

" M. Morrel, I believe ! " said Villefort.

" Yes, sir."

" Come nearer," said the magistrate, with a patronizing wave of the hand, "and tell me to what circumstance I owe the honor of this visit."

" Do you not guess, monsieur ? " asked Morrel.

" Not in the least ; but, if I can serve you in any way, I shall be delighted."

" Everything depends on you."

" Explain yourself, pray."

" Monsieur," said Morrel, recovering his assurance as he proceeded, encouraged by the justice of his cause, " do you recollect that a few days before the landing of his majesty the emperor, I came to intercede for an unfortunate young man, the mate of my ship, who was accused of being concerned in a correspondence with the isle of Elba ? and what was the other day a crime is to-day a title of favor. You then served Louis XVIII., and you did not show any favor — it was your duty; to-day you serve Napoleon, and you ought to protect him — it is equally your duty. I come, therefore, to ask what has become of him."

Villefort made a violent effort.

" What is his name ?" said he; "tell me his name."

" Edmond Dantès."

Villefort would, evidently, have rather stood opposite the muzzle of a pistol at five-and-twenty paces than have heard this name pronounced; but he betrayed no emotion.

"In this way," said Villefort to himself, "I cannot be accused of making the arrest of this young man a personal question."

"Dantès," repeated he, "Edmond Dantès."

"Yes, monsieur."

Villefort opened a large register, then went to a table, from the table turned to his registers, and then, turning to Morrel,

"Are you quite sure you are not mistaken, monsieur?" said he, in the most natural tone in the world.

Had Morrel been a more quick-sighted man, or better versed in these matters, he would have been surprised at the king's procureur answering him on such a subject so entirely out of his line, instead of referring him to the governors of the prison or the prefect of the department. But Morrel, disappointed in his expectations of exciting fear, saw only, where no fear was visible, condescension. Villefort had calculated rightly.

"No," said Morrel, "I am not mistaken. I have known him ten years, and the last four he has been in my service. Do not you recollect, I came about six weeks ago to beseech your clemency, as I come to-day to beseech your justice — you received me very coldly, and answered me rudely? Oh, the royalists were very severe with the Bonapartists in those days."

"Monsieur," returned Villefort, "I was then a royalist, because I believed the Bourbons not only the heirs to the throne but the chosen of the nation. The miraculous return which we have seen proves me mistaken; the genius of Napoleon has conquered; the legitimate monarch is he who is loved by his people."

"That's right!" cried Morrel. "I like to hear you speak thus, and I augur well for Edmond from it."

"Wait a moment," said Villefort, turning over the leaves of a register; "I have it — a sailor, who was about to marry a young Catalan girl. I recollect now, it was a very serious charge."

"How so?"

"You know that when he left here he was taken to the Palais de Justice."

"Well?"

"I made my report to the authorities at Paris, and sent to them the papers found on him,—it was my duty,—and a week after, he was carried off."

"Carried off!" said Morrel. "What can they have done with him?"

"Oh, he has been taken to Fenestrelles, to Pignerol, or to the Iles

Sainte-Marguérite. Some fine morning he will return to assume the command of your vessel."

" Come when he will, it shall be kept for him. But how is it he is not already returned? It seems to me, the first care of the Bonapartist government should be to set at liberty those who have suffered from that of the Bourbons."

" Do not be too hasty, M. Morrel," replied Villefort. " The order of imprisonment came from high authority, and the order for his liberation must proceed from the same source; and, as Napoleon has scarcely been reinstated a fortnight, the letters have not yet been forwarded."

" But," said Morrel, " is there no way of expediting all these formalities? We are victorious; I have friends and some influence; I can obtain the canceling of his arrest."

" There has been no arrest."

" How ? "

" It is sometimes essential to government to cause a man's disappearance without leaving any traces, so that no written forms or documents may defeat their wishes."

" It might be so under the Bourbons, but at present——"

" It is always the same, my dear Morrel, since the reign of Louis XIV., all governments are alike; we have the Bastile to-day. The emperor is more strict in prison discipline than even Louis himself, and the number of prisoners whose names are not on the register is incalculable."

Had Morrel even any suspicions, so much kindness would have dispelled them.

" Well, M. de Villefort, how would you advise me to act? " asked he.

" Petition the minister."

" Oh, I know what that is ; the minister receives two hundred every day, and does not read four."

" That is true; but he will read a petition countersigned and presented by me."

" And will you undertake to deliver it ? "

" With the greatest pleasure. Dantès was then guilty, and now he is innocent; and it is as much my duty to free him as it was to condemn him."

Villefort foresaw the danger of an inquiry, possible but not probable, which might ruin him beyond retrieval.

" But how shall I address the minister ? "

" Sit down there," said Villefort, giving up his place to Morrel, " and write what I dictate."

" Will you be so good ? "

" Certainly. But lose no time; we have lost too much already."

"That is true. Only think that perhaps this poor young man is pining in despair."

Villefort shuddered at this picture of the prisoner cursing him in silence and obscurity, but he was too far gone to recede; Dantès must be crushed beneath the weight of Villefort's ambition.

"I am waiting," said Morrel, pen in hand.

Villefort dictated a petition, in which, from an excellent intention, no doubt, Dantès' services to the Bonapartists were exaggerated, and he was made out one of the most active agents of Napoleon's return. It was evident that at the sight of this document the minister would instantly release him. The petition finished, Villefort read it aloud.

"That will do," said he; "leave the rest to me."

"Will the petition go soon ?"

"To-day."

"Countersigned by you ?"

"The best thing I can do will be to certify the truth of the contents of your petition."

And, sitting down, Villefort wrote the certificate at the bottom.

"What more is to be done ?"

"I will answer for everything."

This assurance charmed Morrel, who took leave of Villefort, and hastened to announce to old Dantès that he would soon see his son.

As for Villefort, instead of sending to Paris, he carefully preserved the petition that so fearfully compromised Dantès, in the case of an event that seemed not unlikely,— that is, a second restoration. Dantès remained a prisoner, and heard not the noise of the fall of Louis XVIII.'s throne, nor the more terrible collapse of the Empire.

Twice during the brief imperial apparition which is called the Hundred Days had Morrel renewed his demand, and twice had Villefort soothed him with promises. At last there was Waterloo, and Morrel came no more: he had done all that was in his power, and any fresh attempt under the second restoration would only compromise himself uselessly.

Louis XVIII. remounted the throne, Villefort demanded and obtained the situation of king's procureur at Toulouse, and a fortnight afterward married Renée, whose father was more influential at court than ever.

Thus Dantès, during the Hundred Days and after Waterloo, remained under bolt and bar, forgotten by God and man.

Danglars comprehended the full extent of the wretched fate that overwhelmed Dantès, and, like all men of small abilities, he termed this *a decree of Providence.* But when Napoleon returned to the imperial throne in Paris, Danglars' heart failed him, and he feared at every

"BE CAREFUL OF YOURSELF, FOR IF YOU ARE KILLED I SHALL BE ALONE."

instant to behold Dantès eager for vengeance. He therefore informed M. Morrel of his wish to quit the sea, and obtained a recommendation from him to a Spanish merchant, into whose service he entered at the end of March,— that is, ten or twelve days after Napoleon's return to the Tuileries. He then left for Madrid, and was no more heard of.

Fernand understood nothing except that Dantès was absent. What had become of him he cared not to inquire. Only, during the respite the absence of his rival afforded him, he reflected, partly on the means of deceiving Mercédès as to the cause of his absence, partly on plans of emigration and abduction, as from time to time he sat sad and motionless on the summit of Cape Pharo, at the spot from whence Marseilles and the village of the Catalans are visible, watching for the apparition of a young and handsome man, who was for him also the messenger of vengeance. Fernand's mind was made up: he would shoot Dantès, and then kill himself. But Fernand was mistaken; a man of his disposition never kills himself, for he constantly hopes.

During this time the Empire made a last appeal, and every man in France capable of bearing arms rushed to obey the summons of his Emperor. Fernand departed with the rest, bearing with him the terrible thought that perhaps his rival was behind him, and would marry Mercédès. Had Fernand really meant to kill himself, he would have done so when he parted from Mercédès. His devotion, his constant attentions, and the compassion he showed for her misfortunes, produced the effect they always produce on noble minds—Mercédès had always had a sincere regard for Fernand, and this was now strengthened by gratitude.

" My brother," said she, as she placed his knapsack on his shoulders, "be careful of yourself, for if you are killed I shall be alone in the world."

These words infused a ray of hope into Fernand's heart. Should Dantès not return, Mercédès might one day be his. Mercédès was left alone to gaze on this bare earth that had never seemed so barren, and the sea that had never seemed so vast. Sometimes, bathed in tears, she wandered, without ceasing, around the little village of the Catalans, sometimes she stood mute and motionless as a statue beneath the burning sun of the South, gazing toward Marseilles; at other times gazing on the sea, and debating as to whether it were not better to cast herself into the abyss of the ocean, and thus end her woes. It was not want of courage that prevented her putting this resolution into execution; but her religious feelings came to her aid and saved her.

Caderousse was, like Fernand, enrolled in the army, but, being married and eight years older, he was merely sent to the coast fortresses. Old Dantès, who was only sustained by hope, lost all hope at Napoleon's downfall.   Five months after he had been separated from his son, **and** almost at the very hour at which he was arrested, he breathed his last in Mercédès' arms.   Morrel paid the expenses of his funeral and **a few** small debts the poor old man had contracted.

There was more than benevolence in this action; there was courage; for to assist, even on his death-bed, the father of so dangerous a Bonapartist as Dantès was stigmatized as a crime.

CHAPTER XIV

YEAR after Louis XVIII.'s restoration, a visit was made by the inspector-general of prisons. Dantès heard from the recesses of his cell the noises made by the preparations for receiving him,—sounds that at the depth where he lay would have been inaudible to any but the ear of a prisoner, who could distinguish the plash of the drop of water that every hour fell from the roof of his dungeon. He guessed something uncommon was passing among the living; but he had so long ceased to have any intercourse with the world, that he looked upon himself as dead.

The inspector visited the cells and dungeons, one after another, of several of the prisoners whose good behavior or stupidity recommended them to the clemency of the government; the inspector inquired how they were fed, and if they had anything to demand.

The universal response was that the fare was detestable, and that they required their freedom.

The inspector asked if they had anything else to demand. They shook their heads! What could they desire beyond their liberty?

The inspector turned smilingly to the governor.

" I do not know what reason government can assign for these useless visits; when you see one prisoner, you see all,—always the same thing,—ill-fed, and innocent. Are there any others?"

" Yes ; the dangerous and mad prisoners are in the dungeons."

"Let us visit them," said the inspector, with an air of fatigue. "I must fulfill my mission. Let us descend."

"Let us first send for two soldiers," said the governor. "The prisoners sometimes, through mere disgust of life, and in order to be sentenced to death, commit acts of useless violence, and you might fall a victim."

"Take all needful precautions," replied the inspector.

Two soldiers were accordingly sent for, and the inspector descended a stair so foul, so humid, so dark, that the very sight affected the eye, the smell, and the respiration.

"Oh!" cried the inspector, "who can live here?"

"A most dangerous conspirator, a man we are ordered to keep the most strict watch over."

"He is alone?"

"Certainly."

"How long has he been there?"

"Nearly a year."

"Was he placed here when he first arrived?"

"No, not until he attempted to kill the turnkey."

"To kill the turnkey?"

"Yes, the very one who is lighting us. Is it not true, Antoine?" asked the governor.

"True enough; he wanted to kill me!" replied the turnkey.

"He must be mad," said the inspector.

"He is worse than that,— he is a devil!" returned the turnkey.

"Shall I complain of him?" demanded the inspector.

"Oh, no; it is useless. Besides, he is almost mad now, and, to judge from our experience here, in another year he will be quite so."

"So much the better for him,— he will suffer less," said the inspector.

He was, as this remark shows, a man full of philanthropy, and in every way fit for his office.

"You are right, sir," replied the governor; "and this remark proves that you have deeply considered the subject. Now, we have in a dungeon about twenty feet distant, and to which you descend by another stair, an old abbé, ancient leader of a party in Italy, who has been here since 1811, and in 1813 he went mad, and the change is astonishing. He used to weep,— he now laughs; he grew thin,— he now grows fat. You had better see him, for his madness is amusing."

"I will see them both," returned the inspector; "I must conscientiously perform my duty."

This was the inspector's first visit: he wished to display his authority.

"Let us visit this one first," added he.

"Willingly," replied the governor; and he signed to the turnkey to open the door. At the sound of the key turning in the lock, and the creaking of the hinges, Dantès, who was crouched in a corner of the dungeon, raised his head. At the sight of a stranger, lighted by two turnkeys, accompanied by two soldiers, and to whom the governor spoke bareheaded, Dantès, who guessed the truth, and that the moment to address himself to the superior authorities was come, sprang forward with clasped hands.

The soldiers presented their bayonets, for they thought he was about to attack the inspector, and the latter recoiled two or three steps. Dantès saw he was represented as a dangerous prisoner. Then, infusing all the humility he possessed into his eyes and voice, he addressed the inspector, and sought to inspire him with pity.

The inspector listened attentively; then, turning to the governor, observed in a low tone:

" He will become religious — he is already more gentle; he is afraid, and retreated before the bayonets—madmen are not afraid of anything; I made some curious observations on this at Charenton."

Then, turning to the prisoner, "What do you demand?" said he.

" I ask what crime I have committed — I ask to be tried before my judges; and I ask, if I am guilty, to be shot; if innocent, to be set at liberty."

" Are you well fed?" said the inspector.

"I believe so — I know not; but that matters little. What matters really, not only to me, but to every functionary of justice, every member of the government, is, that an innocent man should languish in prison, the victim of an infamous denunciation, cursing his murderers."

" You are very humble to-day," remarked the governor. "You are not so always; the other day, for instance, when you tried to kill the turnkey."

" It is true, sir, and I beg his pardon; for he has always been very good to me; but I was mad."

" And you are not so any longer?"

"No! captivity has subdued, broken, annihilated me; I have been here so long."

" So long?— when were you arrested, then?" asked the inspector.

" The 28th of February, 1815, at half-past two in the afternoon."

" To-day is the 30th of June, 1816: why, it is but seventeen months."

" Only seventeen months!" replied Dantès. "Oh, you do not know what is seventeen months in prison! seventeen years,— seventeen ages rather, especially to a man who, like me, had arrived at the summit of his ambition — to a man who, like me, was on the point of marrying a woman he adored, who saw an honorable career open before him, and who loses all in an instant — who sees his prospects destroyed, and is ignorant of the fate of his affianced wife, and whether his aged father be still living! Seventeen months' captivity to a sailor accustomed to the air, the expanse, the immensity of the boundless ocean, is a worse punishment than human crime ever merited. Have pity on me, then, and ask for me, not indulgence, but a trial — let me see my judges; I ask only for a judge; you cannot refuse to bring me before a judge."

" We shall see," said the inspector; then, turning to the governor: " On my word, the poor devil touches me. You must show me the proofs against him."

" Certainly; but you will find terrible notes against him."

" Monsieur," continued Dantès, " I know it is not in your power to release me; but you can forward my petition, can obtain an inquiry, can plead for me — you can have me tried; and that is all I ask."

" Light me," said the inspector.

" Monsieur," cried Dantès, " I can tell by your voice you are touched with pity; tell me at least to hope."

" I cannot tell you that," replied the inspector; " I can only promise to examine into your case."

" Oh, I am free — then I am saved ! "

" Who arrested you ? "

" M. Villefort. See him, and hear what he says."

" M. Villefort is no longer at Marseilles; he is now at Toulouse."

" I am no longer surprised at my detention," murmured Dantès, " since my only protector is removed."

" Had M. de Villefort any cause of personal dislike to you ? "

" None; on the contrary, he was very kind to me."

" I can, then, rely on the notes he has left concerning you ? "

" Entirely."

" That is well; wait patiently, then."

Dantès fell on his knees, and prayed earnestly for the man who had descended to this Hades. The door closed; but this time a fresh inmate was left with Dantès — Hope.

" Will you see the register at once," asked the governor, "or proceed to the other cell ? "

" Let us visit them all," said the inspector. " If I once mounted the stairs, I should never have the courage to descend."

" Ah, this one is not like the other; and his madness is less affecting than the reason of his neighbor."

" What is his folly ? "

" He fancies he possesses an immense treasure. The first year he offered government a million of francs ($200,000) for his release ; the second, two; the third, three; and so on progressively. He is now in his fifth year of captivity; he will ask to speak to you in private, and offer you five millions."

" How curious ! — what is his name ? "

" L'Abbé Faria."

" No. 27," said the inspector.

" It is here; unlock the door, Antoine."

The turnkey obeyed, and the inspector gazed curiously into the chamber of the *mad abbé*, as the prisoner was usually called.

In the center of the cell, in a circle traced with a fragment of

plaster detached from the wall, sat a man whose tattered garments scarcely covered him. He was drawing in this circle geometrical lines, and seemed as much absorbed in his problem as Archimedes when the soldier of Marcellus slew him. He did not move at the sound of the door, and continued his problem until the flash of the torches lighted up with an unwonted glare the somber walls of his cell; then, raising his head, he perceived with astonishment the number of persons in his cell. He hastily seized the coverlid of his bed, and wrapped it round him in order to appear in a more decent state to the strangers.

"What do you demand?" said the inspector.

"I, monsieur!" replied the abbé, with an air of surprise,—"I demand nothing."

"You do not understand," continued the inspector; "I am sent here by government to visit the prisoners, and hear the requests of the prisoners."

"Oh, that is different," cried the abbé; "and we shall understand each other, I hope."

"There, now," whispered the governor, "it is just as I told you,"

"Monsieur," continued the prisoner, "I am the Abbé Faria, born at Rome. I was for twenty years Cardinal Spada's secretary; I was arrested, why I know not, in 1811; since then I have demanded my liberty from the Italian and French government."

"Why from the French government?"

"Because I was arrested at Piombino; and I presume that, like Milan and Florence, Piombino has become the capital of some French department."

The inspector and governor looked at each other with a smile.

"Ah!" said the inspector, "you have not the latest intelligence from Italy."

"They date from the day on which I was arrested," returned the Abbé Faria; "and as the emperor had created the kingdom of Rome for his infant son, I presume that he has realized the dream of Machiavel and Cæsar Borgia, which was to make Italy one vast kingdom."

"Monsieur," returned the inspector, "Providence has fortunately changed this gigantic plan you advocate so warmly."

"It is the only means of rendering Italy happy and independent."

"Very possibly; only I am not come to discuss politics, but to inquire if you have anything to ask or complain of."

"The food is the same as in other prisons,— that is, very bad; the lodging is very unwholesome, but, on the whole, passable for a dungeon; but it is not that which I speak of, but of a secret I have to reveal of the greatest importance."

"We are coming to the point," whispered the governor.

"It is for that reason I am delighted to see you," continued the abbé, "although you have disturbed me in a most important calculation, which, if it succeeded, would possibly change Newton's system. Could you allow me a few words in private?"

" What did I tell you ?" said the governor.

" You knew him," returned the inspector.

" What you ask is impossible, monsieur," continued he, addressing **Faria.**

The Abbé Faria.

" But " said the abbé, "I would speak to you of a large sum, amounting to five millions."

" The very figure you named," whispered, in his turn, the inspector.

" However " continued Faria, perceiving the inspector was about to depart, "it is not absolutely necessary we should be alone; monsieur the governor can be present."

" Unfortunately," said the governor, " I know beforehand what you are about to say; it concerns your treasures, does it not ? "

Faria fixed his eyes on him with an expression that would have convinced any one else of his sanity.

" Doubtless," said he ; " of what else should I speak ? "

" Monsieur l'Inspecteur," continued the governor, " I can tell you the story as well, for it has been dinned in my ears for the last four or five years."

" That proves," returned the abbé, " that you are like the people of Holy Writ, who have eyes and see not, and who have ears and hear not."

" The government does not want your treasures," replied the inspector ; " keep them until you are liberated." The abbé's eyes glistened ; he seized the inspector's hand.

" But what if I am not liberated," cried he, " and am detained here, contrary to all justice, until my death ? What, if I die without revealing my secret ? the treasure will be lost. Had not government better profit by it ? I will offer six millions, and I will content myself with the rest."

" On my word," said the inspector, in a low tone, " had I not been told beforehand this man was mad, I should believe what he says."

" I am not mad ! " replied Faria, with that acuteness of hearing peculiar to prisoners. " The treasure I speak of really exists ; and I offer to sign a treaty with you, by virtue of which you will take me to a spot I shall designate, you shall see the earth dug up under your own eyes, and if I lie, if nothing is found, if I am mad, as you call me, then bring me here again, and I shall die without asking more."

The governor laughed. " Is the spot far from here ? "

" A hundred leagues."

" It is not a bad idea," said the governor. " If every prisoner took it into his head to travel a hundred leagues, and their guardians consented to accompany them, they would have a capital chance of escaping."

" The scheme is well known," said the inspector ; " and M. l'Abbé has not even the merit of its invention."

Then, turning to Faria, " I inquired if you are well fed ? " said he.

" Swear to me," replied Faria, " to free me, if what I tell you prove true, and I will stay here whilst you go to the spot."

" Are you well fed ? " repeated the inspector.

" Monsieur, you run no risk, for, as I told you, I will stay here ; so there is no chance of my escaping."

" You do not reply to my question," replied the inspector impatiently.

" Nor you to mine," cried the abbé. " Accursed be you like the other

"YOU WILL NOT ACCEPT MY GOLD; I WILL KEEP IT FOR MYSELF."

fools who will not believe me! You will not accept my gold; I will keep it for myself. You refuse me my liberty; God will give it me. Go! I have no more to say." And the abbé, casting away his coverlid, resumed his place and continued his calculations.

"What is he doing there!" said the inspector.

"Counting his treasures," replied the governor.

Faria replied to this sarcasm by a glance of profound contempt.

They left the dungeon, and the door closed behind them.

"He has been wealthy once, perhaps," said the inspector.

" Or dreamed he was, and awoke mad."

" After all," said the inspector, with the candor of corruption, " if he had been rich, he would not have been here."

Thus finished the adventure of the Abbé Faria. He remained in his cell, and this visit only increased the belief of his insanity.

Caligula or Nero, those treasure-seekers, those desirers of the impossible, would have accorded to the poor wretch, in exchange for his wealth, the liberty and the air he so earnestly prayed for. But the kings of modern ages, retained within the limits of probability, have neither the courage nor the desire. They fear the ear that hears their orders, and the eye that scrutinizes their actions. They do not feel the divinity that hedges a king; they are men with crowns—that is all. Formerly they believed themselves sprung from Jupiter, and shielded by their birth; but, nowadays, they are not inviolable. It has always been against the policy of despotic governments to suffer the victims of their policy to re-appear. As the Inquisition rarely suffered its victims to be seen with their limbs distorted and their flesh lacerated by torture, so madness is always concealed in its cell, from whence, should it depart, it is conveyed to some gloomy hospital, where the doctor recognizes neither man nor mind in the mutilated being the jailer delivers to him. The very madness of the Abbé Faria, gone mad in prison, condemned him to perpetual captivity.

The inspector kept his word with Dantès: he examined the register, and found the following note concerning him:

Edmond Dantès. $\begin{cases} \textit{Violent Bonapartist ; took an active part in the return} \\ \quad \textit{from Elba.} \\ \textit{The greatest watchfulness and care to be exercised.} \end{cases}$

This note was in a different hand from the rest, which proved it had been added since his confinement. The inspector could not contend against this accusation; he simply wrote, *Nothing to be done.*

This visit had infused new vigor into Dantès; he had, till then, forgotten the date; but now, with a fragment of plaster, he wrote the date, 30th July, 1816; and made a mark every day, in order not to lose his reckoning again. Days and weeks passed away, then months — Dantès still waited; he at first expected to be freed in a fortnight. This fortnight expired; he reflected the inspector would do nothing until his return to Paris, and that he would not reach there until his circuit was finished; he therefore fixed three months; three months passed away, then six more. During these ten months no favorable change had taken place; no consoling news came, his jailer was dumb as usual, and Dantès began to fancy the inspector's visit was but a dream, an illusion of the brain.

At the expiration of a year the governor was changed; he had obtained the government of Ham. He took with him several of his subordinates, and amongst them Dantès' jailer. A fresh governor arrived. It would have been too tedious to acquire the names of the prisoners; he learned their numbers instead. This horrible boarding-house consisted of fifty chambers; their inhabitants were designated by the number of their chamber; and the unhappy young man was no longer called Edmond Dantès,— he was now No. 34.

CHAPTER XV

ANTES passed through all the degrees of misfortune that prisoners, forgotten in their dungeons, suffer. He commenced with pride, a natural consequence of hope and a consciousness of innocence; then he began to doubt his own innocence, which justified in some measure the governor's belief in his mental alienation; and then, falling into the opposite extreme, he supplicated, not Heaven, but his jailer. Heaven, which ought to be the first resort of the unhappy, is the last one, only sought when all others have been tried in vain.

Dantès entreated to be removed from his present dungeon into another, even if it were darker and deeper, for a change, however disadvantageous, was still a change, and would afford him some amusement. He entreated to be allowed to walk about, to have books and instruments. Nothing was granted; no matter, he asked all the same. He accustomed himself to speak to his fresh jailer, although he was, if possible, more taciturn than the former; but still, to speak to a man, even though a mute, was something. Dantès spoke for the sake of hearing his own voice; he had tried to speak when alone, but the sound of his voice terrified him.

Often, before his captivity, Dantès' mind had revolted at the idea of those assemblages of prisoners, composed of thieves, vagabonds, and murderers. He now wished to be amongst them, in order to see some other face besides that of his jailer; he sighed for the galleys, with their infamous costume, their chain, and the brand on the shoulder. The galley-slaves breathed the fresh air of heaven, and saw each other. They were very happy.

He besought the jailer one day to let him have a companion, were it even the mad abbé. The jailer, though rude and hardened by the constant sight of so much suffering, was yet a man. At the bottom of his heart he had often compassionated the unhappy young man who suffered thus; and he laid the request of No. 34 before the governor; but the latter sapiently imagined that Dantès wished to conspire or attempt an escape, and refused his request. Dantès had exhausted all human resources; and he then turned to God.

All the pious ideas that had been so long forgotten, returned; he recollected the prayers his mother had taught him, and discovered a new meaning in every word; for in prosperity prayers seem but a mere assemblage of words, until the day when misfortune comes to explain to the unhappy sufferer the sublime language by which he speaks to God. He prayed and prayed aloud, no longer terrified at the sound of his voice; for he fell into a species of ecstasy and saw God at every word he uttered. He laid every action of his life before the Almighty, proposed tasks to accomplish, and at the end of every prayer introduced the entreaty oftener addressed to man than to God, "Forgive us our trespasses as we forgive them that trespass against us." Spite of his earnest prayers, Dantès remained a prisoner.

Then a gloomy feeling took possession of him. He was simple, and without education; he could not, therefore, in the solitude of his dungeon, and of his own thoughts, reconstruct the ages that had passed, reanimate the nations that had perished, and rebuild the ancient cities that imagination renders so vast and poetic, and that pass before our eyes, illuminated by the fires of heaven, as in Martin's pictures of Babylon. He could not do this, he whose past life was so short, whose present so melancholy, and his future so doubtful. Nineteen years of light to reflect upon in eternal darkness. No distraction could come to his aid; his energetic spirit, that would have exulted in thus revisiting the past, was imprisoned like an eagle in a cage. He clung to one idea — that of his happiness, destroyed, without apparent cause, by an unheard of fatality; he considered and reconsidered this idea, devoured it (thus to speak), as Ugolino devours the skull of the Archbishop Roger in the Inferno of Dante.

Rage succeeded to this. Dantès uttered blasphemies that made his jailer recoil with horror, dashed himself furiously against the walls of his prison; he was in a fury with everything, and chiefly himself, and the least thing — a grain of sand, a straw, or a breath of air — that annoyed him. Then the letter of denunciation that he had seen and that Villefort had showed to him recurred to his mind, and every line seemed visible in fiery letters on the wall, like the *Mene Tekel Upharsin* of Belshazzar. He said that it was the vengeance of man, and not of Heaven, that had thus plunged him into the deepest misery. He devoted these unknown persecutors to the most horrible tortures he could devise in his ardent imagination, and found them all insufficient, because after torture came death, and after death, if not repose, at least that insensibility that resembles it.

By dint of constantly dwelling on the idea that repose was death, and, in order to punish, other tortures than death must be invented, he began to reflect on suicide. Unhappy he, who, on the brink of misfortune, broods over these ideas! It is one of those dead seas that seem clear and smooth to the eye; but he who unwarily ventures within its embrace finds himself entangled in the bituminous deposit that draws him down and swallows him. Once thus ensnared, unless the protecting hand of God snatch him thence, all is over, and his struggles but tend to hasten his destruction. This state of mental anguish is, however, less terrible than the sufferings that precede, and the punishment that awaits it — a sort of consolation that points to the yawning abyss, at the bottom of which is nothingness.

Edmond found some solace in these ideas. All his sorrows, all his sufferings, with their train of gloomy specters, fled from his cell when the angel of death seemed about to enter. Dantès reviewed with composure his past life, and, looking forward with terror to his future existence, chose that middle line that seemed to afford him a refuge.

" Sometimes," said he, " in my voyages, when I was a man and commanded other men, I have seen the heavens become overcast, the sea rage and foam, the storm arise, and, like a monstrous bird, cover the sky with its wings. Then I felt that my vessel was a vain refuge that, like a feather in a giant's hand, trembled and shook before the tempest. Soon the fury of the waves and the sight of the sharp rocks announced the approach of death, and death then terrified me, and I used all my skill and intelligence as a man and a sailor to escape. But I did so because I was happy, because I had not courted death, because this repose on a bed of rocks and seaweed seemed terrible, because I was unwilling that I, a creature made for the service of God, should serve for food to the gulls and vultures. But now it is different: I have lost all that bound me to life; death smiles and invites me to repose; I die after my own manner, I die exhausted and broken-spirited, as I fall asleep when I have paced three thousand times round my cell,— that is thirty thousand steps, or about ten leagues."

No sooner had this idea taken possession of him than he became more composed, arranged his couch to the best of his power, ate little and slept less, and found this existence almost supportable because he felt he could throw it off at pleasure, like a worn-out garment. He had two means of dying: the one was to hang himself with his handkerchief, to the stanchions of the window; the other, to refuse food, and starve himself. But the former means were repugnant to him. Dantès had always entertained the greatest horror of pirates, who are hung up to the yard-arm; he would not die by what seemed an infamous death. He resolved to adopt the second, and began that day to execute his resolve.

Nearly four years had thus passed away; at the end of the second he had ceased to mark the lapse of time. Dantès said, " I wish to die," and had chosen the manner of his death; and, fearful of changing his mind, he had taken an oath to die. "When my morning and evening meals are brought," thought he, "I will cast them out of the window, and I shall be believed to have eaten them."

He kept his word: twice a day he cast out, by the barred aperture, the provisions his jailer brought him—at first gayly, then with deliberation, and at last with regret. Nothing but the recollection of his oath gave him strength to proceed. Hunger rendered these viands, once so repugnant, acceptable to him; he held the plate in his hand for an hour at a time, and gazed on the morsel of bad meat, of tainted fish, of black and moldy bread. It was the last instinct of life, which occasionally vanquished his resolve; then his dungeon seemed less somber, his prospects less desperate. He was still young—he was only four or five and twenty—he had nearly fifty years to live. What unforeseen events might not open his prison door and restore him to liberty? Then he raised to his lips the repast that, like a voluntary Tantalus, he refused himself; but he thought of his oath, and he would not break it. He persisted until, at last, he had not sufficient force to cast his supper out of the loop-hole. The next morning he could not see or hear; the jailer feared he was dangerously ill. Edmond hoped he was dying.

The day passed away thus: Edmond felt a species of stupor creeping over him; the gnawing pain at his stomach had ceased; his thirst had abated; when he closed his eyes he saw myriads of lights dancing before them, like the meteors that play about the marshes. It was the twilight of that mysterious country called Death!

Suddenly, about nine o'clock in the evening, Edmond heard a hollow sound in the wall against which he was lying.

So many loathsome animals inhabited the prison that their noise did not, in general, awake him; but whether abstinence had quickened his faculties, or whether the noise was really louder than usual, Edmond raised his head and listened. It was a continual scratching, as if made by a huge claw, a powerful tooth, or some iron instrument attacking the stones.

Although weakened, the young man's brain instantly recurred to the idea that haunts all prisoners—liberty! This sound came just at the time when all sounds were about to cease for him. It seemed to him that Heaven had at length taken pity on him, and had sent this noise to warn him on the very brink of the abyss. Perhaps one of those beloved ones he had so often thought of was thinking of him, and striving to diminish the distance that separated them.

No! no! doubtless he was deceived, and it was but one of those dreams that forerun death!

Edmond still heard the sound. It lasted nearly three hours; he then heard a noise of something falling, and all was silent.

Some hours afterward it began nearer and more distinct; Edmond became already interested in that labor, which seemed like companionship, when the jailer entered.

For a week that he had resolved to die, and for four days that he put this resolution into execution, Edmond had not spoken to this man, had not answered him when he inquired what was the matter with him, and turned his face to the wall when he looked too curiously at him; but now the jailer might hear this noise and put an end to it, thus destroying a ray of something like hope that soothed his last moments.

The jailer brought him his breakfast. Dantès raised himself up, and in loud tones began to speak on everything: on the bad quality of his food, on the coldness of his dungeon, grumbling and complaining, in order to have an excuse for speaking louder, and wearying the patience of his jailer, who had solicited some broth and white bread for his prisoner, and who had brought it.

Fortunately he fancied Dantès was delirious; and, placing his food on the rickety table, he withdrew. Left alone, Edmond listened, and the sound became more and more distinct.

"There can be no doubt," thought he, "it is some prisoner who is striving to obtain his freedom. Oh, if I were near him, how I would assist him."

Suddenly another idea took possession of his mind, so used to misfortune that it could scarcely understand hope; yet this idea possessed him, that the noise arose from the workmen the governor had ordered to repair the neighboring dungeon.

It was easy to ascertain this; but how could he risk the question? It was easy to call his jailer's attention to the noise, and watch his countenance as he listened; but might he not by this means betray interests far more precious than this short-lived satisfaction? Unfortunately, Edmond's brain was still so feeble that he could not bend his thoughts to anything in particular. He saw but one means of restoring lucidity and clearness to his judgment. He turned his eyes toward the soup his jailer had brought him, rose, staggered toward it, raised the vessel to his lips and drank off the contents with a feeling of indescribable pleasure.

He had the resolution to stop with this. He had often heard that shipwrecked persons had died through having eagerly devoured too much food; Edmond replaced on the table the bread he was about to devour, and returned to his couch — he did not wish to die. He soon felt that his ideas, so vague and intangible, became again collected — he could think, and strengthen his thoughts by reasoning. Then he said to himself:

"I must put this to the test, but without compromising anybody. If it is a workman, I need but knock against the wall, and he will cease to work, in order to find out who is knocking, and why he does so ; but as his occupation is sanctioned by the governor, he will soon resume it. If, on the contrary, it is a prisoner, the noise I make will alarm him, he will cease, and not recommence until he thinks every one is asleep."

Edmond rose again, but this time his legs did not tremble, and his eyes were free from mists; he advanced to a corner of his dungeon, detached a stone, and with it knocked against the wall where the sound came. He struck thrice.

At the first blow the sound ceased as if by magic.

Edmond listened intently : an hour passed, two hours passed, and no sound was heard; all was silent there on the other side of the wall.

Full of hope, Edmond swallowed a few mouthfuls of bread and water, and, thanks to the excellence of his constitution, found himself well-nigh recovered.

The day passed away in utter silence; night came without the noise having recommenced.

"It is a prisoner," said Edmond joyfully. His brain was on fire, and life and energy returned.

The night passed in perfect silence; Edmond did not close his eyes.

In the morning the jailer brought him fresh provisions — he had already devoured those of the previous day; he ate these, listening anxiously for the sound, fearing it had ceased forever; walking round and round his cell, shaking the iron bars of the loop-hole, restoring by exercise vigor and agility to his limbs, and preparing himself thus for his future destiny, as an athlete before entering the arena. At intervals he listened if the noise had not begun again, and grew impatient at the prudence of the prisoner, who did not guess he had been disturbed by a captive as anxious for liberty as himself.

Three days passed — seventy-two long tedious hours, counted minute by minute.

At length, one evening, as the jailer was visiting him for the last time that night, Dantès, as for the hundredth time he glued his ear to the wall, fancied he heard an almost imperceptible movement among the stones. Edmond recoiled from the wall, walked up and down his cell to collect his thoughts, and replaced his ear against the wall.

There could be no doubt something was passing on the other side; the prisoner had discovered the danger, and had substituted the lever for the chisel.

Encouraged by this discovery, Edmond determined to assist the indefatigable laborer. He began by moving his bed, behind which the work seemed to be going on, and sought with his eyes for anything with which he could pierce the wall, penetrate the cement, and displace a stone.

He saw nothing, he had no knife or sharp instrument, the grating

of his window alone was of iron, and he had too often assured himself of its solidity. All his furniture consisted of a bed, a chair, a table, a pail, and a jug. The bed had iron clamps, but they were screwed to the wood, and it would have required a screw-driver to take them off. The table and chair had nothing; the pail had had a handle, but that had been removed.

Dantès had but one resource, which was to break the jug, and with one of the sharp fragments attack the wall. He let the jug fall on his floor, and it broke in pieces.

Dantès concealed two or three of the sharpest fragments in his bed, leaving the rest on the floor. The breaking of his jug was too natural an accident to excite suspicion. Edmond had all the night to work in, but in the darkness he could not do much, and he soon felt his instrument was blunted against something hard; he pushed back his bed and awaited the day,—with hope, patience had returned.

All night he heard the subterranean workman, who continued to mine his way. The day came, the jailer entered. Dantès told him the jug had fallen from his hands in drinking, and the jailer went grumblingly to fetch another, without giving himself the trouble to remove the fragments of the broken one. He returned speedily, recommended the prisoner to be more careful, and departed.

Dantès heard joyfully the key grate in the lock—a sound that hitherto had chilled him to the heart. He listened until the sound of steps died away, and then, hastily displacing his bed, saw, by the faint light that penetrated into his cell, that he had labored uselessly the previous evening in attacking the stone instead of removing the plaster that surrounded it.

The damp had rendered it friable, and Dantès saw joyfully the plaster detach itself,— in small morsels, it is true; but at the end of half an hour he had scraped off a handful. A mathematician might have calculated that in two years, supposing that the rock was not encountered, a passage, twenty feet long and two feet square, might be formed.

The prisoner reproached himself with not having thus employed the hours he had passed in hopes, prayers, and despair. In six years, the time he had been confined, what might he not have accomplished?

This idea imparted new energy, and in three days he had succeeded, with the utmost precaution, in removing the cement and exposing the stone; the wall was formed of rough stones, to give solidity to which were imbedded, at intervals, blocks of hewn stone. It was one of these he had uncovered, and which he must remove from its socket.

Dantès strove to do so with his nails, but they were too weak. The fragments of the jug broke, and after an hour of useless toil, Dantès paused with anguish on his brow.

Was he to be thus stopped at the beginning, and was he to wait inactive until his fellow-workman had completed his toils? Suddenly an idea occurred to him,— he smiled, and the perspiration dried on his forehead.

The jailer always brought Dantès' soup in an iron saucepan; this saucepan contained the soup of a second prisoner; for Dantès had remarked that it was either quite full, or half empty, according as the turnkey gave it to himself or his companion first. The handle of this

saucepan was of iron; Dantès would have given ten years of his life in exchange for it.

The jailer poured the contents of this saucepan into Dantès' plate, who, after eating his soup with a wooden spoon, washed the plate, which thus served for every day. In the evening Dantès placed his plate on the ground near the door; the jailer, as he entered, stepped on it and broke it.

This time he could not blame Dantès. He was wrong to leave it there, but the jailer was wrong not to have looked before him. The jailer, therefore, contented himself with grumbling. Then he looked about him for something to pour the soup into; Dantès' whole furniture consisted of one plate — there was no alternative.

"Leave the saucepan," said Dantés; "you can take it away when you bring me my breakfast."

This advice was to the jailer's taste, as it spared him the necessity of ascending, descending, and ascending again. He left the saucepan.

Dantès was beside himself with joy. He rapidly devoured his food, and after waiting an hour, lest the jailer should change his mind and return, he removed his bed, took the handle of the saucepan, inserted the point between the hewn stone and rough stones of the wall, and employed it as a lever. A slight oscillation showed to Dantès that all went well. At the end of an hour the stone was extricated from the wall, leaving a cavity of a foot and a half in diameter.

Dantès carefully collected the plaster, carried it into the corners of his cell, and covered it with earth, which he scratched up with one of the pieces of his jug. Then, wishing to make the best use of this night, in which chance, or rather his own stratagem, had placed so precious an instrument in his hands, he continued to work without ceasing. At the dawn of day he replaced the stone, pushed his bed against the wall, and lay down. The breakfast consisted of a piece of bread; the jailer entered and placed the bread on the table.

"Well, you do not bring me another plate," said Dantès.

"No," replied the turnkey, "you smash everything. First you break your jug, then you make me break your plate; if all the prisoners followed your example, the government would be ruined. I shall leave you the saucepan, and pour your soup into that. So for the future, perhaps, you will not be so destructive to your furniture."

Dantès raised his eyes to heaven, clasped his hands beneath the coverlid, and prayed. He felt more gratitude for the possession of this piece of iron than he had ever felt for anything. He had, however, remarked that the prisoner on the other side had ceased to labor; no matter, this was a greater reason for proceeding — if his neighbor would not come to him, he would go to him.

All day he toiled on untiringly, and by the evening he had succeeded in extracting ten handfuls of plaster and fragments of stone. When the hour for his jailer's visit arrived, Dantès straightened the handle of the saucepan as well as he could, and placed it in its accustomed place. The turnkey poured his ration of soup into it, together with the fish, for thrice a week the prisoners were made to abstain from meat: this would have been a method of reckoning time, had not Dantès long ceased to do so. Having poured out the soup, the turnkey retired.

Dantès wished to ascertain whether his neighbor had really ceased to work. He listened — all was silent, as it had been for the last three days. Dantès sighed; it was evident that his neighbor distrusted him. However, he toiled on all the night without being discouraged; but after two or three hours he encountered an obstacle. The iron made no impression, but met with a smooth surface; Dantès touched it, and found it was a beam. This beam crossed, or rather blocked up, the hole Dantès had made; it was necessary, therefore, to dig above or under it. The unhappy young man had not thought of this.

"O my God! my God!" murmured he, "I have so earnestly prayed to you, that I hoped my prayers had been heard. After having deprived me of my liberty, after having deprived me of death, after having recalled me to existence, my God! have pity on me, and do not let me die in despair."

"Who talks of God and despair at the same time?" said a voice that seemed to come from beneath the earth, and, deadened by the distance, sounded hollow and sepulchral in the young man's ears. Edmond's hair stood on end, and he rose on his knees.

"Ah!" said he, "I hear a human voice." Edmond had not heard any one speak save his jailer for four or five years; and to a prisoner a jailer is not a man — he is a living door added to his door of oak, a barrier of flesh and blood added to his barriers of iron.

"In the name of Heaven," cried Dantès, "speak again, though the sound of your voice terrifies me."

"Who are you?" said the voice.

"An unhappy prisoner," replied Dantès, who made no hesitation in answering.

"Of what country?"

"A Frenchman."

"Your name?"

"Edmond Dantès."

"Your profession?"

"A sailor."

"How long have you been here?"

"Since the 28th of February, 1815."

"Your crime?"

"I am innocent."

"But of what are you accused?"

"Of having conspired to aid the emperor's return."

"How for the emperor's return? — the emperor is no longer on the throne, then?"

"He abdicated at Fontainebleau in 1814, and was sent to the island of Elba. But how long have you been here that you are ignorant of all this?"

"Since 1811."

Dantès shuddered: this man had been four years longer than himself in prison.

" Do not dig any more," said the voice; " only tell me how high up is your excavation ? "

" On a level with the floor."

" How is it concealed ? "

" Behind my bed."

" Has your bed been moved since you have been a prisoner ? "

" No."

" What does your chamber open on ? "

" A corridor."

" And the corridor ? "

" On a court."

" Alas ! " murmured the voice.

" Oh, what is the matter ? " cried Dantès.

" I am deceived, and the imperfection of my plans has ruined all. An error of a line in the plan has been equivalent to fifteen feet in reality, and I took the wall you are mining for the wall of the fortress."

" But then you would end at the sea ? "

" That is what I hoped."

" And supposing you succeeded ? "

" I should have thrown myself into the sea, gained one of the islands near here,— the Isle de Daume or the Isle de Tiboulen,—and then I was safe."

" Could you have swum so far ? "

" Heaven would have given me strength; but now all is lost."

" All ? "

" Yes; stop up your excavation carefully; do not work any more, and wait until you hear from me."

" Tell me, at least, who you are."

" I am — I am No. 27."

" You mistrust me, then," said Dantès.

Edmond fancied he heard a bitter laugh proceed from the unknown.

" Oh, I am a Christian," cried Dantés, guessing instinctively that this man meant to abandon him. " I swear to you by Him who died for us that I will die rather than breathe one syllable of the truth to our jailers; but, I conjure you, do not abandon me. Let me know you are near, let me hear your voice. If you do abandon me, I swear to you that I will dash my brains out against the wall, and you will have my death to reproach yourself with."

"How old are you ? Your voice is that of a young man."

"I do not know my age, for I have not counted the years I have been here. All I do know is that I was just nineteen when I was arrested, the 28th of February, 1815."

"Not quite twenty-six!" murmured the voice; "at that age he cannot be a traitor."

"Oh! no, no!" cried Dantès. "I swear to you again, rather than betray you they shall hew me to pieces."

"You have done well to speak to me and entreat me, for I was about to form another plan, and leave you; but your age re-assures me. I will not forget you. Expect me."

"When?"

"I must calculate our chances; I will give you the signal."

"But you will not leave me; you will come to me, or you will let me come to you. We will escape, and if we cannot escape we will talk,—you of those whom you love, and I of those whom I love. You must love somebody."

"No, I am alone in the world."

"Then you will love me. If you are young, I will be your comrade; if you are old, I will be your son. I have a father who is seventy if he yet lives; I only love him and a young girl called Mercédès. My father has not yet forgotten me, I am sure; but God alone knows if she loves me still; I shall love you as I loved my father."

"It is well," returned the voice; "to-morrow."

These few words were uttered with an accent that left no doubt of his sincerity; Dantès rose, dispersed the fragments with the same precaution as before, and pushed back his bed against the wall. He then gave himself up to his happiness; he would no longer be alone. He was, perhaps, about to regain his liberty. At the worst, he would have a companion; and captivity that is shared is but half captivity.

All day Dantès walked up and down his cell, his breast throbbing with joy. He sat down occasionally on his bed, pressing his hand on his heart. At the slightest noise he bounded toward the door. Once or twice the thought crossed his mind that he might be separated from this unknown, whom he loved already; and then his mind was made up,—when the jailer moved his bed and stooped to examine the opening, he would kill him with his water-jug. He would be condemned to die, but he was about to die of grief and despair when this miraculous noise recalled him to life.

The jailer came in the evening; Dantès was on his bed. It seemed to him that thus he better guarded the unfinished opening. Doubtless there was a strange expression in his eyes, for the jailer said, "Come, are you going mad again?"

Dantès did not answer; he feared that the emotion of his voice would betray him. The jailer retired, shaking his head. The night came; Dantès hoped that his neighbor would profit by the silence to

FABIA ENTERS DANTÈS' CELL.

address him, but he was mistaken. The next morning, however, just as he removed his bed from the wall, he heard three knocks; he threw himself on his knees.

" Is it you ? " said he ; " I am here."

" Is your jailer gone ? "

" Yes," said Dantès; " he will not return until evening; so that we have twelve hours before us."

" I can work, then," said the voice.

" Oh, yes, yes; this instant, I entreat you."

In an instant the portion of the floor on which Dantès (half buried in the opening) was leaning his two hands, gave way; he cast himself back, whilst a mass of stones and earth disappeared in a hole that opened beneath the aperture he himself had formed. Then from the bottom of this passage, the depth of which it was impossible to measure, he saw appear, first the head, then the shoulders, and lastly the body of a man, who sprang lightly into his cell.

CHAPTER XVI

RUSHING toward the friend so long and ardently desired, Dantès almost carried him toward the window, in order to obtain a better view of his features by the aid of the imperfect light that struggled through the grating of the prison. He was a man of small stature, with hair blanched rather by suffering and sorrow than years. A deep-set, penetrating eye, almost buried beneath the thick gray eyebrow, and a long (and still black) beard reaching down to his breast. The meagerness of his features, furrowed with deep wrinkles, joined to the bold outline of his strongly marked features announced a man more accustomed to exercise his moral faculties than his physical strength. Large drops of perspiration were now standing on his brow, while his garments hung about him in such rags as to render it useless to form a guess as to their primitive description.

The stranger might have numbered sixty or sixty-five years; but a certain vigor in his movements made it probable that he was aged more from captivity than the course of time. He received the enthusiastic greeting of his young acquaintance with evident pleasure, as though his chilled affections seemed rekindled and invigorated by his contact with one so ardent. He thanked him with grateful cordiality for his kindly welcome, although he must at that moment have been suffering bitterly to find another dungeon where he had fondly reckoned on finding liberty.

"Let us first see," said he, "whether it is possible to remove the traces of my entrance here — our future comforts depend upon our jailers being entirely ignorant of it."

Advancing to the opening, he stooped and raised the stone easily in spite of its weight; then, fitting it into its place, he said:

" You removed this stone very carelessly; but I suppose you had no tools to aid you."

" Why," exclaimed Dantès, with astonishment, " do you possess any ? "

" I made myself some; and, with the exception of a file, I have all that are necessary — a chisel, pincers, and lever."

" Oh, how I should like to see these products of your industry and patience."

" Well, in the first place, here is my chisel."

So saying, he displayed a sharp, strong blade, with a handle made of beechwood.

"And with what did you contrive to make that?" inquired Dantès.

"With one of the clamps of my bedstead; and this very tool has sufficed me to hollow out the road by which I came hither, a distance of at least fifty feet."

"Fifty feet!" reëchoed Dantès, with a species of terror.

"Do not speak so loud, young man — don't speak so loud. It frequently occurs in a state prison like this that persons are stationed outside the doors of the cells purposely to overhear the conversation of the prisoners."

"But they believe I am shut up alone here."

"That makes no difference."

"And you say that you penetrated a length of fifty feet to arrive here?"

"I do; that is about the distance that separates your chamber from mine; only, unfortunately, I did not curve aright; for want of the necessary geometrical instruments to calculate my scale of proportion, instead of taking an ellipsis of forty feet, I have made fifty. I expected, as I told you, to reach the outer wall, pierce through it, and throw myself into the sea; I have, however, kept along the corridor on which your chamber opens, instead of going beneath it. My labor is all in vain, for I find that the corridor looks into a court-yard filled with soldiers."

"That's true," said Dantès; "but the corridor you speak of only bounds *one* side of my cell; there are three others — do you know anything of their situation?"

"This one is built against the solid rock, and it would take ten experienced miners, duly furnished with the requisite tools, as many years to perforate it. This adjoins the lower part of the governor's apartments, and were we to work our way through, we should only get into some lock-up cellars, where we must necessarily be recaptured. The fourth and last side of your cell looks out — looks out — stop a minute; now, where does it open to?"

The side which thus excited curiosity was the one in which was fixed the loop-hole by which the light was admitted into the chamber. This loop-hole, which gradually diminished as it approached the outside, until only an opening through which a child could not have passed, was, for better security, furnished with three iron bars, so as to quiet all apprehensions even in the mind of the most suspicious jailer as to the possibility of a prisoner's escape. As the stranger finished his self-put question, he dragged the table beneath the window.

"Climb up," said he to Dantès.

The young man obeyed, mounted on the table, and, divining the intentions of his companion, placed his back securely against the wall, and held out both hands. The stranger, whom as yet Dantès knew only by his assumed title of the number of his cell, sprang up with an agility by no means to be expected in a person of his years, and, light and steady as the bound of a cat or a lizard, climbed from the table to the outstretched hands of Dantès, and from them to his shoulders; then, almost doubling himself in two, for the ceiling of the dungeon prevented his holding himself erect, he managed to slip his head through the top bar of the window, so as to be able to command a perfect view from top to bottom.

An instant afterward he hastily drew back his head, saying, "I thought so!" and, sliding from the shoulders of Dantès as dexterously as he had ascended, he nimbly leaped from the table to the ground.

"What made you say those words?" asked the young man, in an anxious tone, in his turn descending from the table.

The elder prisoner appeared to meditate. "Yes," said he at length, "it is so. This side of your chamber looks out upon a kind of open gallery, where patrols are continually passing, and sentries keep watch day and night."

"Are you sure of that?"

"Certain. I saw the soldier's shako and the top of his musket; that made me draw in my head so quickly, for I was fearful he might also see me."

"Well?" inquired Dantès.

"You perceive then the utter impossibility of escaping through your dungeon?"

"Then——" pursued the young man, eagerly.

"Then," answered the elder prisoner, "the will of God be done!" And as the old man slowly pronounced those words, an air of profound resignation spread itself over his care-worn countenance.

Dantès gazed on the individual who could thus philosophically resign hopes so long and ardently nourished, with an astonishment mingled with admiration.

"Tell me, I entreat of you, who and what you are?" said he at length.

"Willingly," answered the stranger; "if, indeed, you feel any curiosity now that I am powerless to aid you."

"Say not so; you can console and support me by the strength of your own powerful mind."

The stranger smiled a melancholy smile.

"Then listen," said he. "I am the Abbé Faria, and have been imprisoned in this Château d'If since the year 1811; previously to which

I had been confined for three years in the fortress of Fenestrelle. In the year 1811 I was transferred from Piedmont to France. It was at this period I learned that the destiny which seemed subservient to every wish formed by Napoleon had bestowed on him a son, named king of Rome even in his cradle. I was very far then from expecting the change you have just informed me of; namely, that four years afterward, this colossus of power would be overthrown. Then, who reigns in France at this moment — Napoleon II.?"

"No, Louis XVIII.!"

"The brother of Louis XVI.! How inscrutable are the ways of Providence — for what great and mysterious purpose has it pleased Heaven to abase the man once so elevated, and raise up the individual so cast down?"

Dantès' whole attention was riveted on the man who could thus forget his own misfortunes while occupying himself with the destinies of others.

"But so it was," continued he, "in England. After Charles I. came Cromwell; to Cromwell succeeded Charles II., and then James II., who was succeeded by some son-in-law or relation, who became king; then new concessions to the people, a constitution, and liberty! Ah, my friend!" said the abbé, turning toward Dantès, and surveying him with the kindling gaze of a prophet, "mark what I say! You are young, and may see my words come to pass, that such will be the case with France — you will see it, I say."

"Probably, if ever I get out of prison!"

"True," replied Faria, "we are prisoners; but I forget this sometimes, and there are even moments when my mental vision transports me beyond these walls, and I fancy myself at liberty."

"But wherefore are you here?"

"Because in 1807 I meditated the very scheme Napoleon wished to realize in 1811; because, like Machiavel, I desired to alter the political face of Italy, and instead of allowing it to be split up into a quantity of petty principalities, each held by some weak or tyrannical ruler, I sought to form one large, compact, and powerful empire; and, lastly, because I fancied I had found my Cæsar Borgia in a crowned simpleton, who feigned to enter into my views only to betray me. It was projected equally by Alexander VI. and Clement VII., but it will never succeed now, for they attempted it fruitlessly, and Napoleon was unable to complete his work. Italy seems fated to be unlucky."

The old man uttered these last words in a tone of deep dejection, and his head fell listlessly on his breast.

To Dantès all this was perfectly incomprehensible. In the first place, he could not understand a man risking his life and liberty for such unimportant matters as the division of a kingdom; then, again, the persons referred to were wholly unknown to him. Napoleon certainly he knew something of, inasmuch as he had seen and spoken with him; but the other individuals alluded to were strangers to him even by name.

"Pray excuse my questions," said Dantès, beginning to partake of the jailer's opinion touching the state of the abbé's brain, "but are you not the priest who is considered throughout the Château d'If — to — be — ill ?"

"Mad, you mean, don't you ?"

"I did not like to say so," answered Dantès, smiling.

"Well, then," resumed Faria, with a bitter smile, "let me answer your question in full, by acknowledging that I am the poor, mad prisoner of the Château d'If, for many years permitted to amuse the different visitants to the prison with what is said to be my insanity; and, in all probability, I should be promoted to the honor of making sport for the children, if such innocent beings could be found in an abode devoted like this to suffering and despair."

Dantès remained for a short time mute and motionless; at length he said:

"Then you abandon all hope of flight ?"

"I perceive its utter impossibility; and I consider it impious to attempt that which the Almighty evidently does not approve."

"Nay, be not discouraged. Would it not be expecting too much to hope to succeed at your first attempt ? Why not try to find an opening in another direction to that which had so unfortunately failed ?"

"Alas! it shows how little notion you can have of all I have done, if you talk of beginning over again. In the first place, I was four years making the tools I possess, and have been two years scraping and digging out earth, hard as granite itself; then, what toil and fatigue has it not been to remove huge stones I should once have deemed impossible to loosen! Whole days have I passed in these Titanic efforts, considering my labor well repaid if by night-time I had contrived to carry away a square inch of this old cement, as hard as the stones themselves; then, to conceal the mass of earth and rubbish I dug up, I was compelled to break through a staircase and throw the fruits of my labor into the hollow part of it; but the well is now so completely choked up that I scarcely think it would be possible to add another handful of dust without leading to a discovery. Consider also that I fully believed I had accomplished the end and aim of my undertaking, for which I had so exactly husbanded my strength as to make it just hold out to the termination of my enterprise; and, just at the moment when I reckoned upon success, my hopes are forever dashed from me. No, I repeat again, that nothing shall induce me to renew attempts to regain my liberty which the will of God has decreed I shall lose forever."

Dantès held down his head, that his companion might not perceive that the prospect of having a companion prevented him from sympathizing as he ought with the disappointment of the prisoner.

The abbé sunk upon Edmond's bed, while Edmond himself remained standing, lost in a train of deep meditation.

Flight had never once occurred to him. There are, indeed, some things which appear so impossible that the mind does not dwell on them. To undermine the ground for fifty feet — to devote three years to a labor which, if successful, would conduct you to a precipice overhanging the sea — to plunge into the waves at a height of fifty or sixty feet — a hundred feet, perhaps — at the risk of being dashed to pieces against the rocks, should you have been fortunate enough to have escaped the balls from the sentinel's musket; and even, supposing all these perils past, then to have to swim for your life a distance of at least three miles ere you could reach the shore — were difficulties so startling and formidable that Dantès had never even dreamed of such a scheme, but resigned himself to his fate.

But the sight of an old man clinging to life with so desperate a courage gave a fresh turn to his ideas, and inspired him with new courage and energy. An instance was before him of one less adroit, as well as weaker and older, having devised a plan which nothing but an unfortunate mistake in geometrical calculation could have rendered abortive, and of having, with almost incredible patience and perseverance, contrived to provide himself with tools requisite for so unparalleled an attempt. If, then, one man had already conquered the seeming impossibility, why should not he, Dantès, also try to regain his liberty? Faria had made his way through fifty feet of the prison; Dantès resolved to penetrate through double that distance. Faria, at the age of fifty, had devoted three years to the task; he, who was but half as old, would sacrifice six. Faria, a churchman and philosopher, had not shrunk from risking his life by trying to swim a distance of three miles to reach the isles of Daume, Ratonneau, or Lemaire; should a hardy sailor, an experienced diver, like himself, shrink from a similar task; should he, who had so often for mere amusement's sake plunged to the bottom of the sea to fetch up the bright coral-branch, hesitate to swim a distance of three miles? He could do it in an hour, and how many times had he for pure pastime continued in the water for more than twice as long! At once Dantès resolved to follow the example of his companion, and to remember that what has once been done may be done again.

After continuing some time in profound meditation, the young man suddenly exclaimed, "I have found what you were in search of!"

Faria started. "Have you, indeed?" cried he, raising his head with quick anxiety; pray, let me know what it is you have discovered?"

"The corridor through which you have bored your way from the cell you occupy here, extends in the same direction as the outer gallery, does it not?"

" It does ! "

" And is not above fifteen steps from it ? "

" About that ! "

" Well, then, I will tell you what we must do. We must pierce a side opening about the middle of the corridor, as it were the top part of a cross. This time you will lay your plans more accurately; we shall get out into the gallery you have described, kill the sentinel who guards it, and make our escape. All we require to insure success is courage, and that you possess, and strength, which I am not deficient in; as for patience, you have abundantly proved yours—you shall now see me prove mine."

" One instant, my dear friend," replied the abbé; "it is clear you do not understand the nature of the courage with which I am endowed, and what use I intend making of my strength. As for patience, I consider I have abundantly exercised that on recommencing every morning the task of the overnight, and every night beginning again the task of the day. But, then, young man (and I pray of you to give me your full attention), then I thought I could not be doing anything displeasing to the Almighty in trying to set an innocent being at liberty,—one who had committed no offense and merited not condemnation."

" And have your notions changed ? " asked Dantès with much surprise; " do you think yourself more guilty in making the attempt since you have encountered me ? "

" No; neither do I wish to incur guilt. Hitherto I have fancied myself merely waging war against circumstances, not men. I have thought it no sin to bore through a wall or destroy a staircase; but I cannot so easily persuade myself to pierce a heart or take away a life."

A slight movement of surprise escaped Dantès.

" Is it possible," said he, " that where your liberty is at stake you can allow any such scruple to deter you from obtaining it ? "

" Tell me," replied Faria, " what has hindered you from knocking down your jailer with a piece of wood torn from your bedstead, dressing yourself in his clothes, and endeavoring to escape ? "

" Simply that I never thought of such a scheme," answered Dantès.

" Because," said the old man, " the natural repugnance to the commission of such a crime prevented its bare idea from occurring to you; and so it ever is with all simple and allowable things. Our natural instincts keep us from deviating from the strict line of duty. The tiger, whose nature teaches him to delight in shedding blood, needs but the organ of smelling to know when his prey is within his reach; and by following this instinct he is enabled to measure the leap necessary to enable him to spring on his victim; but man, on the contrary, loathes the idea of blood;—not only the laws of social life, but the laws of his nature, recoil from murder."

Dantès remained confused and silent by this explanation of the thoughts which had unconsciously been working in his mind, or, rather,

soul; for there are two distinct sorts of ideas,—those that proceed from the head and those that emanate from the heart.

"Since my imprisonment," said Faria, "I have thought over all the most celebrated cases of escape recorded. Among the many that have failed, I consider there has been precipitation and haste. Those escapes that have been crowned with full success have been long meditated upon, and carefully arranged; such, for instance, as the escape of the Duke de Beaufort from the Château de Vincennes, that of the Abbé

Dubuquoi from For l'Evêque, and Latude's from the Bastile; chance, too, frequently affords opportunities we should never ourselves have thought of. Let us, therefore, wait patiently for some favorable moment, and take advantage of it."

"Ah!" said Dantès, "you might well endure the tedious delay; you were constantly employed in the task you set yourself, and when weary with toil, you had your hopes to refresh and encourage you."

"I assure you," replied the old man, "I did not turn to that source for recreation or support."

"What did you do then?"

"I wrote or studied."

"Were you then permitted the use of pens, ink, and paper?"

"Oh, no!" answered the abbé; "I had none but what I made for myself."

"Do you mean to tell me," exclaimed Dantès, "that you could make all those things?"

"I do, indeed, truly say so."

Dantès gazed with admiration on the abbé; some doubt, however, still lingered in his mind, which was quickly perceived by Faria.

"When you pay me a visit in my cell, my young friend," said he, "I will show you an entire work, the fruits of the thoughts and reflections of my whole life; many of them meditated over in the ruins of the Coliseum of Rome, at the foot of St. Mark's column at Venice, and on the borders of the Arno at Florence, little imagining at the time that they would be arranged in order within the walls of the Château d'If. The work I speak of is called *A Treatise on the Practicability of forming Italy into one General Monarchy*, and will make one large quarto volume."

"And on what have you written this?"

"On two of my shirts. I invented a preparation that makes linen as smooth and as easy to write on as parchment."

"You are, then, a chemist?"

"Somewhat; I knew Lavoisier, and was the intimate friend of Cabanis."

"But for such a work you must have needed books—had you any?"

"I possessed nearly five thousand volumes in my library at Rome; but, after reading them over many times, I found out that with one hundred and fifty well-chosen books a man possesses a complete analysis of all human knowledge, or at least all that is either useful or desirable to be acquainted with. I devoted three years of my life to reading and studying these one hundred and fifty volumes, till I knew them nearly by heart; so that since I have been in prison a very slight effort of memory has enabled me to recall their contents as readily as though the pages were open before me. I could recite you the whole of Thucydides, Xenophon, Plutarch, Livy, Tacitus, Strada, Jornandes, Dante, Montaigne, Shakspere, Spinosa, Machiavel, and Bossuet. Observe, I merely quote the most important names and writers."

"You are acquainted with a variety of languages?"

"Yes, I speak five of the modern tongues,— that is to say, German, French, Italian, English, and Spanish. By the aid of ancient Greek I learned modern Greek; I don't speak it well, but I am studying it now."

"Studying!" repeated Dantès.

"Why, I made a vocabulary of the words I knew; turned, re-turned, and arranged them, so as to enable me to express my thoughts through their medium. I know nearly one thousand words, which is all that is absolutely necessary, although I believe there are nearly one hundred thousand in the dictionaries. I cannot hope to be very fluent, but I certainly shall be understood; and that is all that is needed."

Stronger grew the wonder of Dantès, who almost fancied he had to do with one gifted with supernatural powers. Still hoping to find some imperfection, he added, "Then, if you were not furnished with pens, how did you manage to write the work you speak of?"

"I made myself some excellent ones, which would be universally preferred to all others if once known. You are aware what huge whitings are served to us on *maigre* days. Well, I selected the cartilages of the heads of these fishes, and you can scarcely imagine the delight with which I welcomed the arrival of each Wednesday, Friday, and Saturday, as affording me the means of increasing my stock of pens; for I will freely confess that my historical labors have been my greatest solace and relief. While retracing the past, I forget the present; and while following the free and independent course of historical record, I cease to remember that I am a prisoner."

"But the ink," said Dantès; "how have you procured that?"

"I will tell you," replied Faria. "There was formerly a fire-place in my dungeon, but closed up long ere I became an occupant of this prison. Still, it must have been many years in use, for it was thickly covered with a coating of soot; this soot I dissolved in a portion of the wine brought to me every Sunday, and I assure you a better ink cannot be desired. For very important notes, for which closer attention is required, I have pricked one of my fingers, and written the facts claiming notice in blood."

"And when," asked Dantès, "will you show me all this?"

"Whenever you please," replied the abbé.

"Oh, then, let it be directly!" exclaimed the young man.

"Follow me, then," said the abbé, as he reëntered the subterraneous passage, in which he soon disappeared, followed by Dantès.

CHAPTER XVII

THE ABBÉ'S CHAMBER

FTER having passed, in a stooping position but with toler-able ease, through the subterranean passage, the two friends reached the farther end of the corridor, into which the cell of the abbé opened; from that point the opening became much narrower, barely permitting a man to creep through on his hands and knees. The floor of the abbé's cell was paved, and it had been by raising one of the stones in the most obscure corner that Faria had been able to commence the laborious task of which Dantès had witnessed the completion.

. As he entered the chamber of his friend, Dantès cast around a searching glance, but nothing more than common met his view.

"It is well," said the abbé; "we have some hours before us — it is now just a quarter past twelve o'clock."

Instinctively Dantès turned round to observe by what watch or clock the abbé had been able so accurately to specify the hour.

"Look at this ray of light which enters by my window," said the abbé, "and then observe the lines traced on the wall. Well, by means of these lines, which are in accordance with the double motion of the earth, as well as the ellipse it describes round the sun, I am enabled to ascertain the precise hour with more minuteness than if I possessed a watch; for that might go wrong, while the sun and earth never vary."

This last explanation was wholly lost upon Dantès, who had always imagined, from seeing the sun rise from behind the mountains and set in the Mediterranean, that it moved, and not the earth. A double movement in the globe he inhabited, and of which he could feel nothing, appeared to him perfectly impossible; still, each word that fell from his lips seemed fraught with the wonders of science, as admirably deserving of being brought fully to light as the mines of gold and diamonds he could just recollect having visited during his earliest youth in a voyage he made to Guzerat and Golconda.

" Come," said he to the abbé, " show me the wonderful inventions you told me of."

The abbé, proceeding to the fire-place, raised, by the help of his chisel, a stone, which had been the hearth, beneath which was a cavity of considerable depth, serving as a depository of the articles mentioned to Dantès.

" What do you wish to see first ? " asked the abbé.

" Oh! your great work on the monarchy of Italy ! "

Faria then drew forth from his hiding-place three or four rolls of linen, laid one over the other like the folds of papyrus. These rolls consisted of slips of cloth about four inches wide and eighteen long; they were all carefully numbered and closely covered with writing, so legible that Dantès could easily read it, as well as make out the sense — it being in Italian, a language he, as a Provençal, perfectly understood. " There !" said he, " there is the work complete — I wrote the word *finis* at the end of the sixty-eighth strip about a week ago. I have torn up two of my shirts, and as many handkerchiefs as I was master of, to complete the precious pages. Should I ever get out of prison, and find a printer to publish what I have composed, my reputation is secured."

" I see," answered Dantès. " Now let me behold the curious pens with which you have written your work."

" Look !" said Faria, showing to the young man a slender stick about six inches long, and much resembling the size of the handle of a fine painting brush, to the end of which was tied, by a piece of thread, one of those cartilages of which the abbé had before spoken to Dantès; it was pointed, and divided at the nib like an ordinary pen. Dantès examined it with intense admiration, then looked around to see the instrument with which it had been shaped so correctly into form.

" Ah, I see," said Faria. " My penknife ? That was a master-piece ! I made it, as well as this knife, out of an old iron candlestick."

The penknife was sharp and keen as a razor ; as for the other knife, it possessed the double advantage of being capable of serving either as a dagger or a knife.

Dantès examined the various articles shown to him with the same attention he had bestowed on the curiosities and strange tools exhibited in the shops at Marseilles as the works of the savages in the South Seas, from whence they had been brought by the different trading vessels.

" As for the ink," said Faria," I told you how I managed ; and I only just make it as I require it."

" There is one thing puzzles me still," observed Dantès, " and that is how you managed to do all this by daylight."

" I worked at night also," replied Faria.

" Night ! — why, for Heaven's sake, are your eyes like cats', that you can see to work in the dark ?"

" Indeed they are not ; but a beneficent Creator has supplied man with intelligence and ability to supply his wants. I furnished myself with a light."

" You did ? "

" I separated the fat from the meat served to me, melted it, and made a sort of oil — here is my lamp." So saying, the abbé exhibited a sort of vessel very similar to those employed upon the occasion of public illuminations.

"But how do you procure a light?"

"Oh, here are two flints and a morsel of burnt linen. I feigned a

disorder of the skin, and asked for a little sulphur, which was readily supplied."

Dantès laid the different things he had been looking at gently on the table, and stood with his head drooping, as though overwhelmed by the persevering spirit of such a character.

" You have not seen all yet," continued Faria, " for I did not think it wise to trust all my treasures in the same hiding-place. Let us shut this one up."

Dantès helped him to replace the stone; the abbé sprinkled a little dust over it, rubbed his foot well on it to make it assume the same appearance as the other, and then, going toward his bed, he removed it from the spot it stood in.

Behind the head of the bed, and concealed by a stone fitting in so closely as to defy all suspicion, was a hollow space, and in this space a ladder of cords, between twenty-five and thirty feet in length.

Dantès closely and eagerly examined it; he found it firm, solid, and compact enough to bear any weight.

" Who supplied you with the materials for making this wonderful work?" asked Dantès.

" No one but myself. I tore up several of my shirts, and unraveled the sheets of my bed, during my three years' imprisonment at Fenestrelle; and when I was removed to the Château d'If, I managed to bring the ravelings with me, so that I have been able to finish my work here."

" And was it not discovered that your sheets were unhemmed?"

" Oh, no! for when I had taken out the thread I required, I hemmed the edges over again."

" With what?"

" With this needle!" said the abbé, as, opening his ragged vestments, he showed Dantès a long, sharp fish-bone, with a small, perforated eye for the thread, a small portion of which still remained in it.

" I once thought," continued Faria, " of removing these iron bars, and letting myself down from the window, which, as you see, is somewhat wider than yours, although I should have enlarged it still more preparatory to my flight; however, I discovered that I should merely have dropped into a sort of inner court, and I therefore renounced the project altogether as too full of risk and danger. Nevertheless, I carefully preserved my ladder against one of those unforeseen opportunities of which I spoke just now, and which chance frequently brings about."

While affecting to be deeply engaged in examining the ladder, the mind of Dantès was, in fact, busily occupied by the idea that a person so intelligent, ingenious, and clear-sighted as the abbé might probably be enabled to clear up the dark recesses of his own misfortunes, in which he had in vain sought to distinguish aught.

" What are you thinking of?" asked the abbé smilingly, imputing the deep abstraction in which his visitor was plunged to the excess of his awe and wonder.

" I was reflecting, in the first place," replied Dantès, " upon the enormous degree of intelligence you must have employed to reach the high perfection to which you have attained. What would you not have accomplished free ?"

" Possibly nothing at all; the overflow of my brain would have evaporated in follies; it needs trouble to hollow out various mysterious mines of human intelligence. Pressure is required, you know, to crush the beam: captivity has collected into one single focus all the floating faculties of my mind; they have come into close contact in the narrow space; and you are well aware that from the collision of clouds electricity is produced — from electricity the lightning, from whose flash we have light."

" Alas, no !" replied Dantès. " I know not that these things follow in such natural order. Oh, I am very ignorant ! and you must be blessed indeed to possess the knowledge you have."

The abbé smiled.

" Well," said he, " but you had another subject for your thoughts besides admiration for me; did you not say so just now ?"

" I did !"

" You have told me as yet but one of them,— let me hear the other."

" It was this: that while you had related to me all the particulars of your past life, you were perfectly unacquainted with mine."

" Your life, my young friend, has not been of sufficient length to admit of any very important events."

" It admits of a terrible misfortune which I have not deserved. I would fain know who has been the author of it, that I may no longer accuse Heaven, as I have done, but charge men with my woes."

" Then you profess ignorance of the crime with which you are charged ?"

" I do, indeed; and this I swear by the two beings most dear to me upon earth — my father and Mercédès."

" Come," said the abbé, closing his hiding-place, and pushing the bed back to its original situation, " let me hear your story."

Dantès obeyed, and commenced what he called his history, but which consisted only of the account of a voyage to India, and two or three in the Levant, until he arrived at the recital of his last cruise, with the death of Captain Leclere, and the receipt of a packet to be delivered by himself to the grand-maréchal; his interview with that personage, and his receiving, in place of the packet brought, a letter addressed to M. Noirtier; his arrival at Marseilles, and interview with his father; his affection for Mercédès, and their nuptial fête; his arrest and subsequent examination in the temporary prison of the Palais de Justice, ending in his final imprisonment in the Château d'If.

From the period of his arrival there he knew nothing, not even the length of time he had been imprisoned. His recital finished, the abbé reflected long and earnestly.

"There is," said he, at the end of his meditations, "a clever maxim, which bears upon what I was saying to you some little while ago, and that is, that unless wicked ideas take root in a naturally depraved mind, human nature revolts at crime. Still, from civilization have originated wants, vices, and false tastes, which occasionally stifle within us all good feelings, and lead us into guilt. From this view of things, then, comes the axiom I allude to — that if you wish to discover the author of any bad action, discover the person to whom that bad action could be advantageous. Now, to whom could your disappearance have been serviceable ? "

"To no breathing soul. Why, who could have cared about the removal of so insignificant a person as myself ? "

" Do not speak thus, for your reply evinces neither logic nor philosophy; everything is relative, my dear young friend, from the king who obstructs his successor's immediate possession of the throne, to the occupant of a place for which the supernumary to whom it has been promised ardently longs. Now, in the event of the king's death, his successor inherits a crown; — when the placeman dies, the supernumary steps into his shoes and receives his salary of twelve thousand livres. Well, these twelve thousand livres are his civil list, and are as essential to him as the twelve millions of a king. Every individual, from the highest to the lowest degree, has his place in the ladder of social life, and around him are grouped a little world of interests, composed of stormy passions and conflicting atoms, like the worlds of Descartes; but let us return to your world. You say you were on the point of being appointed captain of the *Pharaon ?* "

"I was."

"And about to become the husband of a young and lovely girl ? "

"True."

"Now, could any one have had any interest in preventing the accomplishment of these two circumstances ? But let us first settle the question as to its being the interest of any one to hinder you from being captain of the *Pharaon*. What say you ? "

"No! I was generally liked on board; and had the sailors possessed the right of electing a captain, their choice would have fallen on me. There was only one person among the crew who had any feeling of ill will toward me. I had quarreled with him some time previously, and had even challenged him to fight me; but he refused."

"Now we are getting on. And what was this man's name ? "

" Danglars."

" What rank did he hold on board ? "

" He was supercargo."

" And had you been captain, should you have retained him in his employment ? "

" Not if the choice had remained with me, for I had frequently observed inaccuracies in his accounts."

" Good again! Now then, tell me, was any person present during your last conversation with Captain Leclere ? "

" No; we were quite alone."

" Could your conversation be overheard by any one ? "

" It might, for the cabin door was open;— and — stay; now I recollect,— Danglars himself passed by just as Captain Leclere was giving me the packet for the grand-maréchal."

" That will do," cried the abbé; " now we are on the right scent. Did you take anybody with you when you put into the port of Elba ? "

" Nobody."

" Somebody there received your packet, and gave you a letter in place of it, I think ? "

" Yes; the grand-maréchal did."

" And what did you do with that letter ? "

" Put it into my pocket-book."

" Ah! indeed! You had your pocket-book with you, then ? Now, how could a pocket-book, large enough to contain an official letter, find sufficient room in the pockets of a sailor ? "

" You are right: I had it not with me,— it was left on board."

" Then it was not till your return to the ship that you placed the letter in the pocket-book ? "

" No."

" And what did you do with this same letter while returning from Porto-Ferrajo to your vessel ? "

" I carried it in my hand."

" So that when you went on board the *Pharaon*, everybody could perceive you held a letter in your hand ? "

" To be sure they could."

" Danglars, as well as the rest ? "

" Yes; he as well as others."

" Now, listen to me, and try to recall every circumstance attending your arrest. Do you recollect the words in which the information against you was couched ? "

" Oh, yes! I read it over three times, and the words sank deeply into my memory."

"Repeat it to me."

Dantès paused a few instants, as though collecting his ideas, then said, "This is it, word for word: 'M. le Procureur du Roi is informed, by a friend to the throne and religion, that an individual, named Edmond Dantès, second in command on board the *Pharaon*, this day arrived from Smyrna, after having touched at Naples and Porto-Ferrajo, has been charged by Murat with a packet for the usurper; again, by the usurper, with a letter for the Bonapartist Club in Paris. This proof of his guilt may be procured by his immediate arrest, as the letter will be found either about his person, at his father's residence, or in his cabin on board the *Pharaon.*' "

The abbé shrugged up his shoulders. "The thing is clear as day," said he; "and you must have had a very unsuspecting nature, as well as a good heart, not to have suspected the origin of the whole affair."

"Do you really think so? Ah, that would indeed be the treachery of a villain!"

"How did Danglars usually write?"

"Oh! extremely well."

"And how was the anonymous letter written?"

"All the wrong way — backward, you know."

Again the abbé smiled. "In fact, it was a disguised hand?"

"I don't know; it was very boldly written, if disguised."

"Stop a bit," said the abbé, taking up what he called his pen, and, after dipping it into the ink, he wrote on a morsel of prepared linen, with his left hand, the first two or three words of the accusation. Dantès drew back, and gazed on the abbé with a sensation almost amounting to terror.

"How very astonishing!" cried he at length. "Why, your writing exactly resembles that of the accusation!"

"Simply because that accusation had been written with the left hand; and I have always remarked one thing——"

"What is that?"

"That whereas all writing done with the right hand varies, that performed with the left hand is invariably similar."

"You have evidently seen and observed everything."

"Let us proceed."

"Oh! yes, yes! Let us go on."

"Now, as regards the second question. Was there any person whose interest it was to prevent your marriage with Mercédès?"

"Yes, a young man who loved her."

"And his name was—— "

"Fernand."

" That is a Spanish name, I think ! "

" He was a Catalan."

" You imagine him capable of writing the letter ? "

" Oh, no! he would more likely have got rid of me by sticking a knife into me."

" That is in strict accordance with the Spanish character; an assassination they will unhesitatingly commit, but an act of cowardice, never."

" Besides," said Dantès, " the various circumstances mentioned in the letter were wholly unknown to him."

" You had never spoken of them yourself to any one ? "

" To no person whatever."

" Not even to your mistress ? "

" No, not even to my betrothed bride."

" Then it is Danglars, beyond a doubt."

" I feel quite sure of it now."

" Wait a little. Pray, was Danglars acquainted with Fernand ? "

" No —— yes, he was. Now I recollect —— "

" What ? "

" To have seen them both sitting at the table together beneath an arbor at Père Pamphile's the evening before the day fixed for my wedding. They were in earnest conversation. Danglars was joking in a friendly way, but Fernand looked pale and agitated."

" Were they alone ? "

" There was a third person with them whom I knew perfectly well, and who had, in all probability, made their acquaintance; he was a tailor named Caderousse, but he was quite intoxicated. Stay! — stay! — How strange that it should not have occurred to me before! Now I remember quite well, that on the table round which they were sitting were pens, ink, and paper. Oh! the heartless, treacherous scoundrels! " exclaimed Dantès, pressing his hand to his throbbing brows.

" Is there anything else I can assist you in discovering, besides the villainy of your friends ? " inquired the abbé.

" Yes, yes," replied Dantès, eagerly; " I would beg of you, who see so completely to the depths of things, and to whom the greatest mystery seems but an easy riddle, to explain to me how it was that I underwent no second examination, was never brought to trial, and, above all, my being condemned without ever having had sentence passed on me."

" That is a more serious matter," responded the abbé. " The ways of justice are frequently too dark and mysterious to be easily penetrated. All we have hitherto done in the matter has been child's play. On this matter, you must give me the most minute information on every point."

" Gladly. So pray begin, my dear abbé, and ask me whatever questions you please; for you see my past life far better than I could do myself."

"In the first place, then, who examined you,— the procureur du roi, his deputy, or a magistrate?"

"The deputy."

"Was he young or old?"

"About six or seven and twenty years of age, I should say."

"To be sure," answered the abbé. "Old enough to be ambitious, but not sufficiently so to have hardened his heart. And how did he treat you?"

"With more of mildness than severity."

"Did you tell him your whole story?"

"I did."

"And did his conduct change at all in the course of your examination?"

"Yes; certainly he did appear much disturbed when he read the letter that had brought me into this scrape. He seemed quite overcome at the danger I was in."

"*You* were in?"

"Yes; for whom else could he have felt any apprehensions?"

"Then you feel quite convinced he sincerely pitied your misfortune?"

"Why, he gave me one great proof of his sympathy, at least."

"And what was that?"

"He burned the sole proof that could at all have criminated me."

"Do you mean the letter of accusation?"

"Oh, no! the letter I was intrusted to convey to Paris."

"Are you sure he burned it?"

"He did so before my eyes."

"Ay, indeed! that alters the case; this man might, after all, be a greater scoundrel than I at first believed."

"Upon my word," said Dantès, "you make me shudder. Is the world filled with tigers and crocodiles?"

"Only remember that two-legged tigers and crocodiles are more dangerous than those that walk on four."

"Never mind, let us go on."

"With all my heart! You tell me he burned the letter in your presence?"

"He did; saying at the same time, 'You see I thus destroy the only proof existing against you.'"

"This action is somewhat too sublime to be natural."

"You think so?"

"I am sure of it. To whom was this letter addressed?"

"To M. Noirtier, No. 13 Rue Coq-Héron, Paris."

"Now, can you conceive any interest your heroic deputy procureur could by possibility have had in the destruction of that letter?"

"Why, he might have had, for he made me promise several times never to speak of that letter to any one; and, more than this, he insisted on my taking a solemn oath never to utter the name mentioned in the address."

"Noirtier!" repeated the abbé; "Noirtier!—I knew a person of that name at the court of the queen of Etruria,—a Noirtier, who had been a Girondin during the Revolution! What was your deputy called?"

"De Villefort!"

The abbé burst into a fit of laughter, while Dantès gazed on him in utter astonishment. "What ails you?" said he, at length.

"Do you see this ray of light?"

"I do."

"Well! I see my way more clearly than you discern that sunbeam. Poor fellow! poor young man! And this magistrate expressed sympathy for you?"

"He did!"

"And the worthy man destroyed your compromising letter?"

"He burned it before me!"

"And then this purveyor for the scaffold made you swear never to utter the name of Noirtier?"

"Certainly."

"Why, you poor, short-sighted simpleton! Can you not guess who this Noirtier was, whose very name he was so careful to keep concealed? This Noirtier was his father!"

Had a thunderbolt fallen at the feet of Dantès, or hell opened before him, he could not have been more completely transfixed with horror than at the words so wholly unexpected. Starting up, he clasped his hands around his head as though to prevent his very brain from bursting, and exclaimed:

"His father! oh, no! not his father, surely!"

"His own father, I assure you," replied the abbé; "his right name was Noirtier de Villefort!"

At this instant a bright light shot through the mind of Dantès, and cleared up all that had been dark and obscure before. The change that had come over Villefort during the examination; the destruction of the letter, the exacted promise, the almost supplicating tones of the magistrate, who seemed rather to implore mercy than denounce punishment,—all returned to his memory. A cry of agony escaped his lips, and he staggered like a drunken man; then he hurried to the opening conducting from the abbé's cell to his own, and said:

"I must be alone, to think over all this."

When he regained his dungeon, he threw himself on his bed, where the turnkey found him at his evening visit, sitting with fixed gaze and contracted features, still and motionless as a statue; but, during these hours of deep meditation, which to him had seemed but as minutes, he had formed a fearful resolution, and bound himself to its fulfillment by a solemn oath.

Dantès was at length roused from his reverie by the voice of Faria, who, having also been visited by his jailer, had come to invite his fellow-sufferer to share his supper. The reputation of being out of his mind, though harmlessly and even amusingly so, had procured for the abbé greater privileges than were allowed to prisoners in general. He was supplied with bread of a finer, whiter description than the usual prison fare, and each Sunday with a small quantity of wine; the present day chanced to be Sunday, and the abbé came, delighted at having such luxuries to offer his new friend.

Dantès followed him; his features had lost their contraction, and now wore their usual expression; but there was that in his whole appearance that bespoke one who had come to a fixed resolve. Faria bent on him his penetrating eye.

"I regret now," said he, "having helped you in your late inquiries, or having given you the information I did."

"Why so ?" inquired Dantès.

"Because it has instilled a new passion in your heart — that of vengeance."

A bitter smile played over the features of the young man. "Let us talk of something else," said he.

Again the abbé looked at him, then mournfully shook his head; but, in accordance with Dantès' request, he began to speak of other matters. The elder prisoner was one of those persons whose conversation, like that of all who have experienced many trials, contained many useful hints as well as sound information; but it was never egotistical, for the unfortunate man never alluded to his own sorrows. Dantès listened with admiring attention to all he said; some of his remarks corresponded with what he already knew, or applied to the sort of knowledge his nautical life had enabled him to acquire. A part of the good abbé's words, however, were wholly incomprehensible to him; but, like those auroræ boreales which light the navigators in northern latitudes, they sufficed to open to the inquiring mind of the listener fresh views and new horizons, illumined by the meteoric flash, enabling him justly to estimate the delight an intellectual mind would have in following this towering spirit in all the giddiest heights of science, moral, social, or philosophical.

" You must teach me a small part of what you know," said Dantès, " if only to prevent your growing weary of me. I can well believe that you would prefer solitude to the company of one as ignorant and uninformed as myself. If you will only agree to my request, I promise you never to mention another word about escaping."

The abbé smiled.

" Alas! my child," said he, " human knowledge is confined within very narrow limits; and when I have taught you mathematics, physics, history, and the three or four modern languages with which I am acquainted, you will know as much as I do myself. Now, it will scarcely require two years for me to communicate to you the stock of learning I possess."

" Two years!" exclaimed Dantès; " do you really believe I can acquire all these things in so short a time ?"

" Not their application, certainly, but their principles you may; to learn is not to know; there are the learners and the learned. Memory makes the one, philosophy the other."

" But can I not learn philosophy as well as other things ?"

" My son, philosophy, as I understand it, is reducible to no rules by which it can be learned; it is the amalgamation of all the sciences, the golden cloud on which Christ placed his feet to remount to heaven."

" Well, then," said Dantès, " tell me what you shall teach me first ? When shall we commence ?"

" Directly, if you will," said the abbé.

And that very evening the prisoners sketched a plan of education, to be entered upon the following day. Dantès possessed a prodigious memory, an astonishing quickness of conception; the mathematical turn of his mind rendered him apt at all kinds of calculation, while his naturally poetical feelings corrected the dry reality of arithmetical computation or the rigid severity of lines. He already knew Italian, and a little of the Romaic dialect, picked up during his different voyages to the East; and by the aid of these two languages he easily comprehended the construction of all the others, so that at the end of six months he began to speak Spanish, English, and German.

In strict accordance with the promise made to the abbé, Dantès never even alluded to flight: it might have been that the delight his studies afforded him supplied the place of liberty; or, probably, the recollection of his pledged word (a point, as we have already seen, to which he paid rigid attention) kept him from reverting to any plan for escape; but, absorbed in the acquisition of knowledge, days, even months, passed by unheeded in one rapid and instructive course; time flew on, and at the end of a year Dantès was a new man. With Faria, on the contrary, Dantès remarked that, spite of the relief his society afforded, he daily grew sadder; one thought seemed incessantly to harass and distract his mind. Sometimes he would fall into long reveries, sigh heavily and involuntarily, then suddenly rise, and, with folded arms, begin pacing the confined space of his dungeon. One day he stopped all at once in the midst of these so often-repeated promenades, and exclaimed:

" Ah, if there were no sentinel ! "

" There shall not be one a minute longer than you please," said Dantès, who had followed the working of his thoughts as accurately as though his brain were inclosed in crystal.

" I have already told you," answered the abbé, " that I loathe the idea of shedding blood."

" Still, in our case, it would be a necessary step to secure our own personal safety and preservation."

" No matter! I could never agree to it."

" Still, you have thought of it ? "

" Incessantly, alas! " cried the abbé.

" And you have discovered a means of regaining our freedom, have you not ? " asked Dantès eagerly.

" I have; if it were only possible to place a deaf and blind sentinel in the gallery beyond us."

" I will undertake to render him both," replied the young man, with an air of determined resolution that made his companion shudder.

" No, no," cried the abbé; " I tell you the thing is impossible; name it no more! "

In vain did Dantès endeavor to renew the subject; the abbé shook his head in token of disapproval, but refused any further conversation respecting it. Three months passed away.

" Do you feel yourself strong ? " inquired the abbé of Dantès. The young man, in reply, took up the chisel, bent it into the form of a horse-shoe, and then as readily straightened it.

" And will you engage not to do any harm to the sentry, except as a last extremity ? "

" I promise on my honor not to hurt a hair of his head, unless positively obliged for our mutual preservation."

" Then," said the abbé, " we may hope to put our design into execution."

" And how long shall we be in accomplishing the necessary work ? "

" At least a year."

" And shall we begin at once ? "

" Directly."

"We have lost a year to no purpose!" cried Dantès.

"Do you consider the last twelve months as wasted?" asked the abbé, in a tone of mild reproach.

"Forgive me!" cried Edmond, blushing deeply; "I am indeed ungrateful to have hinted such a thing."

"Tut, tut!" answered the abbé; "man is but man at last, and you are about the best I have ever known. Come, let me show you my plan."

The abbé then showed Dantès the sketch he had made for their escape. It consisted of a plan of his own cell and that of Dantès, with the corridor which united them. In this passage he proposed to form a tunnel, such as is employed in mines; this tunnel would conduct the two prisoners immediately beneath the gallery where the sentry kept watch; once there, a large excavation would be made, and one of the flag-stones with which the gallery was paved be so completely loosened that at the desired moment it would give way beneath the soldier's feet, who, falling into the excavation below, would be immediately bound and gagged, ere, stunned by the effects of his fall, he had power to offer any resistance. The prisoners were then to make their way through one of the gallery windows, and to let themselves down from the outer walls by means of the abbé's ladder of cords.

The eyes of Dantès sparkled with joy, and he rubbed his hands with delight at the idea of a plan so simple, yet apparently so certain to succeed. That very day the miners commenced their labor, and that with so much more vigor, as it succeeded to a long rest from fatigue and was destined, in all probability, to carry out the dearest wish of the heart of each. Nothing interrupted the progress of their work except the necessity of returning to their respective cells against the hour in which their jailer was in the habit of visiting them; they had learned to distinguish the almost imperceptible sound of his footsteps as he descended toward their dungeons, and, happily, never failed being prepared for his coming. The fresh earth excavated during their present work, and which would have entirely blocked up the old passage, was thrown, by degrees and with the utmost precaution, out of the window in either Faria's or Dantès' cell, the rubbish being first pulverized so finely that the night wind carried it far away without permitting the smallest trace to remain.

More than a year had been consumed in this undertaking, the only tools for which had been a chisel, a knife, and a wooden lever; Faria still continuing to instruct Dantès by conversing with him, sometimes in one language, sometimes in another; at others, relating to him the history of nations and great men who from time to time have left behind them one of those bright tracks called glory. The abbé was a man of the world, and had, moreover, mixed in the first society of the day; he had, too, that air of melancholy dignity which Dantès, thanks to the imitative powers bestowed on him by nature, easily acquired, as well as that outward politeness he had before been wanting in, and which is seldom possessed except by constant intercourse with persons of high birth and breeding.

At the end of fifteen months the tunnel was made, and the excavation completed beneath the gallery, and the two workmen could distinctly hear the measured tread of the sentinel as he paced to and fro over their heads. Compelled, as they were, to await a night sufficiently dark to favor their flight, they were obliged to defer their final attempt till that auspicious moment should arrive; their greatest dread now was lest the stone through which the sentry was doomed to fall should give way before its right time, and this they had in some measure provided against by placing under it, as a kind of prop, a sort of bearer they had discovered among the foundations. Dantès was occupied in arranging this piece of wood when he heard Faria, who had remained in Edmond's cell for the purpose of cutting a peg to secure their rope ladder, call to him in accents of pain and suffering. Dantès hastened to his dungeon, where he found him standing in the middle of the room, pale as death, his forehead streaming with perspiration, and his hands clenched tightly.

"Gracious heavens!" exclaimed Dantès, "what is the matter? what has happened?"

"Quick! quick!" returned the abbé, "listen to what I have to say."

Dantès looked at the livid countenance of Faria, whose eyes were circled by a halo of a bluish cast, his lips were white, and his very hair seemed to stand on end. In his alarm he let fall the chisel he held in his hand.

"For God's sake!" cried Dantès, "tell me what ails you?"

"Alas!" faltered out the abbé, "all is over with me. I am seized with a terrible, perhaps mortal, illness; I can feel that the paroxysm is fast approaching. I had a similar attack the year previous to my imprisonment. This malady admits but of one remedy; I will tell you what that is. Go into my cell as quickly as you can; draw out one of the feet that support the bed; you will find it has been hollowed out; you will find there a small phial half filled with a red-looking fluid. Bring it to me — or rather, no, no! I may be found here; therefore, help me back to my room while I have any strength. Who knows what may happen, or how long the fit may last?"

Spite of the magnitude of the misfortune, Dantès lost not his presence of mind, but descended into the corridor, dragging his unfortunate companion with him; then, half carrying, half supporting him, he man-

"HELP! HELP! I — I — DIE — I —"

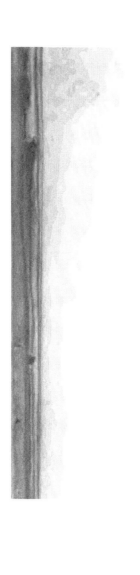

aged to reach the abbé's chamber, when he immediately laid the sufferer on his bed.

"Thanks!" said the poor abbé, shivering in every limb as though emerging from freezing water; "I am seized with a fit of catalepsy; I may, probably, lie still and motionless, uttering neither sigh nor groan. I may fall into convulsions that cover my lips with foam and force from me piercing shrieks. Let no one hear my cries, for if they are heard I should be removed to another part of the prison, and we be separated forever. When I become quite motionless, cold, and rigid as a corpse, then, and not before, you understand, force open my teeth with a chisel, pour from eight to ten drops of the liquor contained in the phial down my throat, and I may perhaps revive."

"Perhaps!" exclaimed Dantès in grief-stricken tones.

"Help! help!" cried the abbé, "I — I — die — I ——"

So sudden and violent was the fit, that the unfortunate prisoner was unable to complete the sentence begun; a cloud came over his brow, dark as a storm at sea, his eyes started from their sockets, his mouth was drawn on one side, his cheeks became purple, he struggled, foamed, and uttered dreadful cries, which Dantès deadened by covering his head with the blanket. The fit lasted two hours; then, more helpless than an infant, and colder and paler than marble, more broken than a reed trampled under foot, he fell, stiffened with a last convulsion, and became livid.

Edmond waited till life seemed extinct in the body of his friend; then, taking up the chisel, he with difficulty forced open the closely fixed jaws, carefully poured the appointed number of drops down the rigid throat, and anxiously awaited the result. An hour passed away without the old man's giving the least sign of returning animation. Dantès began to fear he had delayed too long ere he administered the remedy, and, thrusting his hands into his hair, continued gazing on his friend in an agony of despair. At length a slight color tinged the cheeks, consciousness returned to the dull, open eyeballs, a faint sigh issued from the lips, and the sufferer made a feeble effort to move.

"He is saved! he is saved!" cried Dantès, in a paroxysm of delight.

The sick man was not yet able to speak, but he pointed with evident anxiety toward the door. Dantès listened, and plainly distinguished the approaching steps of the jailer. It was therefore near seven o'clock; but Edmond's anxiety had put all thoughts of time out of his head.

The young man sprang to the entrance, darted through it, carefully drawing the stone over the opening, and hurried to his cell. He had scarcely done so before the door opened and disclosed to the jailer's inquisitorial gaze the prisoner seated as usual on the side of his bed.

Almost before the key had turned in the lock, and before the steps of the jailer had died away in the corridor, Dantès, consumed by anxiety, without any desire to touch the food, hurried back to the abbé's chamber, and, raising the stone by pressing his head against it, was soon beside the sick man's couch. Faria had now fully regained his consciousness, but he still lay helpless and exhausted on his miserable bed.

"I did not expect to see you again," said he, feebly, to Dantès.

"And why not?" asked the young man. "Did you fancy yourself dying?"

"No, I had no such idea; "but, as all was ready for your flight, I considered you were gone."

The deep glow of indignation suffused the cheeks of Dantès.

"And did you really think so meanly of me," cried he, " as to believe I would depart without you?"

"At least," said the abbé, "I now see how wrong such an opinion would have been. Alas, alas! I am fearfully exhausted and debilitated."

"Be of good cheer," replied Dantès; "your strength will return." And as he spoke he seated himself on the bed beside Faria, and tenderly chafed his chilled hands. The abbé shook his head.

"The former of these fits," said he, "lasted but half an hour, at the termination of which I experienced a sensation of hunger, and I rose from my bed without requiring help; now I can neither move my right arm or leg, and my head seems uncomfortable, proving a rush of blood to the brain. The next of these fits will either carry me off or leave me paralyzed for life."

"No, no!" cried Dantès; "you are mistaken — you will not die! And your third attack (if, indeed, you should have another) will find you at liberty. We shall save you another time, as we have done this, only with a better chance, because we shall be able to command every requisite assistance."

"My good Edmond," answered the abbé, "be not deceived. The attack which has just passed away condemns me forever to the walls of a prison. None can fly from their dungeon but those who can walk."

"Well, well, we can wait, say a week, a month, — two, if necessary; by that time you will be quite well and strong; and as it only remains with us to fix the hour and minute, we will choose the first instant that you feel able to swim to execute our project."

"I shall never swim again," replied Faria. "This arm is paralyzed; not for a time, but forever. Lift it, and judge by its weight if I am mistaken."

The young man raised the arm, which fell back by its own weight, perfectly inanimate and helpless. A sigh escaped him.

"You are convinced now, Edmond, are you not?" asked the abbé. "Depend upon it, I know what I say. Since the first attack I experienced of this malady, I have continually reflected on it. Indeed, I expected it, for it is a family inheritance, both my father and grand-

father having been taken off by it. The physician who prepared for me the remedy was no other than the celebrated Cabanis, and he predicted a similar end for me."

"The physician may be mistaken!" exclaimed Dantès. "And as for your poor arm, what difference will that make in our escape? I can take you on my shoulders and swim for both of us."

" My son," said the abbé, " you, who are a sailor and a swimmer, must know as well as I do that a man so loaded would sink ere he had advanced fifty yards in the sea. Cease, then, to allow yourself to be duped by vain hopes that even your own excellent heart refuses to believe in. Here I shall remain till the hour of my deliverance arrives; and that, in all human probability, will be the hour of my death. As for you, who are young and active, delay not on my account, but fly — go — I give you back your promise."

" It is well," said Dantès. " And now hear my determination also." Then, rising and extending his hand with an air of solemnity over the old man's head, he slowly added:

" Here I swear to remain with you so long as life is spared to you."

Faria gazed fondly on his noble-minded but single-hearted young friend, and read in his honest, open countenance ample confirmation of truthfulness as well as sincere, affectionate, and faithful devotion.

" Thanks, my child," murmured the invalid, extending the one hand of which he still retained the use. " Thanks for your generous offer, which I accept as frankly as it was made." Then, after a short pause, he added, " You may one of these days reap the reward of your disinterested devotion. But, as I cannot, and you will not, quit this place, it becomes necessary to fill up the excavation beneath the soldier's gallery; he might, by chance, find out the hollow sound above the excavated ground, and call the attention of his officer to the circumstance. We should be discovered and separated. Go, then, and set about this work, in which, unhappily, I can offer you no assistance; keep at it all night, if necessary, and do not return here to-morrow till after the jailer has visited me. I shall have something of the greatest importance to communicate to you."

Dantès took the hand of the abbé, who smiled encouragingly on him, and retired to his task, filled with a determination to discharge the vow which bound him to his friend.

CHAPTER XVIII

HEN Dantès returned next morning to the chamber of his companion in captivity, he found Faria seated and looking composed. In the ray of light which entered by the narrow window of his cell, he held open in his left hand, of which alone, it will be recollected, he retained the use, a morsel of paper, which, from being constantly rolled into a small compass, had the form of a cylinder, and was not easily kept open. He did not speak, but showed the paper to Dantès.

"What is that?" he inquired.

"Look at it," said the abbé, with a smile.

"I have looked at it with all possible attention," said Dantès, "and I only see a half-burned paper, on which are traces of Gothic characters, traced with a peculiar kind of ink."

"This paper, my friend," said Faria, "I may now avow to you, since I have proved you — this paper is my treasure, of which, from this day forth, one-half belongs to you."

A cold damp started to Dantès' brow. Until this day — and what a space of time! — he had avoided talking to Faria of this treasure, the source whence the accusation of madness against the poor abbé was derived. With his instinctive delicacy Edmond had preferred avoiding any touch on this painful chord, and Faria had been equally silent. He had taken the silence of the old man for a return to reason, and now these few words uttered by Faria, after so painful a crisis, seemed to announce a serious relapse of mental alienation.

"Your treasure?" stammered Dantès. Faria smiled.

"Yes," said he. "You are, indeed, a noble heart, Edmond, and I see by your paleness and your shudder what is passing in your heart at this moment. No; be assured, I am not mad. This treasure exists,

Dantès; and if I have not been allowed to possess it, you will. Yes — you. No one would listen to me or believe me, because they thought me mad; but you, who must know that I am not, listen to me, and believe me afterward, if you will."

"Alas!" murmured Edmond to himself, "this is a terrible relapse! There was only this blow wanting."

Then he said aloud, "My dear friend, your attack has, perhaps, fatigued you; had you not better repose awhile? To-morrow, if you will, I will hear your narrative; but to-day I wish to nurse you carefully. Besides," he said, "a treasure is not a thing we need hurry about."

"On the contrary, we must hurry, Edmond!" replied the old man. "Who knows if to-morrow, or the next day after, the third attack may not come on? and then must not all be finished? Yes, indeed, I have often thought with a bitter joy that these riches, which would make the wealth of a dozen families, will be forever lost to those men who persecute me. This idea was one of vengeance to me, and I tasted it slowly in the night of my dungeon and the despair of my captivity. But now I have forgiven the world for the love of you; now I see you young and full of hope and prospect — now that I think of all that may result to you in the good fortune of such a disclosure, I shudder at any delay, and tremble lest I should not assure to one as worthy as yourself the possession of so vast an amount of hidden treasure."

Edmond turned away his head with a sigh.

"You persist in your incredulity, Edmond," continued Faria. "My words have not convinced you. I see you require proofs. Well, then, read this paper, which I have never shown to any one."

"To-morrow, my dear friend," said Edmond, desirous of not yielding to the old man's madness. "I thought it was understood that we should not talk of that till to-morrow."

"Then we will not talk of it until to-morrow; but read this paper to-day."

"I will not irritate him," thought Edmond, and taking the paper, of which half was wanting, having been burned, no doubt, by some accident, he read:

"' *This treasure, which may amount to two*
of Roman crowns in the most distant a
of the second opening wh
declare to belong to him alo
heir.
"' *25th April, 149*'"

"Well!" said Faria, when the young man had finished reading it.

"Why," replied Dantès, "I see nothing but broken lines and unconnected words, which are rendered illegible by fire."

"Yes, to you, my friend, who read them for the first time; but not for me who have grown pale over them by many nights' study, and have reconstructed every phrase, completed every thought."

"And do you believe you have discovered the concealed sense?"

"I am sure I have, and you shall judge for yourself; but, first listen to the history of this paper."

"Silence!" exclaimed Dantès. "Steps approach —. I go — adieu!"

And Dantès, happy to escape the history and explanation which could not fail to confirm to him his friend's malady, glided like a snake along the narrow passage; whilst Faria, restored by his alarm to a kind of activity, pushed with his foot the stone into its place, and covered it with a mat in order the more effectually to avoid discovery.

It was the governor, who, hearing of Faria's accident from the jailer, had come in person to see him.

Faria sat up to receive him, and continued to conceal from the governor the paralysis that had already half stricken him with death. His fear was lest the governor, touched with pity, might order him to be removed to a prison more wholesome, and thus separate him from his young companion. But, fortunately, this was not the case, and the governor left him, convinced that the poor madman, for whom in his heart he felt a kind of affection, was only affected with a slight indisposition.

During this time, Edmond, seated on his bed with his head in his hands, tried to collect his scattered thoughts. All was so rational, so grand, so logical with Faria, since he had known him, that he could not understand how so much wisdom on all points could be allied to madness in any one. Was Faria deceived as to his treasure, or was all the world deceived as to Faria?

Dantès remained in his cell all day, not daring to return to his friend, thinking thus to defer the moment when he should acquire the certainty that the abbé was mad — such a conviction would be so terrible!

But, toward the evening, after the usual visitation, Faria, not seeing the young man appear, tried to move and get over the distance which separated them. Edmond shuddered when he heard the painful efforts which the old man made to drag himself along; his leg was inert, and he could no longer make use of one arm. Edmond was compelled to draw him toward himself, for otherwise he could not enter by the small aperture which led to Dantès' chamber.

" Here I am, pursuing you remorselessly," he said, with a benignant smile. " You thought to escape my munificence, but it is in vain. Listen to me." Edmond saw there was no escape, and, placing the old man on his bed, he seated himself on the stool beside him.

" You know," said the abbé, " that I was the secretary and intimate friend of Cardinal Spada, the last of the princes of that name. I owe to this worthy lord all the happiness I ever knew. He was not rich, although the wealth of his family had passed into a proverb, and I heard the phrase very often, 'As rich as a Spada.' But he, like public rumor, lived on this reputation for wealth. His palace was my paradise; I instructed his nephews, who are dead; and when he was alone in the world, I returned to him, by an absolute devotion to his will, all he had done for me during ten years. The house of the cardinal had no secrets for me. I had often seen my noble patron annotating ancient volumes, and eagerly searching amongst dusty family manuscripts. One day when I was reproaching him for his unavailing searches, and the kind of prostration of mind that followed them, he looked at me, and, smiling bitterly, opened a volume relating to the History of the City of Rome. There, in the twenty-ninth chapter of the Life of Pope Alexander VI., were the following lines, which I can never forget:

" ' The great wars of Romagna had ended; Cæsar Borgia, who had completed his conquest, had need of money to purchase all Italy. The pope had also need of money to conclude with Louis XII. of France, formidable still, in spite of his recent reverses; and it was necessary, therefore, to have recourse to some profitable speculation, which was a matter of great difficulty in exhausted Italy. His Holiness had an idea. He determined to make two cardinals.'

" By choosing two of the greatest personages of Rome, especially rich men — *this* was the return the Holy Father looked for from his speculation. In the first place, he had to sell the great appointments and splendid offices which the cardinals already held; and then he had the two hats to sell besides. There was a third view in the speculation, which will appear hereafter.

" The pope and Cæsar Borgia first found the two future cardinals; they were Juan Rospigliosi, who held four of the highest dignities of the holy seat, and Cæsar Spada, one of the noblest and richest of the Roman nobility; both felt the high honor of such a favor from the pope. They were ambitious; and these found, Cæsar Borgia soon found purchasers for their appointments. The result was, that Rospigliosi and Spada paid for being cardinals, and eight other persons paid for the offices the cardinals held before their elevation, and thus eight hundred thousand crowns entered into the coffers of the speculators.

" It is time now to proceed to the last part of the speculation. The pope, having almost smothered Rospigliosi and Spada with caresses, having bestowed upon them the insignia of cardinal, and induced them to realize their fortunes, and fix themselves at Rome, the pope and Cæsar Borgia invited the two cardinals to dinner. This was a matter of con-

Marco Spada.

test between the Holy Father and his son. Cæsar thought they could make use of one of the means which he always had ready for his friends; that is to say, in the first place the famous key with which they requested certain persons to go and open a particular cupboard. This key was furnished with a small iron point,—a negligence on the part of the lock-smith. When this was pressed to effect the opening of the cupboard, of which the lock was difficult, the person was pricked by this small point, and died next day. Then there was the ring with the lion's head, which Cæsar wore when he meant to give certain squeezes of the hand. The lion bit the hand thus favored, and at the end of twenty-four hours the bite was mortal.

"Cæsar then proposed to his father, either to ask the cardinals to open the cupboard, or to give each a cordial squeeze of the hand; but Alexander VI. replied to him: 'Whilst we are thinking of those worthy cardinals, Spada and Rospigliosi, let us ask both of them to a dinner. Something tells me that we shall regain this money. Besides, you forget, Cæsar, an indigestion declares itself immediately, whilst a prick or a bite occasions a day or two's delay.' Cæsar gave way before such cogent reasoning; and the cardinals were consequently invited to dinner.

"The table was laid in a vineyard belonging to the pope, near Saint Peter ad Vincula, a charming retreat which the cardinals knew very well by report. Rospigliosi, quite giddy with his dignity, prepared his stomach, and assumed his best looks. Spada, a prudent man, and greatly attached to his only nephew, a young captain of highest prom-ise, took paper and pen, and made his will. He then sent to his nephew to await him in the vicinity of the vineyard; but it appeared the servant did not find him.

"Spada knew the nature of these invitations; since Christianity, so eminently civilizing, had made progress in Rome, it was no longer a centurion who came from the tyrant with a message, 'Cæsar wills that you die,' but it was a legate *à latere*, who came with a smile on his lips to say from the pope, 'His Holiness requests you will dine with him.'

"Spada set out about two o'clock to Saint Peter ad Vincula. The pope awaited him. The first figure that struck the eyes of Spada was that of his nephew, in full costume, and Cæsar Borgia paying him most marked attentions. Spada turned pale, as Cæsar looked at him with an ironical air, which proved that he had anticipated all, and that the snare was well spread.

"They began dinner, and Spada was only able to inquire of his nephew if he had received his message. The nephew replied no, per-fectly comprehending the meaning of the question. It was too late, for he had already drunk a glass of excellent wine, placed for him expressly by the pope's butler. Spada at the same moment saw another bottle approach him, which he was pressed to taste. An hour afterward a physician declared they were both poisoned through eating mushrooms. Spada died on the threshold of the villa; the nephew expired at his own door, making signs which his wife could not comprehend.

"Then Cæsar and the pope hastened to lay hands on the heritage, under pretense of seeking for the papers of the dead man. But the inheritance consisted in this only, a scrap of paper on which Spada had written:

"'I bequeath to my beloved nephew my coffers, my books, and, amongst other, my breviary with gold corners; which I beg he will preserve in remembrance of his affectionate uncle.'

"The heirs sought everywhere, admired the breviary, laid hands on the furniture, and were greatly astonished that Spada, the rich man, was really the most miserable of uncles — no treasures — unless they were those of science, composed in the library and laboratories. This was all: Cæsar and his father searched, examined, scrutinized, but found nothing, or, at least, very little — not exceeding a few thousand crowns in plate, and about the same in ready money; but the nephew had time to say to his wife before he expired:

"'Look well among my uncle's papers; there is a will.'

"They sought even more thoroughly than the august heirs had done, but it was fruitless. There were two palaces and a villa behind the Palatine Hill; but in these days landed property had not much value, and the two palaces and the villa remained to the family as beneath the rapacity of the pope and his son. Months and years rolled on. Alexander VI. died poisoned,—you know by what mistake. Cæsar, poisoned at the same time, escaped with changing his skin like a snake, and assumed a new cuticle, on which the poison left spots, like those we see on the skin of a tiger; then, compelled to quit Rome, he went and got himself killed in obscurity in a night skirmish, scarcely noticed in history.

"After the pope's death and his son's exile, it was supposed the Spada family would again make the splendid figure they had before the cardinal's time; but this was not the case. The Spadas remained in doubtful ease; a mystery hung over this dark affair, and the public rumor was that Cæsar, a better politician than his father, had carried off from the pope the fortune of the cardinals. I say the two, because Cardinal Rospigliosi, who had not taken any precaution, was completely despoiled.

"Up to this time," said Faria, interrupting the thread of his narrative, "this seems to you very ridiculous, no doubt, eh?"   ·

"Oh, my friend," cried Dantès, "on the contrary, it seems as if I were reading a most interesting narrative; go on, I pray of you."

"I will. The family began to feel accustomed to this obscurity. Years rolled on, and amongst the descendants some were soldiers, others diplo-matists; some churchmen, some bankers; some grew rich, and some were ruined. I come now to the last of the family, whose secretary I was — the Comte de Spada. I had often heard him complain of the disproportion of his rank with his fortune; and I advised him to sink all he had in an annuity. He did so, and thus doubled his income. The celebrated breviary remained in the family, and was in his possession. It had been handed down from father to son; for the singular clause of the only will that had been found had rendered it a real *relique*, preserved in the family with superstitious veneration. It was an illuminated book, with beautiful Gothic characters, and so weighty with gold that a servant always carried it before the cardinal on days of great solemnity.

"At the sight of papers of all sorts,— titles, contracts, parchments, which were kept in the archives of the family, all descending from the poisoned cardinal,— I, like twenty servitors, stewards, secretaries before me, in my turn examined the immense bundles of documents; but in spite of the most accurate researches, I found — nothing. Yet I had read, I had even written a precise history of the Borgia family, for the sole purpose of assuring myself whether any increase of fortune had occurred to them on the death of the Cardinal Cæsar Spada; but could only trace the acquisition of the property of the Cardinal Rospigliosi, his companion in misfortune.

"I was then almost assured that the inheritance had neither profited the Borgias nor the family, but had remained unpossessed like the treas-ures of the Arabian Nights, which slept in the bosom of the earth under the eyes of a *génie*. I searched, ransacked, counted, calculated a thou-sand and a thousand times the income and expenditure of the family for three hundred years. It was useless. I remained in my ignorance, and the Comte de Spada in his poverty.

"My patron died. He had reserved from his annuity his family papers, his library, composed of five thousand volumes, and his famous breviary. All these he bequeathed to me, with a thousand Roman crowns, which he had in ready money, on condition that I would have said anniversary masses for the repose of his soul, and that I would draw up a genealogical tree and history of his house. All this I did scrupulously. Be easy, my dear Edmond, we are near the conclusion.

"In 1807, a month before I was arrested, and fifteen days after the death of Comte de Spada, on the 25th of December (you will see pres-ently how the date became fixed in my memory), I was reading, for the thousandth time, the papers I was arranging, for the palace was sold to a stranger, and I was going to leave Rome and settle at Florence, intending to take with me twelve thousand francs I possessed, my library, and famous breviary, when, tired with my constant labor at the same thing, and overcome by a heavy dinner I had eaten, my head dropped on my hands, and I fell asleep about three o'clock in the afternoon.

"I awoke as the clock was striking six. I raised my head; all was in darkness. I rang for a light, but, as no one came, I determined to find one for myself. It was indeed the habit of a philosopher which I should soon be under the necessity of adopting. I took a wax-candle in one hand, and with the other groped about for a piece of paper (my matchbox being empty), with which I proposed to produce a light from the small flame still playing on the embers. Fearing, however, to make use of any valuable piece of paper, I hesitated for a moment, then recollected that I had seen in the famous breviary, which was on the table beside me, an old paper quite yellow with age, and which had served as a marker for centuries, kept there by the superstition of the heirs. I felt for it, found it, twisted it up together, and, putting it into the expiring flame, set light to it.

"But beneath my fingers, as if by magic, in proportion as the fire ascended, I saw yellowish characters appear on the paper. I grasped it in my hand, put out the flame as quickly as I could, lighted my taper in the fire itself, and opened the crumpled paper with inexpressible emotion, recognizing, when I had done so, that these characters had been traced in mysterious and sympathetic ink, only appearing when exposed to the fire: nearly one-third of the paper had been consumed by the flame. It was that paper you read this morning; read it again, Dantès, and then I will complete for you the incomplete words and unconnected sense."

Faria, with an air of triumph, offered the paper to Dantès, who this time read the following words, traced with an ink of a color which most nearly resembled rust:

"'This 25th day of April, 1498, be . . .
Alexander VI. and fearing that not . . .
he may desire to become my heir, and re . . .
and Bentivoglio, who were poisoned . . .
my sole heir, that I have bu . . .
and has visited with me, that is in . . .
island of Monte-Cristo all I poss . . .
jewels, diamonds, gems; that I alone . . .
may amount to nearly two mil . . .
will find on raising the twentieth ro . . .
creek to the east in a right line. Two open . . .
in these caves; the treasure is in the furthest a . . .
which treasure I bequeath and leave en . . .
as my sole heir.
"'25th April, 1498.   *"' Cæs . . .*

"And now," said the abbé, "read this other paper." And he presented to Dantès a second leaf with fragments of lines written on it, which Edmond read as follows:

THE CARDINAL'S SECRETARY.

> .*" '. . . ing invited to dine by his Holiness*
> *. . . content with making me pay for my hat*
> *. . . serves for me the fate of Cardinals Caprara*
> *. . . I declare to my nephew Guido Spada*
> *. . . ried in a place he knows*
> *. . . the caves of the small*
> *. . . essed of ingots, gold, money,*
> *. . . know of the existence of this treasure, which*
> *. . . lions of Roman crowns, and which he*
> *. . . ck from the small*
> *. . . ings have been made*
> *. . . ngle in the second;*
> *. . . tire to him*
> *. . . ar † Spada.' "*

Faria followed him with excited looks.

" And now," he said, when he saw Dantès had read the last line, "put the two fragments together, and judge for yourself." Dantès obeyed, and the conjoined pieces gave the following:

" This 25th day of April, 1498, be . . . ing invited to dine by his Holiness Alexander VI., and fearing that not . . . content with making me pay for my hat, he may desire to become my heir, and re . . . serves for me the fate of Cardinals Caprara and Bentivoglio, who were poisoned, . . . I declare to my nephew, Guido Spada, my sole heir, that I have bu . . . ried in a place he knows, and has visited with me, that is, in . . . the caves of the small island of Monte-Cristo, all I poss . . . essed of ingots, gold, money, jewels, diamonds, gems ; that I alone . . . know of the existence of this treasure, which may amount to nearly two mil . . . lions of Roman crowns, and which he will find on raising the twentieth ro . . . ck from the small creek to the east in a right line. Two open . . . ings have been made in these caves; the treasure is in the furthest a . . . ngle in the second; which treasure I bequeath and leave en . . . tire to him as my sole heir.

" 25th April, 1498.　　　　　　　　　　" Cæs . . . ar † Spada."

" Well, do you comprehend now ? " inquired Faria.

" It is the declaration of Cardinal Spada, and the will so long sought for," replied Edmond, still incredulous.

" Of course ; what else could it be ? "

" And who completed it as it now is ? "

" I did. Aided by the remaining fragment, I guessed the rest; measuring the length of the lines by those of the paper, and divining the hidden meaning by means of what was in part revealed, as we are guided in a cavern by the small ray of light above us."

" And what did you do when you arrived at this conclusion ? "

" I resolved to set out, and did set out, that very instant, carrying with me the beginning of my great work on the unity of Italy; but for some time the imperial police (who at this period, quite contrary to what Napoleon desired so soon as he had a son born to him, wished for a partition of provinces) had their eyes on me; and my hasty departure, the cause of which they were unable to guess, having aroused their suspicions, I was arrested at the very moment I was leaving Piombino.

" Now," continued Faria, addressing Dantès with an almost paternal expression; " now, my dear fellow, you know as much as I do myself. If we ever escape together, half this treasure is yours; if I die here, and you escape alone, the whole belongs to you."

" But," inquired Dantès, hesitating, " has this treasure no more legitimate possessor in this world than ourselves ? "

" No, no, be easy on that score; the family is extinct. The last Comte de Spada, moreover, made me his heir; bequeathing to me this symbolic breviary, he bequeathed to me all it contained: no, no, make your mind satisfied on that point. If we lay hands on this fortune, we may enjoy it without remorse."

" And you say this treasure amounts to——"

" Two millions of Roman crowns; nearly thirteen million francs of our money."

" Impossible ! " said Dantès, staggered at the enormous amount.

" Impossible! and why ? " asked the old man. " The Spada family was one of the oldest and most powerful families of the fifteenth century; and in these times, when all speculation and occupation were wanting, those accumulations of gold and jewels were by no means rare; there are at this day Roman families perishing of hunger, though possessed of nearly a million in diamonds and jewels, handed down as heirlooms, and which they cannot touch."

Edmond thought he was in a dream—he wavered between incredulity and joy.

" I have only kept this secret so long from you," continued Faria, " that I might prove you, and then surprise you. Had we escaped before my attack of catalepsy, I should have conducted you to Monte-Cristo; now," he added, with a sigh, " it is you who will conduct me thither. " Well! Dantès, you do not thank me ? "

" This treasure belongs to you, my dear friend," replied Dantès, " and to you only. I have no right to it. I am no relation of yours."

" You are my son, Dantès," exclaimed the old man. " You are the child of my captivity. My profession condemns me to celibacy. God has sent you to me to console, at one and the same time, the man who could not be a father and the prisoner who could not get free."

And Faria extended the arm of which alone the use remained to him to the young man, who threw himself around his neck and wept bitterly.

CHAPTER XIX

THE THIRD ATTACK

OW that this treasure, which had so long been the object of the abbé's meditations, could insure the future happiness of him whom Faria really loved as a son, it had doubled its value in his eyes, and every day he expatiated on the amount, explaining to Dantès all the good which, with thirteen or fourteen millions of francs, a man could do in these days to his friends; and then Dantès' countenance became gloomy, for the oath of vengeance he had taken recurred to his memory, and he reflected how much ill, in these times, a man with thirteen or fourteen millions could do to his enemies.

The abbé did not know the isle of Monte-Cristo; but Dantès knew it, and had often passed it, situated twenty-five miles from Pianosa, between Corsica and the isle of Elba, and had once touched at it. This island was, always had been, and still is, completely deserted. It is a rock of almost conical form, which seems as though elevated by some volcanic effort from the depth to the surface of the ocean.

Dantès traced a plan of the island to Faria, and Faria gave Dantès advice as to the means he should employ to recover the treasure. But Dantès was far from being as enthusiastic and confident as the old man. It was past a question now that Faria was not a lunatic, and the way in which he had achieved the discovery, which had given rise to the suspicion of his madness, increased the young man's admiration of him; but at the same time he could not believe that that deposit, supposing it had ever existed, still existed; and though he considered the treasure as by no means chimerical, he yet believed it was no longer there.

However, as if fate resolved on depriving the prisoners of their last chance, and making them understand that they were condemned to perpetual imprisonment, a new misfortune befell them: the gallery on the sea side, which had long been in ruins, was rebuilt. They had repaired it completely, and stopped up with vast masses of stone the hole Dantès had partly filled in. But for this precaution, which, it will be remembered, the abbè had suggested to Edmond, the misfortune would have been still greater, for their attempt to escape would have been detected, and they would unfortunately have been separated. Thus a fresh and even stronger door was closed upon them.

" You see," said the young man, with an air of sorrowful resignation, to Faria, " that God deems it right to take from me even what you call my devotion to you. I have promised to remain forever with you, and now I could not break my promise if I would. I shall no more have the treasure than you, and neither of us will quit this prison. But my real treasure is not that, my dear friend, which awaits me beneath the somber rocks of Monte-Cristo, but it is your presence, our living together five or six hours a day, in spite of our jailers; it is those rays of intelligence you have poured into my brain, the languages you have implanted in my memory, and which spring there with all their philological ramifications. These different sciences that you have made so easy to me by the depth of the knowledge you possess of them, and the clearness of the principles to which you have reduced them — this is my treasure, my beloved friend, and with this you have made me rich and happy. Believe me, and take comfort, this is better for me than tons of gold and cases of diamonds, even were they not as problematical as the clouds we see in the morning floating over the sea, which we take for *terra firma,* and which evaporate and vanish as we draw near to them. To have you as long as possible near me, to hear your eloquent voice, which embellishes my mind, strengthens my soul, and makes my whole frame capable of great and terrible things, if I should ever be free, so fills my whole existence, that the despair to which I was just on the point of yielding when I knew you, has no longer any hold over me; and this — this is my fortune — not chimerical, but actual. I owe you my real good, my present happiness; and all the sovereigns of the earth, were they Cæsar Borgias, could not deprive me of this."

Thus, if not actually happy, yet the days these two unfortunates passed together went quickly. Faria, who for so long a time had kept silence as to the treasure, now perpetually talked of it. As he had said, he remained paralyzed in the right arm and the left leg, and had given up all hope of ever enjoying it himself. But he was continually thinking over some means of escape for his young companion, and he enjoyed it for him. For fear the letter might be some day lost or abstracted, he compelled Dantès to learn it by heart; and he thus knew it from one end to the other. Then he destroyed the second portion, assured that if the first were seized, no one would be able to penetrate its real meaning. Whole hours sometimes passed whilst Faria was giving instructions to Dantès — instructions which were to serve him when he was at liberty. Then, once free, from the day and hour and moment when he was so, he could have but one only thought, which was, to gain Monte-Cristo by some means, and remain there alone under some pretext which would give no suspicions; and once there, to endeavor to find the wonderful caverns, and search in the appointed spot. The appointed spot, be it remembered, being the farthest angle in the second opening.

In the meanwhile the hours passed, if not rapidly, at least tolerably. Faria, as we have said, without having recovered the use of his hand and foot, had resumed all the clearness of his understanding; and had gradually, besides the moral instructions we have detailed, taught his youthful companion the patient and sublime duty of a prisoner, who learns to make something from nothing. They were thus perpetually employed,— Faria, that he might not see himself grow old; Dantès, for fear of recalling the almost extinct past which now only floated in his memory like a distant light wandering in the night. All went on as if in existences in which misfortune has deranged nothing, and which glide on mechanically and tranquilly beneath the eye of Providence.

But beneath this superficial calm there were in the heart of the young man, and perhaps in that of the old man, many repressed desires, many stifled sighs, which found vent when Faria was left alone, and when Edmond returned to his cell.

One night Edmond awoke suddenly, believing he heard some one calling him. He opened his eyes and tried to pierce through the gloom. His name, or rather a plaintive voice which essayed to pronounce his name, reached him. He sat up, the sweat of anguish on his brow, and listened. Beyond all doubt the voice came from the cell of his comrade.

"Alas!" murmured Edmond, "can it be?"

He moved his bed, drew up the stone, rushed into the passage, and reached the opposite extremity; the secret entrance was open. By the light of the wretched and wavering lamp, of which we have spoken, Dantès saw the old man, pale, but yet erect, clinging to the bedstead. His features were writhing with those horrible symptoms which he already knew, and which had so seriously alarmed him when he saw them for the first time.

"Alas! my dear friend," said Faria in a resigned tone, "you understand, do you not; and I need not attempt to explain to you?"

Edmond uttered a cry of agony, and, quite out of his senses, rushed toward the door, exclaiming,—"Help! help!"

Faria had just sufficient strength to retain him.

"Silence!" he said, "or you are lost. Think now of yourself; only, my dear friend, act so as to render your captivity supportable or your flight possible. It would require years to renew only what I have done here, and which would be instantly destroyed if our jailers knew we had communicated with each other. Besides, be assured, my dear Edmond, the dungeon I am about to leave will not long remain empty; some other unfortunate being will soon take my place, and to him you will appear like an angel of salvation. Perhaps he will be young, strong, and enduring, like yourself, and will aid you in your escape; whilst I have been but a hindrance. You will no longer have half a dead body tied to you to paralyze all your movements. At length Providence has done something for you; he restores to you more than he takes away, and it was time I should die."

Edmond could only clasp his hands and exclaim,—"Oh, my friend! my friend! speak not thus!" and then resuming all his presence of mind, which had for a moment staggered under this blow, and his strength, which had failed at the words of the old man, he said:

"Oh! I have saved you once, and I will save you a second time."

And raising the foot of the bed, he drew out the phial, still a third filled with the red liquor.

"See!" he exclaimed, "there remains still some of this saving draught. Quick, quick! tell me what I must do this time,— are there any fresh instructions? Speak, my friend, I listen."

"There is not a hope," replied Faria, shaking his head; "but no matter, God wills it that man, whom he has created, and in whose heart he has so profoundly rooted the love of life, should do all in his power to preserve that existence, which, however painful it may be, is yet always so dear."

"Oh! yes, yes!" exclaimed Dantès, "and I tell you you shall yet be saved!"

"Well, then, try. The cold gains upon me. I feel the blood flowing toward my brain. This horrible trembling, which makes my teeth chatter, and seems to dislocate my bones, begins to pervade my whole frame; in five minutes the malady will reach its height, and in a quarter of an hour there will be nothing left of me but a corpse."

"Oh!" exclaimed Dantès, his heart wrung with anguish.

"Do as you did before, only do not wait so long. All the springs of life are now exhausted in me, and death," he continued, looking at his paralyzed arm and leg, "has but half its work to do. If, after having made me swallow twelve drops instead of ten, you see that I do not recover, then pour the rest down my throat. Now lift me on my bed, for I can no longer support myself."

Edmond took the old man in his arms, and laid him on the bed.

"And now, my dear friend," said Faria, "sole consolation of my wretched existence,— you whom Heaven gave me somewhat late, but still gave me, a priceless gift, and for which I am most grateful, at the moment of separating from you forever, I wish you all the happiness and all the prosperity you so well deserve. My son, I bless thee!"

The young man cast himself on his knees, leaning his head against the old man's bed.

"Listen, now, to what I say in this my dying moment. The treasure of the Spadas exists. God grants me that there no longer exists for me distance or obstacle. I see it in the depths of the inner cavern. My eyes pierce the inmost recesses of the earth, and are dazzled at the sight of so much riches. If you do escape, remember that the poor abbé, whom all the world called mad, was not so. Hasten to Monte-Cristo— avail yourself of the fortune— for you have indeed suffered long enough."

A violent shock interrupted the old man. Dantès raised his head and saw Faria's eyes injected with blood. It seemed as if a flow of blood had ascended from the chest to the head.

"Adieu! adieu!" murmured the old man, clasping Edmond's hand convulsively —"adieu!"

"Oh, no — no, not yet," he cried; "do not forsake me! Oh! succor him! Help! help! help!"

"Hush! hush!" murmured the dying man, "that they may not separate us if you save me!"

"You are right. Oh, yes, yes! be assured I shall save you! Besides, although you suffer much, you do not seem in such agony as before."

"Do not mistake! I suffer less because there is in me less strength to endure it. At your age we have faith in life; it is the privilege of youth to believe and hope, but old men see death more clearly. Oh! 'tis here —'tis here — 'tis over— my sight is gone — my reason escapes! Your hand, Dantès! Adieu! adieu!"

And raising himself by a final effort, in which he summoned all his faculties, he said: "Monte-Cristo! forget not Monte-Cristo!" and fell back in his bed.

The crisis was terrible; his twisted limbs, his swollen eyelids, a foam of blood and froth in his lips, a frame quite rigid, was soon extended on this bed of agony, in place of the intellectual being who was there but so lately.

Dantès took the lamp, placed it on a projecting stone above the bed, whence its tremulous light fell with strange and fantastic ray on this discomposed countenance and this motionless and stiffened body. With fixed eyes he awaited boldly the moment for administering the hoped-for restorative.

When he believed the instant had arrived, he took the knife, unclosed the teeth, which offered less resistance than before, counted, one after

the other, twelve drops, and watched; the phial contained, perhaps, twice as much more. He waited ten minutes, a quarter of an hour, half an hour; nothing moved. Trembling, his hair erect, his brow bathed with perspiration, he counted the seconds by the beatings of his heart. Then he thought it was time to make the last trial, and he put the phial to the violet lips of Faria, and without having occasion to force open his jaws, which had remained extended, he poured the whole of the liquid down his throat.

The draught produced a galvanic effect, a violent trembling pervaded the old man's limbs, his eyes opened until it was fearful to gaze upon them, he heaved a sigh which resembled a shriek, and then all this vibrating frame returned gradually to its state of immobility, only the eyes remained open.

Half an hour, an hour, an hour and a half elapsed, and during this time of anguish, Edmond leaned over his friend, his hand applied to his heart, and felt the body gradually grow cold, and the heart's pulsation become more and more deep and dull, until at length all stopped; the last movement of the heart ceased, the face became livid, the eyes remained open, but the look was glazed.

It was six o'clock in the morning, the dawn was just breaking, and its weak ray came into the dungeon, and paled the ineffectual light of the lamp. Singular shadows passed over the countenance of the dead man, which at times gave it the appearance of life. Whilst this struggle between day and night lasted, Dantès still doubted; but as soon as the daylight gained the preëminence, he saw that he was alone with a corpse. Then an invincible and extreme terror seized upon him, and he dared not again press the hand that hung out of bed, he dared no longer to gaze on those fixed and vacant eyes which he tried many times to close, but in vain — they opened again as soon as shut. He extinguished the lamp, carefully concealed it, and then went away, closing as well as he could the entrance to the secret passage by the large stone as he descended.

It was time, for the jailer was coming. On this occasion he began his rounds at Dantès' cell, and on leaving him he went on to Faria's dungeon, where he was taking breakfast and some linen. Nothing betokened that the man knew anything of what had occurred. He went on his way.

Dantès was then seized with an indescribable desire to know what was going on in the dungeon of his unfortunate friend. He therefore returned by the subterraneous gallery, and arrived in time to hear the exclamations of the turnkey, who called out for help. Other turnkeys came, and then was heard the regular tramp of soldiers even when not on duty — behind them came the governor.

Edmond heard the noise of the bed in which they were moving the corpse, heard the voice of the governor, who desired them to throw water on the face; and seeing that, in spite of this application, the prisoner did not recover, sent for the doctor. The governor then went out, and some words of pity fell on Dantès' listening ears, mingled with brutal laughter.

"Well! well!" said one, "the madman has gone to look after his treasure. Good journey to him!"

" With all his millions, he will not have enough to pay for his shroud ! " said another.

" Oh ! " added a third voice, " the shrouds of the Château d'If are not dear ! "

" Perhaps," said one of the previous speakers, " as he was a church-man, they may go to some expense in his behalf."

" They may give him the honors of the sack."

Edmond did not lose a word, but comprehended very little of what was said. The voices soon ceased, and it seemed to him as if the persons had all left the cell. Still he dared not to enter, as they might have left some turnkey to watch the dead. He remained, therefore, mute and motionless, restraining even his respiration. At the end of an hour, he heard a faint noise, which increased. It was the governor, who returned, followed by the doctor and other attendants. There was a moment's silence,— it was evident that the doctor was examining the dead body. The inquiries soon commenced.

The doctor analyzed the symptoms of the malady under which the prisoner had sunk, and declared he was dead. Questions and answers followed in a manner that made Dantès indignant, for he felt that all the world should experience for the poor abbé the love he bore him.

"I am very sorry for what you tell," said the governor, replying to the assurance of the doctor, "that the old man is really dead; for he was a quiet, inoffensive prisoner, happy in his folly, and required no watching."

"Ah!" added the turnkey, "there was no occasion for watching him; he would have stayed here fifty years, I'll answer for it, without any attempt to escape."

"Still," said the governor, "I believe it will be requisite, notwithstanding your certainty, and not that I doubt your science, but for my own responsibility's sake, that we should be perfectly assured that the prisoner is dead."

There was a moment of complete silence, during which Dantès, still listening, felt assured that the doctor was examining and touching the corpse a second time.

"You may make your mind easy," said the doctor; "he is dead. I will answer for that."

"You know, sir," said the governor, persisting, "that we are not content in such cases as this with such a simple examination. In spite of all appearances, be so kind, therefore, as to finish your duty by fulfilling the formalities prescribed by law."

"Let the irons be heated," said the doctor; "but really it is a useless precaution."

This order to heat the irons made Dantès shudder. He heard hasty steps, the creaking of a door, people going and coming, and some minutes afterward a turnkey entered, saying:

"Here is the brazier, lighted."

There was a moment's silence, and then was heard the noise made by burning flesh, of which the peculiar and nauseous smell penetrated even behind the wall where Dantès was listening horrified. At this smell of human flesh carbonized, the damp came over the young man's brow, and he felt as if he should faint.

"You see, sir, he is really dead," said the doctor; "this burn in the heel is decisive. The poor fool is cured of his folly, and delivered from his captivity."

" Wasn't his name Faria ?" inquired one of the officers who accompanied the governor.

" Yes, sir; and, as he said, it was an ancient name. He was, too, very learned, and rational enough on all points which did not relate to his treasure; but on that, indeed, he was obstinate."

" It is the sort of malady which we call monomania," said the doctor.

" You had never anything to complain of ?" said the governor to the jailer who had charge of the abbé.

" Never, sir," replied the jailer, " never ; on the contrary, he sometimes amused me very much by telling me stories. One day, too, when my wife was ill, he gave me a prescription which cured her."

" Ah, ah !" said the doctor, " I was ignorant that I had a colleague ; but I hope, M. le Gouverneur, that you will show him all proper respect in consequence."

" Yes, yes, make your mind easy ; he shall be decently interred in the newest sack we can find. Will that satisfy you ?"

" Must we do this last formality in your presence, sir ?" inquired a turnkey.

" Certainly. But make haste — I cannot stay here all day." Fresh footsteps, going and coming, were now heard, and a moment afterward the noise of cloth being rubbed reached Dantès' ears, the bed creaked on its hinges, and the heavy foot of a man who lifts a weight resounded on the floor ; then the bed again creaked under the weight deposited upon it.

" In the evening !" said the governor.

" Will there be any mass ?" asked one of the attendants.

" That is impossible," replied the governor. The chaplain of the château came to me yesterday to beg for leave of absence, in order to take a trip to Hyères for a week. I told him I would attend to the prisoners in his absence. If the poor abbé had not been in such a hurry, he might have had his requiem."

" Pooh ! pooh !" said the doctor, with the accustomed impiety of persons of his profession, " he is a churchman. God will respect his profession, and not give the devil the wicked delight of sending him a priest." A shout of laughter followed this brutal jest. During this time the operation of putting the body in the sack was going on.

" This evening," said the governor, when the task was ended.

" At what o'clock ?" inquired a turnkey.

" Why, about ten or eleven o'clock."

" Shall we watch by the corpse ?"

" Of what use would it be ? Shut the dungeon as if he were alive — that is all."

Then the steps retreated, and the voices died away in the distance ; the noise of the door, with its creaking hinges and bolts, ceased, and a silence duller than any solitude ensued — the silence of death, which pervaded all, and struck its icy chill through the young man's whole frame.

Then he raised the flag-stone cautiously with his head, and looked carefully round the chamber. It was empty ; and Dantès, quitting the passage, entered it.

CHAPTER XX

THE CEMETERY OF THE CHÂTEAU D'IF

N the bed, at full length, and faintly lighted by the pale ray that penetrated the window, was visible a sack of coarse cloth, under the large folds of which were stretched a long and stiffened form; it was Faria's last winding-sheet — a winding-sheet which, as the turnkey said, cost so little. All, then, was completed. A material separation had taken place between Dantès and his old friend; he could no longer see those eyes which had remained open as if to look even beyond death; he could no longer clasp that hand of industry which had lifted for him the veil that had concealed hidden and obscure things. Faria, the useful and the good companion, with whom he was accustomed to live so intimately, no longer lived but in his memory. He seated himself on the edge of that terrible bed, and fell into a melancholy and gloomy reverie.

Alone! — he was alone again! — again relapsed into silence! — he found himself once again in the presence of nothingness! Alone! — no longer to see, no longer to hear the voice of the only human being who attached him to life! Was it not better, like Faria, to seek the presence of his Maker, and learn the enigma of life at the risk of passing through the mournful gate of intense suffering?

The idea of suicide, driven away by his friend, and forgotten in his presence whilst living, arose like a phantom before him in presence of his dead body.

"If I could die," he said, "I should go where he goes, and should assuredly find him again. But how to die? It is very easy," he continued, with a smile of bitterness; "I will remain here, rush on the first person that opens the door, will strangle him, and then they will guillotine me."

But as it happens that in excessive griefs, as in great tempests, the abyss is found between the tops of the loftiest waves, Dantès recoiled from the idea of this infamous death, and passed suddenly from despair to an ardent desire for life and liberty.

"Die! oh, no," he exclaimed—"not die now, after having lived and suffered so long and so much! Die! yes, had I died years since; but now it would be, indeed, to give way to my bitter destiny. No, I desire to live; I desire to struggle to the very last; I wish to reconquer the happiness of which I have been deprived. Before I die I must not forget that I have my executioners to punish; and perhaps, too—who knows?—some friends to reward. Yet they will forget me here, and I shall die in my dungeon like Faria."

As he said this, he remained motionless, his eyes fixed like a man struck with a sudden idea, but whom this idea fills with amazement. Suddenly he rose, lifted his hand to his brow as if his brain were giddy, paced twice or thrice round his chamber, and then paused abruptly at the bed.

. "Ah! ah!" he muttered, "who inspires me with this thought? Is it thou, gracious God? Since none but the dead pass freely from this dungeon, let me assume the place of the dead!"

Without giving himself time to reconsider his decision, and, indeed, that he might not allow his thoughts to be distracted from his desperate resolution, he bent over the appalling sack, opened it with the knife which Faria had made, drew the corpse from the sack, and transported it along the gallery to his own chamber, laid it on his couch, passed round its head the rag he wore at night round his own, covered it with his counterpane, once again kissed the ice-cold brow, and tried vainly to close the resisting eyes, which glared horribly; turned the head toward the wall, so that the jailer might, when he brought his evening meal, believe that he was asleep, as was his frequent custom; returned along the gallery, pushed the bed against the wall, returned to the other cell, took from the hiding-place the needle and thread, flung off his rags, that they might feel naked flesh only beneath the coarse sackcloth, and getting inside the sack, placed himself in the posture in which the dead body had been laid, and sewed up the mouth of the sack withinside.

The beating of his heart might have been heard, if by any mischance the jailers had entered at that moment. Dantès might have waited until the evening visit was over, but he was afraid the governor might change his resolution, and order the dead body to be removed earlier. In that case his last hope would have been destroyed.

Now his project was settled under any circumstances, and he hoped thus to carry it into effect. If during the time he was being conveyed the grave-diggers should discover that they were conveying a live instead of a dead body, Dantès did not intend to give them time to recognize him, but, with a sudden cut of the knife, he meant to open the sack from top to bottom, and, profiting by their alarm, escape; if they tried to catch him, he would use his knife.

If they conducted him to the cemetery and laid him in the grave, he would allow himself to be covered with earth, and then, as it was night, the grave-diggers could scarcely have turned their backs, ere he would have worked his way through the soft soil and escape, hoping that the weight would not be too heavy for him to support. If he was deceived in this, and the earth proved too heavy, he would be stifled, and then, so much the better,— all would be over.

Dantès had not eaten since the previous evening, but he had not thought of hunger or thirst, nor did he now think of it. His position was too precarious to allow him even time to reflect on any thought but one.

The first risk that Dantès ran was, that the jailer, when he brought him his supper at seven o'clock, might perceive the substitution he had effected: fortunately, twenty times at least, from misanthropy or fatigue, Dantès had received his jailer in bed, and then the man placed his bread and soup on the table, and went away without saying a word. This time the jailer might not be silent as usual, but speak to Dantès, and seeing that he received no reply, go to the bed, and thus discover all.

When seven o'clock came, Dantès' agony really commenced. His hand placed upon his heart was unable to repress its throbbings, whilst, with the other, he wiped the perspiration from his temples. From time to time shudderings ran through his whole frame, and compressed his heart as if it were in an icy vise. Then he thought he was going to die. Yet the hours passed on without any stir in the château, and Dantès felt he had escaped the first danger: it was a good augury.

At length, about the hour the governor had appointed, footsteps were heard on the stairs. Edmond felt that the moment had arrived, and summoning up all his courage, held his breath, happy if at the same time he could have repressed in like manner the hasty pulsation of his arteries. They stopped at the door—there were two steps, and Dantès guessed it was the two grave-diggers who came to seek him. This idea was soon converted into certainty, when he heard the noise they made in putting down the hand-bier.

The door opened, and a dim light reached Dantès' eyes through the coarse sack that covered him; he saw two shadows approach his bed, a third remaining at the door with a torch in his hand. Each of these two men, approaching the ends of the bed, took the sack by its extremities.

"He's heavy, though, for an old and thin man," said one, as he raised the head.

"They say every year adds half a pound to the weight of the bones," said another, lifting the feet.

"Have you tied the knot?" inquired the first speaker.

"What would be the use of carrying so much more weight?" was the reply; "I can do that when we get there."

"Yes, you're right," replied the companion.

"What's the knot for?" thought Dantès.

They deposited the supposed corpse on the bier. Edmond stiffened himself in order to play his part of a dead man, and then the party, lighted by the man with the torch, who went first, ascended the stairs. Suddenly he felt the fresh and sharp night air, and Dantès recognized the *Mistral.* It was a sudden sensation, at the same time replete with delight and agony.

The bearers advanced twenty paces, then stopped, putting their bier down on the ground. One of them went away, and Dantès heard his shoes on the pavement.

"Where am I then?" he asked himself.

"Really, he is by no means a light load!" said the other bearer, sitting on the edge of the hand-barrow.

Dantès' first impulse was to escape, but fortunately he did not attempt it.

"Light me, you sir," said the other bearer, "or I shall not find what I am looking for."

The man with the torch complied, although not asked in the most polite terms.

"What can he be looking for?" thought Edmond. "The spade, perhaps."

An exclamation of satisfaction indicated that the grave-digger had found the object of his search. "Here it is at last," he said, "not without some trouble, though."

"Yes," was the answer, "but it has lost nothing by waiting."

As he said this, the man came toward Edmond, who heard a heavy and sounding substance laid down beside him, and at the same moment a cord was fastened round his feet with sudden and painful violence.

"Well, have you tied the knot?" inquired the grave-digger, who was looking on.

"Yes, and pretty tight too, I can tell you," was the answer.

"Move on, then." And the bier was lifted once more, and they proceeded.

They advanced fifty paces farther, and then stopped to open a door, then went forward again. The noise of the waves dashing against the rocks on which the château is built reached Dantès' ear distinctly as they progressed.

"Bad weather!" observed one of the bearers; "not a pleasant night for a dip in the sea."

"Why, yes, the abbé runs a chance of being wet," said the other; and then there was a burst of brutal laughter.

Dantès did not comprehend the jest, but his hair stood erect on his head.

" Well, here we are at last," said one of them.

" A little farther—a little farther," said the other. " You know very well that the last was stopped on his way, dashed on the rocks, and the governor told us next day that we were careless fellows."

They ascended five or six more steps, and then Dantès felt that they took him one by the head and the other by the heels, and swung him to and fro.

" One!" said the grave-diggers, " two! three, and away!"

And at the same instant Dantès felt himself flung into the air like a wounded bird, falling, falling, with a rapidity that made his blood curdle. Although drawn downward by the same heavy weight which hastened his rapid descent, it seemed to him as if the time were a century. At last, with a terrific dash, he entered the ice-cold water, and as he did so he uttered a shrill cry, stifled in a moment by his immersion beneath the waves.

Dantès had been flung into the sea, into whose depths he was dragged by a thirty-six pound shot tied to his feet.

The sea is the cemetery of the Château d'If.

CHAPTER XXI.

ANTÈS, although giddy and almost suffocated, had yet suffi-cient presence of mind to hold his breath; and as his right hand (prepared as he was for every chance) held his knife open, he rapidly ripped up the sack, extricated his arm, and then his body; but, in spite of all his efforts to free himself from the bullet, he felt it dragging him down still lower. He then bent his body, and by a desperate effort severed the cord that bound his legs, at the moment he was suffocating. With a vigorous spring he rose to the sur-face of the sea, whilst the bullet bore to its depths the sack that had so nearly become his shroud.

Dantès merely paused to breathe, and then dived again, in order to avoid being seen. When he arose a second time, he was fifty paces from where he had first sunk. He saw overhead a black and tempestu-ous sky, over which the wind was driving the fleeting vapors that occa-sionally suffered a twinkling star to appear; before him was the vast expanse of waters, somber and terrible, whose waves foamed and roared as if before the approach of a storm. Behind him, blacker than the sea, blacker than the sky, rose, like a threatening phantom, the giant of granite, whose projecting crags seemed like arms extended to seize their prey; and on the highest rock was a torch that lighted two figures.

He fancied these two forms were looking at the sea; doubtless these strange grave-diggers had heard his cry. Dantès dived again, and remained a long time beneath the water. This manœuvre was already familiar to him, and usually attracted a crowd of spectators in the bay before the lighthouse at Marseilles who, with one accord, pro-nounced him the best swimmer in the port. When he re-appeared the light had disappeared.

It was necessary to lay out a course. Ratonneau and Pomègue are the nearest isles of all those that surround the Château d'If; but Ratonneau and Pomègue are inhabited, together with the islet of Daume; Tiboulen or Lemaire were the most secure. The isles of Tiboulen and Lemaire are a league from the Château d'If; Dantès, nevertheless, determined to make for them. But how could he find his way in the darkness of the night?

At this moment he saw before him, like a brilliant star, the lighthouse of Planier. By swimming straight to this light, he kept the isle of Tiboulen a little on the left; by turning to the left, therefore, he would find it. But, as we have said, it was at least a league from the Château d'If to this island. Often in prison Faria had said to him, when he saw him idle and inactive:

"Dantès, you must not give way to this listlessness; you will be drowned if you seek to escape, and your strength has not been properly exercised and prepared for exertion."

These words rang in Dantès' ears, even beneath the waves; he hastened to cleave his way through them to see if he had not lost his strength. He found with pleasure that his captivity had taken away nothing of his power, and that he was still master of that element on whose bosom he had so often sported as a boy.

Fear, that relentless pursuer, doubled Dantès' efforts. He listened if any noise was audible; each time that he rose over the waves his looks scanned the horizon, and strove to penetrate the darkness. Every wave seemed a boat in his pursuit, and he redoubled exertions that increased his distance from the château, but the repetition of which weakened his strength. He swam on still, and already the terrible château had disappeared in the darkness. He could not see it, but he *felt* its presence.

An hour passed, during which Dantès, excited by the feeling of freedom, continued to cleave the waves.

"Let us see," said he, "I have swum above an hour, but, as the wind is against me, that has retarded my speed; however, if I am not mistaken, I must be close to the isle of Tiboulen. But what if I were mistaken?"

A shudder passed over him. He sought to tread water, in order to rest himself; but the sea was too violent, and he felt that he could not make use of this means of repose.

"Well," said he, "I will swim on until I am worn out, or the cramp seizes me, and then I shall sink." And he struck out with the energy of despair.

Suddenly the sky seemed to him to become darker and more dense, and compact clouds lowered toward him; at the same time he felt a violent pain in his knee. His imagination, with its inconceivable rapidity, told him a ball had struck him, and that in a moment he would hear the report; but he heard nothing. Dantès put out his hand, and felt resistance; he then drew up his leg, and felt the land, and in an instant guessed the nature of the object he had taken for a cloud.

Before him rose a mass of strangely formed rocks, that resembled nothing so much as a vast fire petrified at the moment of its most fervent combustion. It was the isle of Tiboulen. Dantès rose, advanced a few steps, and, with a fervent prayer of gratitude, stretched himself on the granite, which seemed to him softer than down. Then, in spite of the wind and rain, he fell into the deep sweet sleep of those worn out by fatigue; whose soul is still awake with the consciousness of unexpected good fortune. At the expiration of an hour Edmond was awakened by the roar of the thunder. The tempest was unchained and let loose in all its fury; from time to time a flash of lightning stretched across the heavens like a fiery serpent, lighting up the clouds that rolled on like the waves of an immense chaos.

Dantès with his sailor's eye had not been deceived — he had reached the first of the two isles, which was, in reality, Tiboulen. He knew that it was barren and without shelter; but when the sea became more calm, he resolved to plunge into its waves again, and swim to Lemaire, equally arid, but larger, and consequently better adapted for concealment.

An overhanging rock offered him a temporary shelter, and scarcely had he availed himself of it when the tempest burst forth in all its fury. Edmond felt the rock beneath which he lay tremble; the waves, dashing themselves against the granite rock, wetted him with their spray. In safety, as he was, he felt himself become giddy in the midst of this war of the elements and the dazzling brightness of the lightning. It seemed to him that the island trembled to its base, and that it would, like a vessel at anchor, break her moorings, and bear him off into the center of the storm.

He then recollected that he had not eaten or drunk for four and twenty hours. He extended his hands, and drank greedily of the rainwater that had lodged in a hollow of the rock. As he rose, a flash of lightning, that seemed as if the whole of the heavens were opened, illumined the darkness. By its light, between the isle of Lemaire and Cape Croiselle, a quarter of a league distant, Dantès saw, like a specter, a fishing-boat driven rapidly on by the force of the winds and waves. A second after, he saw it again, approaching nearer with terrible speed. Dantès cried at the top of his voice to warn them of their danger, but they saw it themselves. Another flash showed him four men clinging to the shattered mast and the rigging, while a fifth clung to the broken rudder. The men he beheld saw him, doubtless, for their cries were carried to his ears by the wind. Above the splintered mast a sail rent to tatters was flapping; suddenly the ropes that still held it gave way, and it disappeared in the darkness of the night like a vast sea-bird.

At the same moment a violent crash was heard, and cries of distress. Perched like a sphinx on the summit of the rock, Dantès saw, by the lightning, the vessel in pieces; and amongst the fragments were visible the agonized features of the unhappy sailors. Then all became dark again. The dreadful spectacle had lasted only the time of the lightning-flash.

Dantes ran down the rocks at the risk of being himself dashed to pieces; he listened, he strove to examine, but he heard and saw nothing — all human cries had ceased, and the tempest alone continued to rage and foam. By degrees the wind abated, vast gray clouds rolled toward the west, and the blue firmament appeared studded with bright stars. Soon a red streak toward the east became visible in the horizon, the waves whitened, a light played over them, and gilded their foaming crest with gold. It was day.

Dantès stood silent and motionless before this vast spectacle, as if he saw it for the first time, for since his captivity he had forgotten it. He turned toward the fortress, and looked both at the sea and the land. The gloomy building rose from the bosom of the ocean with that imposing majesty of inanimate objects that seems at once to watch and to command. It was about five o'clock. The sea continued to grow calmer.

"In two or three hours," thought Dantès, "the turnkey will enter my chamber, find the body of my poor friend, recognize it, seek for me in vain, and give the alarm. Then the passage will be discovered; the men who cast me into the sea, and who must have heard the cry I uttered, will be questioned. Then boats filled with armed soldiers will pursue the wretched fugitive. The cannon will warn every one to refuse shelter to a man wandering about naked and famished. The police of Marseilles will be on the alert by land, whilst the governor pursues me by sea. I am cold, I am hungry. I have lost even the knife that saved me. I am at the mercy of the first boor who would like to make twenty francs by giving me up; I have neither strength, ideas, nor courage. O my God! I have suffered enough, surely. Have pity on me, and do for me what I am unable to do for myself."

As Dantès (his eyes turned in the direction of the Château d'If) uttered this prayer in a kind of delirium, he saw appear, at the extremity of the isle of Pomègue, like a bird skimming over the sea, a small bark, with its lateen sail, that the eye of a sailor alone could recognize as a Genoese tartan. She was coming out of Marseilles harbor, and was standing out to sea rapidly, her sharp prow cleaving through the waves.

"Oh!" cried Edmond, "to think that in half an hour I could join her, did I not fear being questioned, detected, and conveyed back to Marseilles! What can I do? What story can I invent? Under pretext of trading along the coast, these men, who are in reality smugglers, will prefer selling me to doing a good action. I must wait. But I cannot — I am starving. In a few hours my strength will be utterly exhausted; besides, perhaps I have not been missed at the fortress; the alarm has not been given. I can pass as one of the sailors wrecked last night. This story will pass current, for there is no one left to contradict me."

As he spoke, Dantès looked toward the spot where the fishing vessel had been wrecked, and started. The red cap of one of the sailors hung to a point of the rock, and some beams that had formed part of the vessel's keel floated at the foot of the crags. In an instant Dantès' plan was formed. He swam to the cap, placed it on his head, seized one of the beams, and struck out so as to cross the line the vessel was taking.

"I am saved!" murmured he. And this conviction restored his strength.

He soon perceived the vessel, which, having the wind right ahead, was tacking between the Château d'If and the tower of Planier. For an instant he feared lest the bark, instead of keeping in shore, should stand out to sea, as she would have done if bound for Corsica or Sardinia; but he soon saw by her manœuvres that she wished to pass, like most vessels bound for Italy, between the islands of Jaros and Calaseraigne.

However, the vessel and the swimmer insensibly neared one another, and in one of its tacks the bark approached within a quarter of a mile of him. He rose on the waves, making signs of distress; but no one on board perceived him, and the vessel stood on another tack. Dantès would have cried out, but he reflected that the wind and the dash of the waves would drown his voice.

It was then he rejoiced at his precaution in taking the beam, for without it he would have been unable, perhaps, to reach the vessel — certainly to return to shore, should he be unsuccessful in attracting attention.

Dantès, although almost sure as to what course the bark would take, had yet watched it anxiously until it tacked and stood toward him. Then he advanced; but before they had met, the vessel again changed her direction. By a violent effort he rose half out of the water, waving his cap, and uttering a loud shout of distress peculiar to sailors, that seems the cry of some spirit of the deep. This time he was both seen and heard, and the tartan instantly steered toward him. At the same time, he saw they were about to lower the boat.

An instant after, the boat, rowed by two men, advanced rapidly toward him. Dantès abandoned the beam, which he thought now useless, and swam vigorously to meet them. But he had reckoned too much upon his strength, and then he felt how serviceable the beam had been to him. His arms grew stiff, his legs had lost their flexibility, and he was almost breathless.

He uttered a second cry. The two sailors redoubled their efforts, and one of them cried in Italian, "Courage!"

The word reached his ear as a wave which he no longer had the strength to surmount passed over his head. He rose again to the surface, supporting himself by one of those desperate efforts a drowning man makes, uttered a third cry, and felt himself sink again, as if the fatal bullet were again tied to his feet. The water passed over his head, and through it the sky seemed livid. A violent effort again brought him to the surface. He felt as if something seized him by the hair, but he saw and heard nothing. He had fainted.

When he opened his eyes, Dantès found himself on the deck of the tartan. His first care was to see what direction they were pursuing. They were rapidly leaving the Château d'If behind. Dantès was so exhausted that the exclamation of joy he uttered was mistaken for a sigh.

As we have said, he was lying on the deck. A sailor was rubbing his limbs with a woolen cloth; another, whom he recognized as the one who had cried out "Courage!" held a gourd full of rum to his mouth; whilst the third, an old sailor, at once the pilot and captain, looked on with that egotistical pity men feel for a misfortune that they have escaped yesterday and which may overtake them to-morrow.

A few drops of rum restored suspended animation, whilst the friction of his limbs restored their elasticity.

"Who are you?" said the pilot, in bad French.

"I am," replied Dantès, in bad Italian, "a Maltese sailor. We were coming from Syracuse laden with grain. This storm of last night overtook us at Cape Morgiou, and we were wrecked on these rocks."

"Where do you come from?"

"From these rocks that I had the good luck to cling to whilst our captain was lost. My three comrades are drowned, and I am the sole survivor. I saw your ship, and fearful of being left to perish on the desolate island, I swam off on a fragment of the vessel in order to try and gain your bark. You have saved my life, and I thank you," continued Dantès. "I was lost when one of your sailors caught hold of my hair."

"It was I," said a sailor of a frank and manly appearance; "and it was time, for you were sinking."

"Yes," returned Dantès, holding out his hand, "I thank you again."

"I almost hesitated though," replied the sailor; "you looked more like a brigand than an honest man, with your beard six inches and your hair a foot long."

Dantès recollected that his hair and beard had not been cut all the time he was at the Château d'If.

"Yes," said he, "I made a vow to our Lady del Pie de la Grotto not to cut my hair or beard for ten years if I were saved in a moment of danger; but to-day the vow expires."

"Now, what are we to do with you?" said the captain.

"Alas! anything you please. My captain is dead; I have barely escaped; but I am a good sailor. Leave me at the first port you make; I shall be sure to find employment."

"Do you know the Mediterranean?"

"I have sailed over it since my childhood."

"You know the best harbors?"

"There are few ports that I could not enter or leave with my eyes blinded."

"I say, captain," said the sailor who had cried "Courage!" to Dantès, "if what he says is true, what hinders his staying with us?"

"If he says true," said the captain doubtingly. "But in his present condition he will promise anything, and take his chance of keeping it afterward."

"I will do more than I promise," said Dantès.

"We shall see," returned the other, smiling.

"Where are you going to?" asked Dantès.

"To Leghorn."

"Then, why, instead of tacking so frequently, do you not sail nearer the wind?"

"Because we should run straight on to the island of Rion."

"You shall pass it by twenty fathoms."

"Take the helm, and let us see what you know."

The young man took the helm, ascertaining by a slight pressure if the vessel answered the rudder, and seeing that, without being a first-rate sailor, she yet was tolerably obedient.

"To the braces," said he. The four seamen, who composed the crew, obeyed, whilst the pilot looked on. "Haul taut."

They obeyed.

"Belay." This order was also executed; and the vessel passed, as Dantès had predicted, twenty fathoms to the right.

"Bravo!" said the captain.

"Bravo!" repeated the sailors. And they all regarded with astonishment this man, whose eye had recovered an intelligence and his body a vigor they were far from suspecting.

"You see," said Dantès, quitting the helm, "I shall be of some use to you, at least, during the voyage. If you do not want me at Leghorn, you can leave me there; and I will pay you out of the first wages I get, for my food and the clothes you lend me."

"Ah," said the captain, "we can agree very well, if you are reasonable."

"Give me what you give the others, and all will be arranged," returned Dantès.

"That's not fair," said the seaman who had saved Dantès; "for you know more than we do."

"What is that to you, Jacopo?" returned the captain. "Every one is free to ask what he pleases."

"That's true," replied Jacopo; "I only made a remark."

"Well, you would do much better to lend him a jacket and a pair of trousers, if you have them."

"No," said Jacopo; "but I have a shirt and a pair of trousers."

"That is all I want," interrupted Dantès. Jacopo dived into the hold and soon returned with what Edmond wanted.

"Now, then, do you wish for anything else?" said the patron.

"A piece of bread and another glass of the capital rum I tasted, for I have not eaten or drunk for a long time." He had not tasted food for forty hours. A piece of bread was brought, and Jacopo offered him the gourd.

"Port your helm," cried the captain to the steersman. Dantès glanced to the same side as he lifted the gourd to his mouth; but his hand stopped.

"Halloa! what's the matter at the Château d'If?" said the captain.

A small white cloud, which had attracted Dantes' attention, crowned the summit of the bastion of the Château d'If. At the same moment the faint report of a gun was heard. The sailors looked at one another.

"What is this?" asked the captain.

"A prisoner has escaped from the Château d'If; and they are firing the alarm gun," replied Dantès.

The captain glanced at him; but he had lifted the rum to his lips,

THE FAINT REPORT OF A GUN WAS HEARD.

and was drinking it with so much composure, that his suspicions, if he had any, died away.

"Pretty strong rum!" said Dantès, wiping his brow with his sleeve.

"At any rate," murmured the captain, "if it be, so much the better, for I have made a rare acquisition."

Jacopo.

Under pretense of being fatigued, Dantès asked to take the helm; the steersman, enchanted to be relieved, looked at the captain, and the latter by a sign indicated that he might abandon it to his new comrade. Dantès could thus keep his eyes on Marseilles.

"What is the day of the month ?" asked he of Jacopo, who sat down beside him.

"The 28th of February !"

"In what year ?"

"In what year ! you ask me in what year ?"

"Yes," replied the young man, "I ask you in what year ?"

"You have forgotten, then ?"

"I have been so frightened last night," replied Dantès, smiling, "that I have almost lost my memory. I ask you what year is it ?"

"The year 1829," returned Jacopo.

It was fourteen years, day for day, since Dantès' arrest. He was nineteen when he entered the Château d'If; he was thirty-three when he escaped. A sorrowful smile passed over his face; he asked himself what had become of Mercédès, who must believe him dead. Then his eyes lighted up with hatred as he thought of the three men who had caused him so long and wretched a captivity. He renewed against Danglars, Fernand, and Villefort the oath of implacable vengeance he had made in his dungeon.

This oath was no longer a vain menace; for the fastest sailer in the Mediterranean would have been unable to overtake the little tartan that, with every stitch of canvas set, was flying before the wind to Leghorn.

CHAPTER XXII

ANTÈS had not been a day on board before he had an insight into the persons with whom he sailed. Without having been in the school of the Abbé Faria, the worthy master of *La Jeune Amélie* (the name of the Genoese tartan) knew a smattering of all the tongues spoken on the shores of that large lake called the Mediterranean, from the Arabic to the Provençal; and this, whilst it spared him interpreters, persons always troublesome and frequently indiscreet, gave him great facilities of communication, either with the vessels he met at sea, with the small barks sailing along the coast, or with those persons without name, country, or apparent calling who are always seen on the quays of seaports, and who live by those hidden and mysterious means which we must suppose come in a right line from Providence, as they have no visible means of existence. We may thus suppose that Dantès was on board a smuggling lugger.

In the first instance the master had received Dantès on board with a certain degree of mistrust. He was very well known to the custom-house officers of the coast; and as there was between these worthies and himself an exchange of the most cunning stratagems, he had at first thought that Dantès might be an emissary of these illustrious executors of rights and duties, who employed this ingenious means of penetrating some of the secrets of his trade. But the skillful manner in which Dantès had manœuvred the little bark had entirely re-assured him; and then, when he saw the light smoke floating like a plume above the bastion of the Château d'If, and heard the distant explosion, he was instantly struck with the idea that he had on board his vessel one for whom, like the goings in and comings out of kings, they accord salutes of cannons. This made him less uneasy, it must be owned, than if the new-comer had proved a custom-house officer; but this latter supposition also disappeared like the first, when he beheld the perfect tranquillity of his recruit.

Edmond thus had the advantage of knowing what the owner was, without the owner knowing who he was; and however the old sailor and his crew tried to "pump" him, they extracted nothing more from him; giving accurate descriptions of Naples and Malta, which he knew as well as Marseilles, and persisting stoutly in his first statement. Thus the Genoese, subtle as he was, was duped by Edmond, in whose favor his mild demeanor, his nautical skill, and his admirable dissimulation pleaded. Moreover, it is possible that the Genoese was one of those shrewd persons who know nothing but what they should know, and believe nothing but what they should believe.

It was thus, in this reciprocal position, that they reached Leghorn. Here Edmond was to undergo another trial; it was to see if he should recognize himself, never having beheld his own features for fourteen years. He had preserved a tolerably good remembrance of what the youth had been, and was now to find what the man had become. His comrades believed that his vow was fulfilled. As he had twenty times touched at Leghorn before, he remembered a barber in the Rue Saint-Ferdinand; he went there to have his beard and hair cut. The barber gazed in amazement at this man with the long hair and beard, thick and black as it was, and resembling one of Titian's glorious heads. At this period it was not the fashion to wear so large a beard and hair so long; now a barber would only be surprised if a man gifted with such advantages should consent voluntarily to deprive himself of them. The Leghorn barber went to work without a single observation.

When the operation was concluded, when Edmond felt his chin was completely smooth, and his hair reduced to its usual length, he requested a looking-glass in which he might see himself. He was now, as we have said, three-and-thirty years of age, and his fourteen years' imprisonment had produced a great moral change in his appearance.

Dantès had entered the Château d'If with the round, open, smiling face of a young and happy man with whom the early paths of life have been smooth, and who relies on the future as a natural deduction of the past. This was now all changed. His oval face was lengthened, his smiling mouth had assumed the firm and marked lines which betoken resolution; his eyebrows were arched beneath a large and thoughtful wrinkle; his eyes were full of melancholy; and from their depths occasionally sparkled gloomy fires of misanthropy and hatred; his complexion, so long kept from the sun, had now that pale color which produces, when the features are encircled with black hair, the aristocratic beauty of the man of the north; the deep learning he had acquired had besides diffused over his features the rays of extreme intellect; and he had also acquired, although previously a tall man, that vigor which a frame possesses which has so long concentrated all its force within itself.

To the elegance of a nervous and slight form had succeeded the solidity of a rounded and muscular figure. As to his voice, prayers, sobs, and imprecations had changed it now into a soft and singularly touching tone, and now into a sound rude and almost hoarse.

Moreover, being perpetually in twilight or darkness, his eyes had acquired that singular faculty of distinguishing objects in the night common to the hyena and the wolf. Edmond smiled when he beheld himself; it was impossible that his best friend — if, indeed, he had any friend left — could recognize him; he could not recognize himself.

The master of *La Jeune Amélie*, who was very desirous of retaining amongst his crew a man of Edmond's value, had offered to him some advances out of his future profits, which Edmond had accepted. His next care on leaving the barber's who had achieved his first metamorphosis was to enter a shop and buy a complete sailor's suit — a garb, as we all know, very simple, and consisting of white trousers, a striped shirt, and a cap.

It was in this costume, and bringing back to Jacopo the shirt and trousers he had lent him, that Edmond re-appeared before the patron of *La Jeune Amélie*, who had made him tell his story over and over again before he could believe him, or recognize in the neat and trim sailor the man with thick and matted beard, his hair tangled with sea-weed, and his body soaking in sea-brine, whom he had picked up naked and nearly drowned. Attracted by his prepossessing appearance, he renewed his offers of an engagement to Dantès; but Dantès, who had his own projects, would not agree for a longer time than three months.

La Jeune Amélie had a very active crew, very obedient to their captain, who lost as little time as possible. He had scarcely been a week at Leghorn before the hold of his vessel was filled with painted muslins, prohibited cottons, English powder, and tobacco on which the crown had forgotten to put its mark. The master was to get all this out of Leghorn free of duties, and land it on the shores of Corsica, where certain speculators undertook to forward the cargo to France.

They sailed; Edmond was again cleaving the azure sea which had been the first horizon of his youth, and which he had so often dreamed of in prison. He left Gorgone on his right and La Pianosa on his left, and went toward the country of Paoli and Napoleon.

The next morning going on deck, which he always did at an early hour, the patron found Dantès leaning against the bulwarks gazing with intense earnestness at a pile of granite rocks, which the rising sun tinged with rosy light. It was the isle of Monte-Cristo.

La Jeune Amélie left it three-quarters of a league to the larboard and kept on for Corsica. Dantès thought, as they passed thus closely the island whose name was so interesting to him, that he had only to leap into the sea and in half an hour he would be on the promised land. But then what could he do without instruments to discover his treasure, without arms to defend himself? Besides, what would the sailors say? What would the patron think? He must wait.

Fortunately, Dantès had learned how to wait; he had waited fourteen years for his liberty, and now he was free he could wait at least six months or a year for wealth. Would he not have accepted liberty without riches if it had been offered to him? Besides, were not those riches chimerical?—offspring of the diseased brain of the poor Abbé Faria, had they not died with him? It is true, this letter of the Cardinal

Spada was singularly circumstantial, and Dantès repeated to himself, from one end to the other, the letter, of which he had not forgotten a word.

The evening came on, and Edmond saw the island pass through every change of tint that twilight brings with it, and disappear in the darkness from all eyes; but he, with his gaze accustomed to the gloom of a prison, continued to see it after all the others, for he remained last upon deck. The next morn broke off the coast of Aleria; all day they coasted, and in the evening saw some fires lighted on land; by the arrangement of these fires they no doubt recognized the signals for landing, for a ship's lantern was hung up at the mast-head instead of the streamer, and they neared the shore within gunshot. Dantès remarked that at this time, too, the patron of *La Jeune Amélie* had, as he neared the land, mounted two small culverines, which, without making much noise, can throw a ball, of four to the pound, a thousand paces or so.

But on this occasion the precaution was superfluous, and everything proceeded with the utmost smoothness and politeness. Four shallops came off with very little noise alongside the bark, which, no doubt, in acknowledgment of the compliment, lowered her own shallop into the sea, and the five boats worked so well that by two o'clock in the morning all the cargo was out of *La Jeune Amélie* and safe on shore. The same night, such a man of regularity was the master of *La Jeune Amélie* that the profits were shared out, and each man had a hundred Tuscan livres, or about fifteen dollars.

But the voyage was not ended. They turned the bowsprit toward Sardinia, where they intended to take in a cargo, which was to replace what had been discharged. The second operation was as successful as the first. *La Jeune Amélie* was in luck. This new cargo was destined for the coast of the Duchy of Lucca, and consisted almost entirely of Havana cigars, sherry, and Malaga wines.

There they had a bit of a skirmish with the custom-house; the *gabelle* was, in truth, the everlasting enemy of *La Jeune Amélie*. A custom-house officer was laid low, and two sailors were wounded; Dantès was one of the latter, a ball having touched him in the left shoulder. Dantès was almost glad of this affray, and almost pleased at being wounded, for they were rude lessons which taught him with what eye he could view danger, and with what endurance he could bear suffering.

He had contemplated danger with a smile, and when wounded had exclaimed with the great philosopher, "Pain, thou art not an evil."

He had, moreover, looked upon the custom-house officer wounded to death, and, whether from heat of blood produced by the rencontre, or the chill of human sentiment, this sight had made but slight impression upon him; Dantès was on the way he desired to follow, and was moving toward the end he wished to achieve; his heart was in a fair way of petrifying in his bosom. Jacopo, seeing him fall, had believed him killed, and rushing toward him raised him up, and then attended to him with all the kindness of an attached comrade.

This world was not then so good as Voltaire's Doctor Pangloss believed it, neither was it so wicked as Dantès thought it, since this man, who had nothing to expect from his comrade but the inheritance of his share of the prize-money, testified so much sorrow when he saw him fall. Fortunately, as we have said, Edmond was only wounded, and with certain herbs gathered at certain seasons, and sold to the smugglers by the old Sardinia women, the wound soon closed. Edmond then resolved to try Jacopo, and offered him in return for his attention a share of his prize-money, but Jacopo refused it indignantly.

It resulted, therefore, from this kind of sympathetic devotion which Jacopo had bestowed on Edmond from the first time he saw him, that Edmond felt for Jacopo a certain degree of affection. But this sufficed for Jacopo, who already instinctively felt that Edmond had a right to superiority of position — a superiority which Edmond had concealed from all others. And from this time the kindness which Edmond showed him was enough for the brave seaman.

Then in the long days on board ship, when the vessel, gliding on with security over the azure sea, required nothing, thanks to the favorable wind that swelled her sails, but the hand of the helmsman, Edmond, with a chart in his hand, became the instructor of Jacopo, as the poor Abbé Faria had been his tutor. He pointed out to him the bearings of the coast, explained to him the variations of the compass, and taught him to read in that vast book opened over our heads which they call heaven, and where God writes in azure with letters of diamonds.

And when Jacopo inquired of him, "What is the use of teaching all these things to a poor sailor like me?" Edmond replied: "Who knows? You may one day be the captain of a vessel. Your fellow-countryman, Bonaparte, became emperor." We had forgotten to say that Jacopo was a Corsican.

Two months and a half elapsed in these trips, and Edmond had become as skillful a coaster as he had been a hardy seaman; he had formed an acquaintance with all the smugglers on the coast, and learned all the masonic signs by which these half-pirates recognize each other. He had passed and repassed his isle of Monte-Cristo twenty times, but not once had he found an opportunity of landing there.

He then formed a resolution. This was, as soon as his engagement with the master of *La Jeune Amélie* ended, he would hire a small bark on his own account — for in his several voyages he had amassed a hundred piastres — and under some pretext land at the isle of Monte-Cristo. Then he would be free to make his researches, not perhaps entirely at liberty, for he would be doubtless watched by those who accompanied him. But in this world we must risk something. Prison had made Edmond prudent, and he was desirous of running no risk whatever. But in vain did he rack his imagination; fertile as it was, he could not devise any plan for reaching the wished-for isle without being accompanied thither.

Dantès was tossed about on these doubts and wishes, when the skipper, who had great confidence in him, and was very desirous of retaining him in his service, took him by the arm one evening and led him to a tavern on the Via del' Oglio, where the leading smugglers of Leghorn used to congregate. It was here they discussed the affairs of the coast. Already Dantès had visited this maritime bourse two or three times, and seeing all these hardy free-traders, who supplied the whole coast for nearly two hundred leagues in extent, he had asked himself what power might not that man attain who should give the impulse of his will to all these contrary and diverging links. This time it was a great matter that was under discussion, connected with a vessel laden with Turkey carpets, stuffs of the Levant, and cashmeres. It was requisite to find some neutral ground on which an exchange could be made, and then to try and land these goods on the coast of France. If successful, the profit would be enormous; there would be a gain of fifty or sixty piastres each for the crew.

The master of *La Jeune Amélie* proposed as a place of landing the isle of Monte-Cristo, which, being completely deserted, and having neither soldiers nor revenue officers, seemed to have been placed in the midst of the ocean since the time of the heathen Olympus by Mercury, the god of merchants and robbers, classes which we in modern times have separated, if not made distinct, but which antiquity appears to have included in the same category.

At the mention of Monte-Cristo Dantès started with joy; he rose, to conceal his emotion, and took a turn round the smoky tavern, where all the languages of the known world were jumbled in the *lingua franca.*

When he again joined the two persons who had been discussing, it had been decided that they should touch at Monte-Cristo, and set out on the following night. Edmond, being consulted, was of opinion that the island offered every possible security, and that great enterprises to be well done should be done quickly.

Nothing then was altered in the plan arranged, and orders were given to get under weigh next night, and, wind and weather permitting, to gain, the day after, the waters of the neutral isle.

THE ISLE OF MONTE-CRISTO.

CHAPTER XXIII

THUS, at length, by one of those pieces of unlooked-for good fortune which sometimes occur to those on whom misfortune has for a long time pressed heavily, Dantès was about to arrive at his wished-for opportunity by simple and natural means, and land in the island without incurring any suspicion. One night only separated him from his departure so ardently wished for.

The night was one of the most feverish that Dantes had ever passed, and during its progress all the charms, good and evil, passed in turn through his brain. If he closed his eyes, he saw the letter of Cardinal Spada written on the wall in characters of flame; if he slept for a moment, the wildest dreams haunted his fancy. He descended into grottoes paved with emeralds, with panels of rubies, and the roof glowing with diamond stalactites. Pearls fell drop by drop, as subterranean waters filter in their caves. Edmond, amazed, wonderstruck, filled his pockets with the radiant gems and then returned to daylight, when he discovered that his prizes were all converted into common pebbles. He then endeavored to reënter these marvelous grottoes, but then beheld them only in the distance; and now the way wound in endless spirals, and then the entrance became invisible, and in vain did he tax his memory for the magic and mysterious word which opened the splendid caverns of Ali Baba to the Arabian fisherman. All was useless; the treasure disappeared, and had again reverted to the genii from whom for a moment he had hoped to carry it off.

The day came at length, and was almost as feverish as the night had been, but it brought reason to aid his imagination, and Dantès was then enabled to arrange a plan which had hitherto been vague and unsettled in his brain. Night came, and with it the preparation for departure, and these preparations served to conceal Dantès' agitation. He had by degrees assumed such authority over his companions that he was almost like a commander on board; and as his orders were always clear, distinct, and easy of execution, his comrades obeyed him with promptitude and pleasure.

The old captain did not interfere, for he too had recognized the superiority of Dantès over the crew and himself. He saw in the young man his natural successor, and regretted that he had not a daughter, that he might have bound Edmond to him by a distinguished alliance.

At seven o'clock in the evening all was ready, and at ten minutes past seven they doubled the lighthouse just as the beacon was kindled. The sea was calm, and, with a fresh breeze from the south-east, they sailed beneath a bright blue sky, in which God also lighted up in turn his beacon-lights, each of which is a world. Dantès told them that all hands might turn in, and he would take the helm. When the Maltese (for so they called Dantès) had said this, it was sufficient, and all went to their cots contentedly.

This frequently happened. Dantès, flung back from solitude into the world, frequently experienced a desire for solitude; and what solitude is at the same time more complete, more poetical, than that of a bark floating isolated on the sea during the obscurity of the night, in the silence of immensity, and under the eye of Heaven?

Now, on this occasion the solitude was peopled with his thoughts, the night lighted up by his illusions, and the silence animated by his anticipations. When the master awoke, the vessel was hurrying on with all her canvas set, and every sail full with the breeze. They were making nearly ten knots an hour. The isle of Monte-Cristo loomed large in the horizon. Edmond resigned the bark to the master's care, and went and lay down in his hammock; but, in spite of a sleepless night, he could not close his eyes for a moment.

Two hours afterward he came on deck, as the boat was about to double the isle of Elba. They were just abreast of Mareciana, and beyond the flat but verdant isle of La Pianosa. The peak of Monte-Cristo, reddened by the burning sun, was seen against the azure sky. Dantès desired the helmsman to put down his helm, in order to leave La Pianosa on the right hand, as he knew that he should thus decrease the distance by two or three knots. About five o'clock in the evening the island was quite distinct, and everything on it was plainly perceptible, owing to that clearness of the atmosphere which is peculiar to the light which the rays of the sun cast at its setting.

Edmond gazed most earnestly at the mass of rocks, which gave out all the variety of twilight colors, from the brightest rose to the deepest blue; and from time to time his cheeks flushed, his brow became purple,

and a mist passed over his eyes.　Never did gamester whose whole fortune is staked on one cast of the die experience the anguish which
Edmond felt in his paroxysms of hope.

Night came, and at ten o'clock they anchored.　*La Jeune Amélie*
was the first at the rendezvous.　In spite of his usual command over
himself, Dantès could not restrain his impetuosity.　He was the first
who jumped on shore; and had he dared, he would, like Lucius Brutus,
have "kissed his mother earth."　It was dark; but at eleven o'clock the
moon rose in the midst of the ocean, whose every wave she silvered, and
then, "ascending high," played in floods of pale light on the rocky hills
of this second Pelion.

The island was familiar to the crew of *La Jeune Amélie*,— it was one
of her halting-places.　As to Dantès, he had passed it on his voyages to
and from the Levant, but never touched at it.　He questioned Jacopo.

"Where shall we pass the night ? " he inquired.

"Why, on board the tartan," replied the sailor.

"Should we not be better in the grottoes."

"What grottoes ? "

"Why, the grottoes — caves of the island."

"I do not know of any grottoes," replied Jacopo.

A cold damp sprang to Dantès' brow.

"What! are there no grottoes at Monte-Cristo ? " he asked.

"None."

For a moment Dantès was speechless; then he remembered that
these caves might have been filled up by some accident, or even stopped
up, for the sake of greater security, by Cardinal Spada.　The point was,
then, to discover the lost opening.　It was useless to search at night, and
Dantès therefore delayed all investigation until the morning.　Besides,
a signal made half a league out at sea, to which *La Jeune Amélie* replied
by a similar signal, indicated that the moment had arrived for business.

The boat that now arrived, assured by the answering signal that all
was right, soon came in sight, white and silent as a phantom, and cast
anchor within a cable's length of shore.

Then the landing began.　Dantès reflected as he worked on the
shout of joy which, with a single word, he could produce from amongst
all these men, if he gave utterance to the one unchanging thought that
was whispering in his ear and in his heart; but, far from disclosing this
precious secret, he almost feared that he had already said too much,
and by his restlessness and continual questions, his minute observations and evident preoccupation, had aroused suspicions.　Fortunately,
as regarded this circumstance at least, with him the painful past
reflected on his countenance an indelible sadness; and the glimmer-

ings of gayety seen beneath this cloud were indeed but transitory flashes.

No one had the slightest suspicion; and when next day, taking a fowling-piece, powder, and shot, Dantès testified a desire to go and kill some of the wild goats that were seen springing from rock to rock, his excursion was construed into a love of sport or a desire for solitude. However, Jacopo insisted on following him; and Dantès did not oppose this, fearing if he did so that he might incur distrust. Scarcely, however, had he gone a quarter of a league than, having killed a kid, he begged Jacopo to take it to his comrades, and request them to cook it, and when ready to let him know by firing a gun. This and some dried fruits, and a flask of the wine of Monte Pulciano, was the bill of fare.

Dantès went forward, looking behind and round about him from time to time. Having reached the summit of a rock, he saw, a thousand feet beneath him, his companions, whom Jacopo had rejoined, and who were all busy preparing the repast which Edmond's skill as a marksman had augmented with a capital dish.

Edmond looked at them for a moment with the sad and soft smile of a man superior to his fellows.

"In two hours' time," said he, "these persons will depart richer by fifty piastres each, to go and risk their lives again by endeavoring to gain fifty more such pieces; then they will return with a fortune of six hundred francs, and waste this treasure in some city with the pride of sultans and the insolence of nabobs. At this moment Hope makes me despise their riches, which seem to me contemptible. Yet perchance to-morrow deception will so act on me, that I shall, on compulsion, consider such a contemptible possession as the utmost happiness. Oh, no!" exclaimed Edmond, "that will not be. The wise, unerring Faria could not be mistaken in this one thing. Besides, it were better to die than to continue to lead this low and wretched life."

Thus Dantès, who but three months before had no desire but liberty, had now not liberty enough, and panted for wealth. The cause was not in Dantès, but in Providence, who, whilst limiting the power of man, has filled him with boundless desires.

Meanwhile, by a way between two walls of rock, following a path worn by a torrent, and which, in all probability, human foot had never before trod, Dantès approached the spot where he supposed the grottoes must have existed. Keeping along the coast, and examining the smallest object with serious attention, he thought he could trace on certain rocks marks made by the hand of man.

Time, which incrusts all physical substances with its mossy mantle, as it invests all things moral with its mantle of forgetfulness, seemed to

have respected these signs, traced with a certain regularity, and probably with the design of leaving traces. Occasionally these marks disappeared beneath tufts of myrtle, which spread into large bushes laden
with blossoms, or beneath parasitical lichen. It was thus requisite that

Edmond should push the branches on one side or remove the mosses in
order to retrace the indicating marks which were to be his guides in
this labyrinth. These signs had renewed the best hopes in Edmond's
mind. Why should it not have been the cardinal who had first traced

them, in order that they might, in the event of a catastrophe, which he could not foresee would have been so complete, serve as a guide for his nephew? This solitary place was precisely suited for a man desirous of burying a treasure. Only, might not these betraying marks have attracted other eyes than those for whom they were made? and had the dark and wondrous isle indeed faithfully guarded its precious secret?

It seemed, however, to Edmond, who was hidden from his comrades by the inequalities of the ground, that at sixty paces from the harbor the marks ceased; nor did they terminate at any grotto. A large round rock, placed solidly on its base, was the only spot to which they seemed to lead. Edmond reflected that perhaps instead of having reached the end he might have only touched on the beginning, and he therefore turned round and retraced his steps.

During this time his comrades had prepared the repast, had got some water from a spring, spread out the fruit and bread, and cooked the kid. Just at the moment when they were taking it from the spit, they saw Edmond, who, light and daring as a chamois, was springing from rock to rock, and they fired a musket to give the signal agreed upon. The sportsman instantly changed his direction, and ran quickly toward them. But at the moment when they were all following with their eyes his agile bounds with a rashness which gave them alarm, Edmond's foot, as if to justify their fears, slipped, and they saw him stagger on the edge of a rock and disappear. They all rushed toward him, for all loved Edmond, in spite of his superiority; yet Jacopo reached him first.

He found Edmond stretched bleeding and almost senseless. He had rolled down a height of twelve or fifteen feet. They poured some drops of rum down his throat, and this remedy, which had before been so beneficial to him, produced the same effect as formerly. Edmond opened his eyes, complained of great pain in his knee, a feeling of heaviness in his head, and severe pains in his loins. They wished to carry him to the shore, but when they touched him, although under Jacopo's directions, he declared, with heavy groans, that he could not bear to be moved.

It may be supposed that Dantès did not now think of his dinner, but he insisted that his comrades, who had not his reasons for fasting, should have their meal. As for himself, he declared that he had only need of a little rest, and that when they returned he should be easier. The sailors did not require much urging. They were hungry, and the smell of the roasted kid was very savory, and your tars are not very ceremonious. An hour afterward they returned. All that Edmond had been able to do was to drag himself about a dozen paces forward to lean against a moss-grown rock.

But, far from being easier, Dantès' pains had appeared to increase in violence. The old skipper, who was obliged to sail in the morning in order to land his cargo on the frontiers of Piedmont and France, between Nice and Fréjus, urged Dantès to try and rise. Edmond made great exertions in order to comply; but at each effort he fell back, moaning and turning pale.

"He has broken his ribs," said the commander, in a low voice. "No matter; he is an excellent fellow, and we must not leave him. We will try and carry him on board the tartan."

Dantès declared, however, that he would rather die where he was than undergo the agony caused by the slightest movement he made.

"Well," said the master, "let what may happen, it shall never be said that we deserted a good comrade like you. We will not go till evening."

This very much astonished the sailors, although not one opposed it. The master was so strict that this was the first time they had ever seen him give up an enterprise, or even delay an arrangement. Dantès would not allow that any such infraction of regular and proper rules should be made in his favor.

"No, no," he said to the master, "I was awkward, and it is just that I pay the penalty of my clumsiness. Leave me a small supply of biscuit, a gun, powder, and balls to kill the kids or defend myself at need, and a pickaxe to build me something like a shed if you delay in coming back for me."

"But you'll die of hunger," said the sailor.

"I would rather do so," was Edmond's reply, "than suffer the inexpressible agonies which the slightest motion brings on."

The captain turned toward his vessel, which was undulating in the small harbor, and, with her sails partly set, was ready for sea when all her toilette should be completed.

"What are we to do, Maltese?" asked the captain. "We cannot leave you here so, and yet we cannot stay."

"Go, go!" exclaimed Dantès.

"We shall be absent at least a week," said the patron, "and then we must run out of our course to come here and take you up again."

"Why," said Dantès, "if in two or three days you hail any fishing-boat, desire them to come here to me. I will pay twenty-five piastres for my passage back to Leghorn. If you do not come across one, return for me." The captain shook his head.

"Listen, Captain Baldi; there's one way of settling this," said Jacopo. "Do you go, and I will stay and take care of the wounded man."

"And give up your share of the venture," said Edmond, "to remain with me?"

"Yes," said Jacopo, "and without any hesitation."

" You are a good fellow," replied Edmond, " and Heaven will recompense you for your generous intentions; but I do not wish any one to stay with me. A day or two's rest will set me up, and I hope I shall find amongst the rocks certain herbs most excellent for contusions."

A singular smile passed over Dantès' lips; he squeezed Jacopo's hand warmly; but nothing could shake his determination to remain — and remain alone.

The smugglers left with Edmond what he had requested and set sail; but not without turning about several times, and each time making signs of a cordial leave-taking, to which Edmond replied with his hand only, as if he could not move the rest of his body.

When they had disappeared, he said with a smile : " 'Tis strange that it should be amongst such men that we find proofs of friendship and devotion." Then he dragged himself cautiously to the top of a rock, from which he had a full view of the sea, and thence he saw the tartan complete her preparations for sailing, weigh anchor, and, balancing herself as gracefully as a water-fowl ere it takes to the wing, set sail.

At the end of an hour she was completely out of sight; at least, it was impossible for the wounded man to see her any longer from the spot where he was. Then Dantès rose more agile and light than the kid amongst the myrtles and shrubs of these wild rocks, took his gun in one hand, his pickaxe in the other, and hastened toward the rock on which the marks he had noted terminated.

" And now," he exclaimed, remembering the tale of the Arabian fisherman, which Faria had related to him, " now, Open Sesame!"

CHAPTER XXIV

HE sun had nearly reached the third of his course, and his warm and vivifying rays fell full on the rocks, which seemed themselves sensible of the heat. Thousands of grasshoppers, hidden in the bushes, chirped with a monotonous and continuous note; the leaves of the myrtle and olive trees waved and rustled in the wind. At every step that Edmond took on the burning granite, he disturbed the lizards glittering with the hues of the emerald; afar off he saw the wild goats, which sometimes attracted sportsmen, bounding from crag to crag. In a word, the isle was inhabited, yet Edmond felt himself alone, guided by the hand of God.

He felt an indescribable sensation somewhat akin to dread — that dread of the daylight which even in the desert makes us fear we are watched and observed.

This feeling was so strong, that at the moment when Edmond was about to commence his labor, he stopped, laid down his pickaxe, seized his gun, mounted to the summit of the highest rock, and from thence gazed round in every direction.

But it was not upon poetic Corsica, the very houses of which he could distinguish; nor on almost unknown Sardinia; nor on the isle of Elba, with its historical associations; nor upon the imperceptible line that to the experienced eye of a sailor alone revealed the coast of Genoa the proud, and Leghorn the commercial, that he gazed. It was at the brigantine that had left in the morning, and the tartan that had just set sail, that Edmond fixed his eyes.

The first was just disappearing in the straits of Bonifacio; the other, following an opposite direction, was about to round the island of Corsica.

This sight re-assured him. He then looked at the objects near him. He saw himself on the highest point of the cone-like isle, a statue on this vast pedestal,—on land not a human being, on sea not a sail; whilst the blue ocean beat against the base of the island and covered it with a fringe of foam. Then he descended with cautious and slow step, for he dreaded lest an accident similar to that he had so adroitly feigned should happen in reality.

Dantès, as we have said, had traced back the marks in the rock; and he had noticed that they led to a small creek, hidden like the bath of some ancient nymph. This creek was sufficiently wide at its mouth, and deep in the center, to admit of the entrance of a small vessel of the speronare class, which would be perfectly concealed from observation.

Then, following the clew that, in the hands of the Abbé Faria, had been so skillfully used to guide him through the Dædalian labyrinth of probabilities, he thought that the Cardinal Spada, anxious not to be watched, had entered the creek, concealed his little bark, followed the line marked by the notches in the rock, and at the end of it had buried his treasure. It was this idea that had brought Dantès back to the circular rock. One thing only perplexed Edmond, and destroyed his theory. How could this rock, which weighed several tons, have been lifted to this spot without the aid of many men?

Suddenly an idea flashed across his mind. Instead of raising it, thought he, they have lowered it. And he sprang upon the rock in order to look for the base on which it had formerly stood.

He soon perceived that a slope had been formed, and the rock had slid along this until it stopped at the spot it now occupied. A stone of ordinary size had served as a wedge; flints and pebbles had been scattered around it, so as to conceal the break: this species of masonry had been covered with earth, and grass and weeds had grown there, moss had clung to the stones, myrtle-bushes had taken root, and the old rock seemed fixed to the earth.

Dantès raised the earth carefully, and detected, or fancied he detected, the ingenious artifice. He attacked this wall, cemented by the hand of Time, with his pickaxe. After ten minutes' labor the wall gave way, and a hole large enough to insert the arm was opened.

Dantès went and cut the strongest olive-tree he could find, stripped off its branches, inserted it in the hole, and used it as a lever. But the rock was too heavy and too firmly wedged to be moved by any one man, were he Hercules himself. Dantés reflected that he must attack this wedge. But how?

He cast his eyes around, and saw the horn full of powder which his friend Jacopo had left him. He smiled; the infernal invention would serve him for this purpose.

With the aid of his pickaxe Dantès dug, between the upper rock and the one that supported it, a mine similar to those formed by pioneers when they wish to spare human labor, filled it with powder, then made a fuse, by pulling threads from his handkerchief and rolling them in the powder.   He lighted it and retired.

The explosion was instantaneous: the upper rock was lifted from its base by the terrific force of the powder; the lower one flew into pieces; thousands of insects escaped from the aperture Dantès had previously formed, and a huge snake, like the guardian demon of the treasure, rolled himself along on his blue convolutions and disappeared. Dantès approached the upper rock, which now, without any support, leaned toward the sea. The intrepid treasure-seeker walked round it, and, selecting the spot from whence it appeared most easy to attack it, placed his lever in one of the crevices, and strained every nerve to move the mass.

The rock, already shaken by the explosion, tottered on its base. Dantès redoubled his efforts; he seemed like one of the ancient Titans, who uprooted the mountains to hurl against the father of the gods. The rock yielded, rolled, bounded, and finally disappeared in the ocean.

On the spot it had occupied was visible a circular place, and which exposed an iron ring let into a square flag-stone.

Dantès uttered a cry of joy and surprise; never had a first attempt been crowned with more perfect success. He would fain have continued, but his knees trembled, his heart beat so violently, and his eyes became so dim, that he was forced to pause.

This feeling lasted but for the time of a flash. Edmond inserted his lever in the ring, and exerting all his strength, the flag-stone yielded, and disclosed a kind of stair that descended until it was lost in the increasing obscurity of a subterraneous grotto.

Any one else would have rushed on with a cry of joy. Dantès turned pale, hesitated, and reflected.

"Come," said he to himself, "be a man. I am accustomed to adversity. I must not be cast down by the discovery that I have been deceived. What, then, would be the use of all I have suffered? The heart breaks when, after having been extravagantly elated by the warm breath of hope, it relapses into cold reality. Faria has dreamed this; the Cardinal Spada buried no treasure here; perhaps he never came here, or if he did, Cæsar Borgia, the intrepid adventurer, the stealthy and indefatigable plunderer, has followed him, discovered his traces, pursued as I have done, like me raised the stone, and descending before me, has left me nothing."

He remained motionless and pensive, his eyes fixed on the somber aperture that was open at his feet.

"Now that I expect nothing, now that I no longer entertain the slightest hopes, the end of this adventure becomes a simple matter of curiosity."

And he remained again motionless and thoughtful.

"Yes, yes; this is an adventure worthy a place in the lights and shades of the life of this royal bandit, in the tissue of strange events that compose the checkered web of his existence; this fabulous event has formed but a link of a vast chain. Yes, Borgia has been here, a torch in one hand, a sword in the other, whilst within twenty paces, at the foot of this rock, perhaps two guards kept watch on land, sea, and sky, whilst their master descended as I am about to descend, dispelling the darkness before his terrible and flaming arm."

"But what was the fate of these guards who thus possessed his secret?" asked Dantès of himself.

"The fate," replied he, smiling, "of those who buried Alaric, and were interred with the corpse."

"Yet, had he come," thought Dantès, "he would have found the treasure, and Borgia, he who compared Italy to an artichoke, which he could devour leaf by leaf, knew too well the value of time to waste it in replacing this rock. I will go down."

Then he descended— a smile on his lips, and murmuring that last word of human philosophy, "Perhaps!"

But instead of the darkness and the thick and mephitic atmosphere he had expected to find, Dantès saw a dim and bluish light, which, as well as the air, entered, not merely by the aperture he had just formed, but by the interstices and crevices of the rock which were invisible from without, and through which he could distinguish the blue sky and the waving branches of the evergreen oaks, and the tendrils of the creepers that grew from the rocks.

After having stood a few minutes in the cavern, the atmosphere of which was rather warm than damp, and free from earthy smell, Dantès' eye, habituated as it was to darkness, could pierce even to the remotest angles of the cavern, which was of granite that sparkled like diamonds.

"Alas!" said Edmond, smiling, "these are the treasures the cardinal has left; and the good abbé, seeing in a dream these glittering walls, has indulged in fallacious hopes."

But he called to mind the words of the will, which he knew by heart: "In the farthest angle of the second opening," said the cardinal's will.

He had only found the first grotto; he had now to seek the second. Dantès commenced his search. He reflected that this second grotto must, doubtless, penetrate deeper into the isle; he examined the stones, and sounded one part of the wall where he fancied the opening existed, masked for precaution's sake.

The pickaxe sounded for a moment with a dull sound that covered Dantès' forehead with large drops of perspiration. At last it seemed to him that one part of the wall gave forth a more hollow and deeper echo; he eagerly advanced, and with the quickness of perception that no one but a prisoner possesses, saw that it was there, in all probability, that the opening must be.

However, he, like Cæsar Borgia, knew the value of time; and, in order to avoid a fruitless toil, he sounded all the other walls with his pickaxe, struck the earth with the butt of his gun, and finding nothing that appeared suspicious, returned to that part of the wall whence issued the consoling sound he had before heard.

He again struck it, and with greater force. Then a singular sight presented itself. As he struck the wall, a species of stucco similar to that used as the ground of frescoes detached itself, and fell to the ground in flakes, exposing a large white stone like common ashlar. The aperture of the rock had been closed with another sort of stones, then this stucco had been applied, and painted to imitate granite. Dantès struck with the sharp end of his pickaxe, which entered some way between the interstices of the stone.

It was there he must dig.

But by some strange phenomenon of the human organization, in proportion as the proofs that Faria had not been deceived became stronger, so did his heart give way, and a feeling of discouragement steal over him. This last proof, instead of giving him fresh strength, deprived him of it; the pickaxe descended, or rather fell; he placed it on the ground, passed his hand over his brow, and remounted the stairs, alleging to himself, as an excuse, a desire to be assured that no one was watching him, but in reality because he felt he was ready to faint.

The isle was deserted, and the sun seemed to cover it with its fiery glance; afar off a few small fishing-boats studded the bosom of the blue ocean.

Dantès had tasted nothing, but he thought not of hunger at such a moment; he hastily swallowed a few drops of rum, and again entered the cavern.

The pickaxe that had seemed so heavy, was now like a feather in his grasp; he seized it and attacked the wall. After several blows he perceived that the stones were not cemented, but merely placed one upon the other, and covered with stucco; he inserted the point of his pickaxe, and using the handle as a lever, soon saw with joy the stone turn as if on hinges, and fall at his feet.

He had nothing more to do now, but with the iron tooth of the pickaxe to draw the stones toward him one by one. The first aperture was sufficiently large to enter, but by waiting, he could still cling to hope, and retard the certainty of deception. At last, after fresh hesitation, Dantès entered the second grotto.

The second grotto was lower and more gloomy than the former; the air that could only enter by the newly formed opening had that mephitic smell Dantès was surprised not to find in the first. He waited in order to allow pure air to revive this dead atmosphere, and then entered.

At the left of the opening was a dark and deep angle. But to Dantès' eye there was no darkness. He glanced round this second grotto; it was, like the first, empty.

The treasure, if it existed, was buried in this corner. The time had at length arrived; two feet of earth to remove was all that remained for Dantès between supreme joy and supreme despair.

He advanced toward the angle, and summoning all his resolution, attacked the ground with the pickaxe. At the fifth or sixth blow the pickaxe struck against an iron substance. Never did funeral knell, never did alarm-bell produce a greater effect on the hearer. Had Dantès found nothing he could not have become more ghastly pale.

He again struck his pickaxe into the earth, and encountered the same resistance, but not the same sound.

"It is a casket of wood bound with iron," thought he.

At this moment a shadow passed rapidly before the opening; Dantès seized his gun, sprang through the opening, and mounted the stair. A wild goat had passed before the mouth of the cave, and was feeding at a little distance. This would have been a favorable occasion to secure his dinner; but Dantès feared lest the report of his gun should attract attention.

He reflected an instant, cut a branch of a resinous tree, lighted it at the fire at which the smugglers had prepared their breakfast, and descended with this torch.

He wished to see all. He approached the hole he had formed with the torch, and saw that he was not deceived, and his pickaxe had in reality struck against iron and wood.

In an instant a space three feet long by two feet broad was cleared, and Dantès could see an oaken coffer, bound with cut steel; in the midst of the lid he saw engraved on a silver plate, which was still untarnished, the arms of the Spada family — viz., a sword, *en pale*, on an oval shield, like all the Italian armorial bearings, and surmounted by a cardinal's hat.

Dantès easily recognized them, Faria had so often drawn them for him. There was no longer any doubt the treasure was there; no one would have been at such pains to conceal an empty casket. In an instant he had cleared every obstacle away, and he saw successively the lock, placed between two padlocks, and the two handles at each end, all carved as things were carved at that epoch, when art rendered the commonest metals precious.

Dantès seized the handles, and strove to lift the coffer; it was impossible.

He sought to open it; lock and padlock were closed: these faithful guardians seemed unwilling to surrender their trust.

Dantès inserted the sharp end of the pickaxe between the coffer and the lid, and, pressing with all his force on the handle, burst open the fastenings with a crash. The hinges yielded in their turn, and fell, still holding in their grasp fragments of the planks, and all was open.

A vertigo seized Edmond; he cocked his gun and laid it beside him. He then closed his eyes as children do in order to perceive in the

ALONE WITH THESE COUNTLESS, THESE UNHEARD-OF FABULOUS TREASURES.

shining night of their own imagination more stars than are visible in the firmament; then he re-opened them, and stood motionless with amazement.

Three compartments divided the coffer. In the first, blazed piles of golden coin; in the second, bars of unpolished gold, which possessed nothing attractive save their value, were ranged; in the third, half-full, Edmond grasped handfuls of diamonds, pearls, and rubies, which as they fell on one another in a glittering cascade, sounded like hail against glass.

After having touched, felt, examined these treasures of gold and gems, Edmond rushed through the caverns like a man seized with frenzy; he leaped on a rock, from whence he could behold the sea. He was alone. Alone with these countless, these unheard-of fabulous treasures! Was he awake, or was it but a dream? Was it a transient vision, or was he face to face with reality?

He would fain have gazed upon his gold, and yet he felt that he had not strength enough; for an instant he leaned his head in his hands as if to prevent his senses from leaving him, and then rushed madly about the rocks of Monte-Cristo without following — not a road, for there is no road in the island — any definite course, terrifying the wild goats and scaring the sea-fowls with his wild cries and gestures; then he returned, and, still unable to believe the evidence of his senses, rushed through the first grotto into the second, and found himself before this mine of gold and jewels.

This time he fell on his knees, and, clasping his hands convulsively, uttered a prayer intelligible to God alone. He soon felt himself calmer and more happy, for now only he began to credit his felicity.

He then set himself to work to count his fortune. There were a thousand ingots of gold, each weighing from three pounds; then he piled up twenty-five thousand crowns, each worth about twenty dollars of our money, and bearing the effigies of Alexander VI. and his predecessors; and he saw that the compartment was not half empty. And he measured ten double-handfuls of precious stones, many of which, mounted by the most famous workmen, were valuable for their execution.

Dantès saw the light gradually disappear; and fearing to be surprised in the cavern, left it, his gun in his hand. A piece of biscuit and a small quantity of wine formed his supper; then he replaced the stone, stretched himself upon it, and snatched a few hours' sleep, lying over the mouth of the cave.

This night was one of those delicious and yet terrible ones, of which this man of paralyzing emotions had already passed two or three in his lifetime.

CHAPTER XXV

AYLIGHT, for which Dantès had so waited with open eyes, again dawned. With the first beams of day Dantès rose, climbed, as on the previous evening, up the most elevated precipices of the island, to search the horizon around, but, as on previous evening, all was deserted.

Returning to the entrance of the cave, he raised the stone, filled his pockets with precious stones, put the box together as well as he could, covered with earth which he trod down, sprinkled fresh sand over the spot to give it everywhere a similar appearance; then, quitting the grotto, he replaced the stone, heaping on it large and small rocks, filling the interstices with earth, into which he planted wild myrtle and flowering thorn; then carefully watering these new plantations, he scrupulously effaced every trace of foot-mark and impatiently awaited the return of his companions. To wait at Monte-Cristo for the purpose of watching, as a dragon watches a useless treasure, over the most incalculable riches that had thus fallen into his possession satisfied not the cravings of his heart, which yearned to return to dwell among mankind, and to assume the rank, power, and influence which wealth, the first and greatest force at the disposal of man, alone can bestow.

On the sixth day the smugglers returned. From a distance Dantès recognized the cut and manner of sailing of *La Jeune Amélie,* and dragging himself, like wounded Philoctetes, toward the landing-place, he met his companions with an assurance that, although considerably better, he still suffered. He then inquired how they had fared in their trip. The smugglers had, indeed, been successful in landing their cargo, but they had scarcely done so when they received intelligence that a guardship had just quitted the port of Toulon, and was crowding all sail toward them; this obliged them to fly with all speed; when they could but lament the absence of Dantès, whose superior skill in the management of a vessel would have availed them so materially. In fact, the chasing vessel had almost overtaken them when night came on, and, by doubling the Cape of Corsica, they eluded pursuit. Upon the whole,

however, the trip had been sufficiently successful; while the crew, and particularly Jacopo, expressed regrets at Dantès not having been with them so as to be an equal sharer with themselves in the profits, amounting to no less a sum than fifty piastres each.

Edmond preserved his self-command, not even smiling at the enumeration of all the benefits he would have reaped had he been able to quit the isle; but, as *La Jeune Amélie* had merely come to Monte-Cristo to fetch him away, he embarked that same evening, and proceeded with the captain to Leghorn.

Arrived at Leghorn, he repaired to the house of a Jew, a dealer in precious stones, to whom he disposed of four of his smallest diamonds, for five thousand francs each. The Jew might have asked how a sailor became possessor of such objects; but he took good care not to do so, as he made a thousand francs on each.

The following day Dantès presented Jacopo with an entirely new vessel, accompanying the gift by one hundred piastres, that he might provide himself with a crew, upon conditions of his going to Marseilles for the purpose of inquiring after an old man named Louis Dantès, residing in the Allées de Meilhan, and also a young female called Mercédès, an inhabitant of the Catalan village.

Jacopo could scarcely believe his senses, but Dantès told him that he had merely been a sailor from whim, because his family did not allow him the money necessary for his support; but that on his arrival at Leghorn he had come into possession of a large fortune, left him by an uncle, whose sole heir he was. The superior education of Dantès gave an air of such probability to this statement that it never once occurred to Jacopo to doubt its accuracy.

The term for which Edmond had engaged to serve on board *La Jeune Amélie* having expired, Dantès took leave of the captain, who at first tried to retain him as one of the crew, but, having been told the history of the legacy, he ceased to importune him further.

The succeeding morning Jacopo set sail for Marseilles, with directions from Dantès to join him at the island of Monte-Cristo.

The same day Dantès departed without saying where he was going; he took leave of the crew of *La Jeune Amélie* after distributing a splendid gratuity, and of the captain with a promise to let him hear of him some day or other. Dantès went to Genoa.

At the moment of his arrival a small yacht was being tried in the bay, by order of an Englishman, who, having heard that the Genoese were the best builders of the Mediterranean, wanted a yacht built there. The price agreed upon with the Englishman was forty thousand francs. Dantès offered sixty thousand francs, upon condition of being allowed to take immediate possession of it. The Englishman had gone upon a tour through Switzerland, and was not expected back in less than three weeks or a month, by which time the builder reckoned upon being able to complete another. Dantès led the builder to a Jew, retired to a small back parlor, and the Jew counted out to the shipbuilder the sum of sixty thousand francs.

The builder then offered his services in providing a crew, but this Dantès declined with many thanks, saying he was accustomed to cruise about quite alone; the only thing the builder would oblige him in would be to contrive a secret closet in the cabin at his bed's head, the closet to

contain three divisions, so constructed as to be concealed from all but himself. He gave the size of these divisions, which were executed next day.

Two hours afterward Dantès sailed from the port of Genoa, amid the gaze of a crowd curious to see the Spanish nobleman who preferred managing his vessel himself.   He acquitted himself admirably; without quitting the tiller, he made his little vessel perform every movement he chose to direct: his bark seemed, indeed, possessed of intelligence, so promptly did it obey the slightest impulse given; and Dantès confessed to himself that the Genoese deserved their high reputation in the art of ship-building.

The spectators followed the little vessel with their eyes so long as it remained visible; they then turned their conjectures upon her probable destination.   Some insisted she was making for Corsica; others, the isle of Elba; others offered bets to any amount that she was bound for Spain; others, to Africa; but no one thought of Monte-Cristo.

He arrived at the close of the second day; his bark had proved herself a first-class sailer, and had come the distance from Genoa in thirty-five hours.   Dantès had carefully noted the general appearance of the shore, and, instead of landing at the usual place, he dropped anchor in the little creek.   The isle was utterly deserted, no one seemed to have landed since he left it: his treasure was just as he had left it.

On the following morning he commenced the removal of his riches, and deposited it in the secret compartments of his hidden closet.

A week passed by.   Dantès employed it in manœuvring his yacht round the island, studying it as a horseman studies his horse, till at the end of that time he was perfectly conversant with its good and bad qualities.   The former Dantès proposed to augment, the latter to remedy.

Upon the eighth day of his being on the island he discerned a small vessel crowding all sail toward Monte-Cristo.   He recognized the bark of Jacopo.   He immediately signaled it.   His signal was returned, and in two hours afterward the bark lay beside his yacht.

A mournful answer awaited each of Edmond's eager inquiries.   Old Dantès was dead, and Mercédès had disappeared.

Dantès listened to these tidings with calmness; but, leaping ashore, he signified his desire to be quite alone.   In a couple of hours he returned.   Two of the men from Jacopo's bark came on board the yacht to assist in navigating it, and he commanded she should be steered direct to Marseilles.   For his father's death he was prepared; but what became of Mercédès?

Without divulging his secret, Dantès could not give sufficiently clear instructions to an agent.   There were, besides, other particulars he was desirous of ascertaining, and those were of a nature he alone could investigate.   His looking-glass had assured him, during his stay at Leghorn, that he ran no risk of recognition; added to which, he had now the means of adopting any disguise he thought proper.   One fine

morning, then, his yacht, followed by the little bark, boldly entered the
port of Marseilles, and anchored exactly opposite the memorable spot
from whence, on a never-to-be-forgotten night, he had been put on
board the boat for the Château d'If.

Dantès could not view without a shudder the gendarme who accompanied the health officers; but with that perfect self-possession he had
acquired, Dantès presented an English passport he had obtained at Leghorn, and, by means of this document, found no difficulty in landing.

The first object that attracted the attention of Dantès, as he landed
on the Cannebière, was one of the crew belonging to the *Pharaon.* This

man had served under him, and furnished a sure test of the change in his appearance. Going straight toward him, he commenced a variety of questions, to which the man replied without a word or look implying his having the slightest idea of ever having seen before the individual with whom he was then conversing.

Giving the sailor a piece of money in return for his civility, Dantès proceeded onward; but ere he had gone many steps he heard the man loudly calling him to stop.

Dantès instantly turned to meet him.

"I beg your pardon, sir," said the honest fellow, "but I believe you made a mistake: you intended to give me a two-franc piece, and see, you gave me a double Napoleon."

"Thank you, my good friend. I see that I have made a mistake; but by way of rewarding your honest spirit, I give you another double Napoleon, that you may drink to my health, with your messmates."

So extreme was the surprise of the sailor, that he was unable even to thank Edmond, whose receding figure he continued to gaze after, saying to himself, "Ah, that's one of those nabobs from India."

Dantès, meanwhile, continued his route. Each step he trod oppressed his heart with fresh emotion: his first and most indelible recollections were there: not a corner, not a street, not a crossing that he passed but seemed filled with dear and cherished reminiscences. At the end of the Rue de Noailles, a view of the Allées de Meilhan was obtained. At this spot his knees tottered under him, he had almost fallen beneath the wheels of a vehicle. Finally, he found himself at the door of the house in which his father had lived.

The nasturtiums and other plants, which his parent had delighted to train before his window, had all disappeared from the upper part of the house.

Leaning against a tree, he remained long gazing on those windows, then he advanced to the door, and inquired whether there were any chambers to be let. Though answered in the negative, he begged so earnestly to be permitted to visit those on the fifth floor, that the concierge went up to the present possessors and asked permission for a gentleman to be allowed to look at them. The tenants of the humble lodging were a young couple who had been scarcely married a week, and the sight sent a pang through his heart.

Nothing in the two small chambers recalled his father; the very paper was different, while the articles of antiquated furniture with which the rooms had been filled in Edmond's time had all disappeared; the four walls alone remained as he had left them.

The bed was placed as the former owner had been accustomed to have his; and, spite of his efforts to prevent it, the eyes of Edmond were suffused in tears as he reflected that on that spot his parent had expired, calling for his son.

The young couple gazed with astonishment at the sight of their

visitor's emotion, and the large tears which streamed down his immovable features; but they felt the sacredness of his grief, and kindly refrained from questioning him as to its cause, while, with instinctive delicacy, they left him to indulge his sorrow alone. When he withdrew from the scene of his painful recollections, they both accompanied him down-stairs, telling him that he could come again whenever he pleased, and that their poor dwelling should ever be open to him.

As Edmond passed the door of similar rooms on the fourth floor, he paused to inquire whether Caderousse the tailor still dwelt there; but he received for reply, that the man in question had got into difficulties, and at the present time kept a small inn on the route from Bellegarde to Beaucaire.

Having obtained the address of the person to whom the house in the Allées de Meilhan belonged, Dantès next proceeded thither, and, under the name of Lord Wilmore (the same appellation as that contained in his passport), purchased the small dwelling for the sum of 25,000 francs, at least 10,000 more than it was worth; but had its owner asked ten times the sum he did, it would unhesitatingly have been given.

The very same day the occupants of the apartments on the fifth floor of the house were informed by the notary who had arranged the transfer, that the new landlord gave them their choice of any of the rooms in the house, without the least increase of rent, upon condition of their giving him possession of the two chambers they inhabited.

This strange event occupied for a whole week the inhabitants of the Allées de Meilhan, and caused a thousand guesses, not one of which came near the truth. But that which puzzled the brains of all was the circumstance of the same stranger who had visited the Allées de Meilhan being seen in the evening walking in the little village of the Catalans, and afterward observed to enter a poor fisherman's hut, and to pass more than an hour in inquiring after persons who had either been dead or gone away for more than fifteen or sixteen years.

But on the following day the family from whom all these particulars had been asked received a handsome present, consisting of an entirely new fishing-boat, with a full supply of excellent nets.

The honest fellows would gladly have poured out their thanks to their benefactor; but they had seen him, on quitting the hut, merely give some orders to a sailor, and then, springing lightly on horseback, quit Marseilles by the Porte d'Aix.

"YOU ARE WELCOME, SIR," SAID CADEROUSSE.

CHAPTER XXVI

THE AUBERGE OF PONT DU GARD

UCH of my readers as have made a pedestrian excursion to the south of France may perchance have noticed, midway between the town of Beaucaire and the village of Bellegarde, a small roadside inn, from the front of which hung, creaking and flapping in the wind, a sheet of tin covered with a caricature resemblance of the Pont du Gard. This little inn stood on the left-hand side of the grand route, turning its back on the Rhone. It also boasted of what in Languedoc is styled a garden, consisting of a small plot of ground, a full view of which might be obtained from a door immediately opposite the grand portal by which travelers were ushered in. In this garden the few dingy olives and stunted fig-trees spread their dusty foliage. Between them grew a scanty supply of garlic, tomatoes, and schalots; while, like a forgotten sentinel, a tall pine raised its melancholy head in one of the corners, while its head, spreading out like a fan, was burned by the scorching sun of thirty degrees.

All these trees, great or small, were turned in the direction to which the Mistral blows, one of the three curses of Provence, the others being the Durance and the Parliament.

In the surrounding plain, which resembled a dusty lake, were scattered a few stalks of wheat, raised, no doubt, out of curiosity by the agriculturists, serving each one as a perch for a grasshopper, who follows, with his shrill, monotonous cry the travelers lost in the desert.

For nearly the last eight years the small auberge had been kept by a man and his wife, with two servants; one, answering to the name of Trinette, was the chambermaid, while the other, named Pecaud, was the stableman. This staff was quite large enough, for a canal recently made between Beauclaire and Aiguemortes superseded the heavy wagons by the towed barge, and the diligence by the packet-boat. And, as though to add to the daily misery which this prosperous canal inflicted on the unfortunate aubergiste, whose utter ruin it was fast accomplishing, it was situated not a hundred steps from the forsaken inn, of which we have given so faithful a description.

The aubergiste himself was a man of from forty to fifty-five years of age, tall, strong, and bony, a perfect specimen of the natives of those southern latitudes. He had the dark, sparkling, and deep-set eye, curved nose, and teeth white as those of a carnivorous animal; his hair, which, spite of the light touch time had as yet left on it, seemed as though it refused to assume any other color than its own, was like his beard, which he wore under his chin, thick and curly, and but slightly mingled with a few silvery threads. His naturally dark complexion had assumed a still further shade of brown from the habit the unfortunate man had acquired of stationing himself from morn till eve at the threshold of his door, in eager hope that some traveler, either equestrian or pedestrian, might bless his eyes; but his expectations were useless. Yet there he stood, day after day, exposed to the rays of the sun, with no other protection for his head than a red handkerchief twisted around it, after the manner of the Spanish muleteers. This aubergiste was our old acquaintance Caderousse.

His wife, on the contrary, whose maiden name had been Madeleine Radelle, was pale, meagre, and sickly-looking. Born in the neighborhood of Arles, she had shared in the beauty for which its females are proverbial; but that beauty had gradually withered beneath the influence of one of those slow fevers so prevalent in the vicinity of the waters of the Aiguemortes and the marshes of Camargue. She remained nearly always sitting shivering in her chamber, situated on the first floor; either lolling in her chair, or extended on her bed, while her husband kept his daily watch at the door — a duty he performed with so much greater willingness, since his helpmate never saw him without breaking out into bitter invectives against her lot, to all of which her husband would calmly return an unvarying reply, couched in these philosophic words:

"Cease to grieve about it, La Carconte. It is God's pleasure."

The sobriquet of La Carconte had been bestowed on Madeleine Radelle from the circumstance of her having been born in a village so called, situated between Salon and Lanbèse; and as a custom existed among the inhabitants of that part, of calling every one by a nickname in place of a name, her husband had bestowed on her the name of La Carconte in place of Madeleine, too sweet and euphonious for him to pronounce.

Still, let it not be supposed that amid this affected resignation to the will of Providence, the unfortunate aubergiste did not writhe under the double misery of seeing the hateful canal carry off alike his customers and profits, and the daily implication of his peevish partner's murmurs and lamentations.

Like other dwellers of the south, he was a man of sober habits and moderate desires, but fond of external show. During the days of his prosperity, not a *fête*, festivity, or ceremonial took place without himself and wife being there in the picturesque costume of the men of the south of France, bearing equal resemblance to the style of the Catalans and of the Andalusians; while La Carconte displayed the charming fashion prevalent among the females of Arles, a mode of attire borrowed equally from Greece and Arabia.   But, by degrees, watch-chains, necklaces, many-colored scarfs, embroidered bodices, velvet vests, elegantly-worked stockings, striped gaiters, and silver buckles for the shoes, all disappeared; and Gaspard Caderousse, unable to appear abroad in his pristine splendor, had given up any further participation in these pomps and vanities, both for himself or wife, although a bitter feeling of envious discontent filled his mind as the sound of mirth and merry music from the joyous revelers reached even the miserable hostelry to which he still clung, more for the shelter than the profit it afforded.

On the present day, Caderousse was, as usual, at his place of observation before the door, his eyes glancing listlessly from a piece of closely-shaven grass on which some fowls were pecking, to the deserted road, the two extremities of which pointed respectively north and south, when he was roused by the shrill voice of his wife.   He proceeded, grumbling, to the floor above — taking care to set the entrance-door wide open, as it were, to invite travelers not to pass by.

At the moment Caderousse went in, the road on which he so eagerly strained his sight was void and lonely as a desert at midday.   There it lay stretched out, white and endless, and one could understand that no traveler, free to choose his own time, would venture into that frightful Sahara, with its sides bordered by meagre trees.

Nevertheless, had Caderousse but retained his post a few minutes longer, he might have seen approaching from the direction of Bellegarde a man and horse, between whom the kindest and most amiable understanding appeared to exist.   The horse was of Hungarian breed, and ambled along with that easy pace peculiar to that race of animals. His rider was a priest, dressed in black, and wearing a three-cornered hat; and, spite of the ardent rays of a noonday sun, the pair came on at a tolerably smart trot.

Having arrived before the door, the horse stopped, but whether for his own pleasure or that of his rider would have been difficult to say. In either case, the priest, dismounting, led his steed by the bridle, which he prepared to hitch to a handle that projected from a half-fallen door; then with a red cotton handkerchief from his pocket he wiped away the perspiration that streamed from his brow, and, advancing to the door, struck thrice with the end of his iron-shod stick.

At this unusual sound, a huge black dog came rushing to meet the daring assailant of his ordinarily tranquil abode, snarling and displaying his sharp white teeth with a determined hostility that abundantly

proved how little he was accustomed to society. At that moment a
heavy footstep shook the wooden staircase, down which the host, bowing and scraping, descended to the door where the priest stood.

"You are welcome, sir," cried the astonished Caderousse. "Now, then,

Margotin, will you be quiet? Pray don't heed him, sir!—he only barks,
he never bites! I make no doubt a glass of good wine would be acceptable this dreadfully hot day!" Then perceiving for the first time the
description of traveler he had to entertain, Caderousse hastily exclaimed:
"A thousand pardons, your reverence! I really did not observe whom I

had the honor to receive under my poor roof. What would you please to have, M. l'Abbé? I am at your service."

The priest gazed on him with a searching gaze—there even seemed a disposition to court a similar scrutiny on the part of the aubergiste; then, remarking in the countenance of the latter no other expression than surprise at receiving no answer, he deemed it as well to terminate this dumb show, and therefore said, speaking with a strong Italian accent:

"You are, I presume, M. Caderousse?"

"Your reverence is quite correct," answered the host, even more surprised at the question than he had been by the silence; "I am Gaspard Caderousse, at your service."

"Gaspard Caderousse!" rejoined the priest. "Yes, that agrees both with the baptismal appellation and surname of the individual I allude to. You formerly lived, I believe, in the Allées de Meilhan, on the fourth floor of a small house situated there?"

"I did."

"Where you followed the business of a tailor?"

"True, till the trade fell off. Then, it is so very hot at Marseilles, that people will end in not wearing clothes at all. But, talking of heat, is there nothing I can offer you by way of refreshment?"

"Yes, let me have a bottle of your best wine, and then, with your permission, we will resume our conversation where we left off."

"As you please, M. l'Abbé," said Caderousse, who, anxious not to lose the present opportunity of finding a customer for one of the few bottles of vin de Cahors still remaining in his possession, hastily raised a trap-door in the floor of the apartment they were in, which served both as parlor and kitchen.

Upon his returning, at the expiration of five minutes, he found the abbé seated on a species of stool, leaning his elbow on a table, while Margotin, whose animosity seemed appeased by the traveler having pronounced the unusual command for refreshments, had crept up to him, his long, skinny neck resting on his lap, while his dim eye was fixed on his face.

"Are you quite alone?" inquired the guest, as Caderousse placed before him the bottle of wine and a glass.

"Quite, quite alone," replied the man—"or at least all but so, M. l'Abbé; for my poor wife, who is the only person in the house besides myself, is laid up with illness, and unable to render me the least assistance, poor thing!"

"You are married, then?" said the priest, with a species of interest, glancing round as he spoke at the scanty style of the fittings-up of the apartment.

"Ah, M. l'Abbé," said Caderousse, with a sigh, "it is easy to perceive I am not a rich man; but in this world a man does not thrive the better for being honest." The abbé fixed on him a searching, penetrating glance.

"I can say that," replied the aubergiste, sustaining the abbé's gaze,

with one hand on his heart and nodding his head; "I can boast with truth of being an honest man; and that is more than every one can say nowadays."

"So much the better for you, if what you assert be true," said the abbé; "for I am firmly persuaded that, sooner or later, the good will be rewarded, and the wicked punished."

"Such words as those belong to your profession, M. l'Abbé," answered

Caderousse, " and you do well to repeat them; but," added he, with a bitter expression, " one is not forced to believe them, all the same."

" You are wrong to speak thus," said the abbé; " and perhaps I may, in my own person, be able to prove to you what I assert."

" What mean you ?" inquired Caderousse, with a look of surprise.

" In the first place, it is requisite I should be satisfied you are the person I am in search of."

" What proofs do you require ?"

" Did you, in the year 1814 or 1815, know a sailor named Edmond Dantès ?"

" Did I ? I should think I did. Poor dear Edmond ! Why, Edmond Dantès and myself were intimate friends ! " exclaimed Caderousse, whose countenance assumed an almost purple hue, as he caught the penetrating gaze of the abbé fixed on him, while the clear, calm eye of the questioner seemed to cover him with confusion.

" Yes," said the priest, " the young man did bear the name of Edmond."

" Bear the name ! " repeated Caderousse, becoming excited and eager. " Why, he was so called as truly as I bear that of Gaspard Caderousse ; but, M. l'Abbé, tell me, I pray, what has become of poor Edmond. Did you know him ? Is he alive and at liberty ? Is he prosperous and happy ? "

" He died a more wretched, hopeless, heart-broken prisoner than the felons who pay the penalty of their crimes at the galleys of Toulon."

A deadly paleness succeeded the deep suffusion which had before spread itself over the countenance of Caderousse, who turned away, and the priest observed him wiping away the tears from his eyes with the corner of the red handkerchief twisted round his head.

" Poor fellow ! poor fellow ! " murmured Caderousse. " Well, there, M. l'Abbé, is another proof that none but the wicked prosper. Ah," continued Caderousse, speaking in the highly-colored language of the South, " the world grows worse and worse. Let heaven rain down two days of powder and one hour of fire, and let all be ended ! "

" You speak as though you had loved this young Dantès," observed the abbé.

" And so I did," replied Caderousse; " though once, I confess, I envied him his good fortune. But I swear to you, M. l'Abbé, I swear to you, by everything a man holds dear, I have, since then, deeply and sincerely lamented his unhappy fate."

There was a brief silence, during which the fixed, searching eye of the abbé was employed in scrutinizing the agitated features of the aubergiste.

" You knew the poor lad, then ? " continued Caderousse.

" I was merely called to see him when on his dying-bed, that I might administer to him the consolations of religion."

" And of what did he die ? " asked Caderousse in a choking voice.

"Of what, think you, do men die in prison, when they die in their

thirtieth year, unless it be of the prison itself ? " Caderousse wiped away the large beads of perspiration that gathered on his brow.

" But the strangest part of the story is," resumed the abbé, that Dantès, even in his dying moments, swore by his crucified Redeemer that he was utterly ignorant of the cause of his imprisonment."

" And so he was," murmured Caderousse. " How should he have

been otherwise? Ah! M. l'Abbé, the poor fellow told you the truth."

"And for that reason, he besought me to clear up the mystery he had never been able to penetrate, and to rehabilitate his memory should any foul spot have fallen on it."

And here the look of the abbé, becoming more and more fixed, semed to rest on the gloomy depression which spread over the countenance of Caderousse.

"A rich Englishman," continued the abbé, "his companion in misfortune, who had been released from prison during the Second Restoration, was possessed of a diamond of immense value: this precious jewel he bestowed on Dantès upon quitting the prison, as a mark of his gratitude for the care with which Dantès had nursed him in a severe illness. Instead of employing this diamond in attempting to bribe his jailers, who might only have taken it and then betrayed him to the governor, Dantès carefully preserved it, for, in the event of his getting out of prison, the produce of such a diamond would have sufficed to make his fortune."

"Then, I suppose," asked Caderousse, with eager, glowing looks, "that it was a stone of immense value?"

"Why, everything is relative," answered the abbé. "To one in Edmond's position the diamond certainly was of great value. It was estimated at 50,000 francs."

"Fifty thousand francs!" exclaimed Caderousse, "why it must have been as large as a nut."

"No," replied the abbé, "but you shall judge for yourself; I have it with me."

The sharp gaze of Caderousse was instantly directed toward the priest's garments, as though hoping to discover the talked-of treasure.

Calmly drawing forth from his pocket a small box covered with black shagreen, the abbé opened it, and displayed to the delighted eyes of Caderousse the sparkling jewel it contained, set in a ring of admirable workmanship.

"And that diamond," cried Caderousse, "you say, is worth 50,000 francs?"

"It is, without the setting, which is also valuable," replied the abbé, as he closed the box, and returned it to his pocket, while its brilliant hues seemed to dance in Caderousse's imagination.

"But how comes this diamond in your possession, M. l'Abbé? Did Edmond make you his heir?"

"No, merely his testamentary executor. When dying, the unfortunate youth said to me, 'I once possessed three dear friends, besides the maiden to whom I was betrothed; and I feel convinced all four unfeignedly grieved over my loss. The name of one of the four friends I allude to is Caderousse.'" The aubergiste shivered.

"'Another of the number,'" continued the abbé, without seeming to notice the emotion of Caderousse, "'is called Danglars; and the third, spite of being my rival, entertained a very sincere affection for me.'"

A fiendish smile played over the features of Caderousse, who was about to break in upon the abbé's speech, when the latter, waving his hand, said : "Allow me to finish first, and then, if you have any observations to make, you can do so afterward. 'The third of my friends, although my rival, was much attached to me,— his name was Fernand; that of my betrothed was——' Stay, stay," continued the abbé, "I have forgotten what he called her."

"Mercédès," cried Caderousse.

"True," said the abbé, with a stifled sigh, "Mercédès it was."

"Go on," urged Caderousse.

"Bring me a *carafe* of water," said the abbé.

Caderousse quickly performed the stranger's bidding; and after pouring some into a glass and slowly swallowing its contents, the abbé said, as he placed his glass on the table:

"Where did we leave off?"

"Oh, that the betrothed of Edmond was called Mercédès."

"To be sure. 'Well, then,' said Dantès,— for you understand, I repeat his words just as he uttered them—'you will go to Marseilles.' Do you understand?"

"Perfectly."

"'For the purpose of selling this diamond; the produce of which you will divide into five equal parts, and give an equal portion to the only persons who have loved me upon earth.'"

"But why into five parts?" asked Caderousse; "you only mentioned four persons."

"Because the fifth is dead, as I hear. The fifth sharer in Edmond's bequest was his own father."

"Too true, too true!" ejaculated Caderousse, almost suffocated by the contending passions which assailed him, "the poor old man did die."

"I learned so much at Marseilles," replied the abbé, making a strong effort to appear indifferent; "but from the length of time that has elapsed since the death of the elder Dantès, I was unable to obtain any particulars of his end. Do you know anything about his death?"

"I do not know who could if I could not," said Caderousse. "Why, I lived almost on the same floor with the poor old man. Ah, yes! about a year after the disappearance of his son the old man died."

"Of what did he die?"

"Why, the doctors called his complaint an internal inflammation, I believe; his acquaintances say he died of grief; but I, who saw him in his dying moments, I say he died of ——"

Caderousse paused.

"Of what?" asked the priest, anxiously and eagerly.

"Why, of downright starvation."

"Starvation!" exclaimed the abbé, springing from his seat. "Why, the vilest animals are not suffered to die by such a death as that. The very dogs that wander houseless and homeless in the streets find some pitying hand to cast them a mouthful of bread; and that a man, a Christian, should be allowed to perish of hunger in the midst of other men equally Christians with himself, is too horrible for belief. Oh, it is impossible! — utterly impossible!"

"What I have said, I have said," answered Caderousse.

"And you are a fool for having said anything about it," said a voice from the top of the stairs. "Why should you meddle with what does not concern you?"

The two male speakers turned round quickly, and perceived the sickly countenance of La Carconte leaning over the rail of the staircase;— attracted by the sound of voices, she had feebly dragged herself down the stairs, and, seated on the lower step, she had listened to the foregoing conversation.

"Mind your own business, wife," replied Caderousse, sharply. "This gentleman asks me for information, which common politeness will not permit me to refuse."

"Prudence requires you to refuse," retorted La Carconte. "How do you know the motives that person may have for trying to extract all he can from you?"

"I assure you, madame," said the abbé, "that my intentions are good, and that your husband can incur no risk, provided he answers me candidly."

"Ah, that's all very fine," retorted the woman. "Nothing is easier than to begin with fair promises and assurances of nothing to fear; then, some fine day trouble comes on the unfortunate wretches, without one knowing whence."

"Nay, nay, my good woman. No evils will be occasioned by me, I promise you."

Some inarticulate sounds escaped La Carconte, then letting her head, which she had raised, again droop on to her lap, she commenced her usual aguish trembling, leaving the two speakers to resume the conversation, but still remaining herself so placed as to be able to hear every word. Again the abbé had been obliged to swallow a draught of water to calm his emotions.

"It appears, then," he resumed, "that the miserable old man you were telling me of was forsaken by every one, as he perished by so dreadful a death."

"Why, I do not mean," continued Caderousse, "that Mercédès the Catalan and M. Morrel forsook him; but somehow the poor old man had contracted a profound hatred of Fernand — the very person," added Caderousse, with a bitter smile, "that you named just now as being one of Dantès' friends."

"And was he not so?" asked the abbé.

"Gaspard! Gaspard!" murmured the woman, from her seat on the stairs, "mind what you are saying!"

Caderousse made no reply to these words, but addressing the abbé, said:

"Can a man be faithful to another whose wife he covets? But Dantès had a heart of gold; he believed everybody's professions of friendship. Poor Edmond! but it was a happy thing he never knew it, or he might have found it more difficult, when on his deathbed, to pardon them. And, whatever people may say," continued Caderousse, in his native language, which was not altogether devoid of rude poetry, "I cannot help being more frightened at the idea of the malediction of the dead than the hatred of the living."

"Weak-minded coward!" exclaimed La Carconte.

"Do you, then, know in what manner Fernand injured Dantès?" inquired the abbé of Caderousse.

"Do I? No one better."

"Speak out then; say what it was!"

"Gaspard!" cried La Carconte, "do as you like, you are the master; but, if you are guided by me, you will have nothing to say."

"Well, well, wife," replied Caderousse, "I do not know but what you are right!"

"Then you are determined to say nothing?" said the abbé."

"Why, what good would it do?" asked Caderousse. "If the poor lad were living, and came to me to beg I would candidly tell which were his true and which his false friends, why, perhaps I should not hesitate. But you tell me he is no more, and therefore can have nothing to do with hatred or revenge; so let all such feelings be buried with him."

"You prefer, then," said the abbé, "allowing me to bestow on men you say are false and treacherous, the reward intended for faithful friendship?"

"That is true enough," returned Caderousse; "besides, what would it be to them? no more than a drop of water in the ocean."

"And remember, husband," chimed in La Carconte, "that these two men could crush you with a wave of the hand!"

"How so?" inquired the abbé. "Are these persons, then, so rich and powerful?"

"Do you not know their history?"

"I do not. Pray relate it to me!"

Caderousse seemed to reflect for a few instants, then said:

"No, truly; it would take up too much time."

"Well, my good friend," returned the abbé, in a tone that indicated utter indifference on his part, "just as you please; I respect your scruples, so let the matter end. I had a simple formality to discharge; I shall sell the diamond."

So saying, the abbé again drew the small box from his pocket, opened it, and flashed the stone before the dazzled gaze of Caderousse.

"Wife, wife!" cried he, in a hoarse voice, "come and see it."

"Diamond!" exclaimed La Carconte, rising and descending to the chamber with a tolerably firm step; "what diamond are you talking about?"

"Why, did you not hear all we said?" inquired Caderousse. "It is a beautiful diamond left by poor Edmond Dantès, to be sold, and the money divided among his father, Mercédès, his betrothed bride, Fernand, Danglars, and myself. The jewel is worth at least 50,000 francs."

"Oh, what a splendid jewel!" cried the astonished woman.

"The fifth part of the produce of this stone belongs to us, then, does it not?" asked Caderousse.

"It does," replied the abbé; "with the addition of an equal division of that part intended for the elder Dantès, which I conceive myself at liberty to share equally with the four surviving persons."

"And wherefore among us four?" inquired Caderousse.

"As being the four friends of Edmond."

"I don't call those friends who betray and ruin you," murmured the wife, in her turn, in a low, muttering voice.

"Of course not!" rejoined Caderousse, quickly; "no more do I; and that was what I was observing just now. It is a sacrilegious profanation to reward treachery, perhaps crime."

"Remember," answered the abbé, calmly, as he replaced the jewel in the pocket of his cassock, "it is your fault, not mine. You will have the goodness to furnish me with the address of both the friends of Edmond, in order that I may execute his last wishes."

The agitation of Caderousse became extreme, and large drops of perspiration rolled from his heated brow. As he saw the abbé rise from his seat and go toward the door, as though to ascertain if his horse were sufficiently refreshed to continue his journey, Caderousse and his wife exchanged looks of deep meaning with each other.

"There, you see, wife," said the former, "this splendid diamond might all be ours, if we chose!"

"Do you believe it?"

"Why, surely a man of his holy profession would not deceive us!"

"Well," replied La Carconte, "do as you like. For my part, I wash my hands of the affair."

So saying, she once more climbed the staircase leading to her chamber, all shivering, and her teeth rattling, spite of the intense heat of the weather. Arrived at the top stair, she turned round and called out in a warning tone, to her husband. "Gaspard, consider well what you are about to do!"

"I have both reflected and decided," answered he.

La Carconte then entered her chamber, the floor of which creaked beneath her heavy, uncertain tread, as she proceeded toward her arm-chair, into which she fell as though exhausted.

"Well," asked the abbé, as he returned to the apartment below, "what have you made up your mind to do?"

"To tell you all I know," was the reply.

"I certainly think you act wisely in so doing," said the priest. "Not because I have the least desire to learn anything you may desire to conceal from me, but simply if, through your assistance, I could distribute the legacy according to the wishes of the testator, why, so much the better, — that is all."

"I trust, indeed, such will be the case," replied Caderousse, his eyes sparkling and his face flushed with the hope of obtaining all himself.

"Now, then, begin, if you please," said the abbé; "I am all attention."

"Stop a minute," answered Caderousse; "we might be interrupted in the most interesting part of my recital, which would be a pity; and it is as well that your visit hither should be made known only to ourselves."

With these words he went stealthily to the door, which he closed, and by way of still greater precaution, bolted and barred it, as he was accustomed to do at night.

During this time the abbé had chosen his place for listening to the tale. He removed his seat into a corner, where he himself would be in deep shadow, while the light would be fully thrown on the narrator; then, with head bent down and hands clasped, or rather clenched together, he prepared to give his whole attention to Caderousse, who seated himself on the little stool, exactly opposite to him.

"Remember, I did not urge you to this," said the trembling voice of La Carconte, as though through the flooring of her chamber she viewed the scene that was enacting below.

"Enough, enough!" replied Caderousse; "say no more about it; I will take all the consequences upon myself."

He then commenced as follows:

CHAPTER XXVII

THE RECITAL

"FIRST," said Caderousse, "sir, I must ask you to make me a promise."

"What is that?" inquired the abbé.

"Why, if you ever make use of the details I am about to give you, that you will never let any one know that it was I who supplied them; for the persons of whom I am about to talk are rich and powerful, and if they only laid the tips of their fingers on me, I should break to pieces like glass."

"Make yourself easy, my friend," replied the abbé. "I am a priest, and confessions die in my breast. Recollect, our only desire is to carry out, in a fitting manner, the last wishes of our friend. Speak, then, without reserve, as without hatred; tell the truth, the whole truth. I do not know, never may know, the persons of whom you are about to speak; besides, I am an Italian, and not a Frenchman, and belong to God, and not to man; and I retire to my convent, which I have only quitted to fulfill the last wishes of a dying man."

This last assurance seemed to give Caderousse courage.

"Well, then, under these circumstances," said Caderousse, "I will, indeed I ought to, undeceive you as to the friendship which poor Edmond believed so sincere and unquestionable."

"Begin with his father, if you please," said the abbé; "Edmond talked to me a great deal about the old man, for whom he had the deepest love."

"The history is a sad one, sir," said Caderousse, shaking his head; "perhaps you know all the earlier part of it?"

"Yes," answered the abbé; "Edmond related to me everything until the moment when he was arrested in a small cabaret close to Marseilles."

"At La Réserve! Oh, yes! I can see it all before me this moment."

" Was it not his betrothal feast ?"

" It was; and the feast that began so gayly had a very sorrowful ending: a commissary of police, followed by four soldiers, entered, and Dantès was arrested."

" Yes, and up to this point I know all," said the priest. " Dantès himself only knew that which personally concerned him, for he never beheld again the five persons I have named to you, nor heard mention of any one of them."

" Well, when Dantès was arrested, M. Morrel hastened to obtain the particulars, and they were very sad. The old man returned alone to his home, folded up his wedding suit with tears in his eyes, and paced up and down his chamber the whole day, and would not go to bed at all, for I was underneath him and heard him walking the whole night; and for myself, I assure you I could not sleep either, for the grief of the poor father gave me great uneasiness, and every step he took went to my heart as really as if his foot had pressed against my breast.

" The next day Mercédès came to implore the protection of M. de Villefort. She did not obtain it, however, and went to visit the old man ;— when she saw him so miserable and heart-broken, having passed a sleepless night, and not touched food since the previous day, she wished him to go with her that she might take care of him; but the old man would not consent. ' No,' was the old man's reply, ' I will not leave this house, for my poor dear boy loves me better than anything in the world; and if he gets out of prison he will come and see me the first thing, and what would he think if I did not wait here for him ?' I heard all this from the window, for I was anxious that Mercédès should persuade the old man to accompany her, for his footsteps over my head night and day did not leave me a moment's repose."

" But did you not go upstairs and try to console the poor old man ?" asked the abbé.

"Ah, sir," replied Caderousse, " we cannot console those who will not be consoled, and he was one of these; besides, I know not why, but he seemed to dislike seeing me. One night, however, I heard his sobs, and I could not resist my desire to go up to him, but when I reached his door he was no longer weeping, but praying. I cannot now repeat to you, sir, all the eloquent words and piteous supplications he made use of; it was more than piety, it was more than grief; and I, who am no canter, and hate the Jesuits, said then to myself, ' It is really well that I am all alone, and I am very glad that I have not any children; for if I were a father, and felt such excessive grief as the old man does, and did not find in my memory or heart all he is now saying, I should throw myself into the sea at once, for I could not bear it.' "

" Poor father ! " murmured the priest.

" From day to day he lived on alone, and more and more solitary. Often M. Morrel and Mercédès came to see him, but his door was closed; and, although I was certain he was at home, he would not make any answer. One day, when, contrary to his custom, he had admitted Mercédès, and the poor girl, in spite of her own grief and despair, endeavored to console him, he said to her. ' Be assured, my dear daughter, he is dead ; and instead of our awaiting him, it is he who is awaiting us; I am quite happy, for I am the oldest, and of course shall see him first.'

" However well disposed a person may be, why, you see, we leave off after a time seeing persons who make one melancholy, and so at last old Dantès was left all to himself, and I only saw from time to time strangers go up to him and come down again with some bundle they tried to hide; but I guessed what these bundles were, and he sold by degrees what he had to pay for his subsistence. At length, the poor old fellow reached the end of all he had; he owed three-quarters' rent, and they threatened to turn him out; he begged for another week, which was granted to him. I know this, because the landlord came into my apartment when he left his.

" For the three first days I heard him walking about as usual, but on the fourth I heard him no longer. I then resolved to go up to him, at all risks. The door was closed, but I looked through the keyhole, and saw him so pale and haggard, that believing him very ill, I went and told M. Morrel, and then ran on to Mercédès. They both came immediately, M. Morrel bringing a doctor, and the doctor said it was an affection of the stomach, and ordered him a limited diet. I was there too, and I never shall forget the old man's smile at this prescription.

" From that time he opened his door; he had an excuse for not eating any more, as the doctor had put him on a diet. "

The abbé uttered a kind of groan.

" The story interests you, does it not, sir ? " inquired Caderousse.

" Yes," replied the abbé ; " it is very affecting."

" Mercédès came again, and she found him so altered that she was even more anxious than before to have him taken to her own abode. This was M. Morrel's wish also, who would fain have conveyed the old man against his consent; but the old man resisted, and cried so, that they were actually frightened. Mercédès remained, therefore, by his bedside, and M. Morrel went away, making a sign to the Catalane that he had left his purse on the chimney-piece; but, availing himself of the doctor's order, the old man would not take any sustenance. At length (after nine days' despair and fasting) the old man died, cursing those who had caused his misery, and saying to Mercédès,—' If you ever see my Edmond again, tell him I die blessing him.' "

The abbè rose from his chair, made two turns round the chamber, and pressed his trembling hand against his parched throat.

"And you believe he died ——"

"Of hunger, sir, of hunger," said Caderousse. "I am as certain of it as that we two are Christians."

The abbé, with a shaking hand, seized a glass of water that was standing by him half full, swallowed it at one gulp, and then resumed his seat with red eyes and pale cheeks.

"This was, indeed, a horrid event," said he, in a hoarse voice.

"The more so, sir, as it was men's and not God's doing."

"Tell me of those men," said the abbé, "and remember too," he added, in a voice that was nearly menacing in its tone, "you have promised to tell me everything. Tell me, therefore, who are these men who have killed the son with despair, and the father with famine ?"

"Two men jealous of him, sir: one from love, and the other ambition,—Fernand and Danglars."

"Say, how was this jealousy manifested ?"

"They denounced Edmond as a Bonapartist agent."

"Which of the two denounced him ? Which was the real delinquent ?"

"Both, sir; one with a letter, and the other put it in the post."

"And where was this letter written ?"

"At La Réserve, the day before the festival of the betrothing."

"'Twas so, then — 'twas so, then," murmured the abbé. "Oh, Faria, Faria! how well did you judge men and things !"

"What did you please to say, sir ?" asked Caderousse.

"Nothing, nothing," replied the priest; "go on."

"It was Danglars who wrote the denunciation with his left hand, that his writing might not be recognized, and Fernand who put it in the post."

"But," exclaimed the abbé, suddenly, "you were there yourself."

"I !" said Caderousse, astonished; "who told you I was there ?"

The abbé saw he had overshot the mark, and he added, quickly:

"No one; but in order to have known everything so well, you must have been an eye-witness."

"True, true!" said Caderousse, in a choking voice, "I was there."

"And did you not remonstrate against such infamy ?" asked the abbé; "if not, you were an accomplice."

"Sir," replied Caderousse, "they had made me drink to such an excess that I nearly lost all perception. I saw everything through a cloud. I said all that a man in such a state could say; but they both assured me that it was a jest they were carrying on, and a perfectly harmless jest."

"Next day — next day, sir, you must have seen plain enough what they had been doing; yet you said nothing, though you were present when Dantès was arrested."

"Yes, sir, I was there, and very anxious to speak! but Danglars restrained me. 'If he should really be guilty,' said he, 'and did really

put in to the isle of Elba; if he is really charged with a letter for the Bonapartist committee at Paris, and if they find this letter upon him, those who have supported him will pass for his accomplices.' I confess I had my fears of the police in the state in which politics then were, and I confess that I held my tongue. It was cowardly, I confess, but it was not criminal."

"I comprehend—you allowed matters to take their course; that was all."

"Yes, sir," answered Caderousse, "and my remorse preys on me night and day. I often ask pardon of God, I swear to you, because this action, the only one with which I have seriously to reproach myself in all my life, is no doubt the cause of my abject condition. I am expiating a moment of selfishness, and thus it is I always say to my wife, when she complains, 'Hold your tongue, woman; it is the will of God.'"

And Caderousse bowed his head with every sign of real repentance.

"Well, sir," said the abbé, "you have spoken unreservedly; and thus to accuse yourself is to deserve pardon."

"Unfortunately, Edmond is dead, and has not pardoned me."

"He was ignorant," said the abbé.

"But he knows it all now," interrupted Caderousse; "they say the dead know everything."

There was a brief silence. The abbé rose and paced up and down pensively, and then resumed his seat.

"You have two or three times mentioned a M. Morrel," he said; "who was he?"

"The owner of the *Pharaon*, and patron of Dantès."

"And what part did he play in this sad drama?" inquired the abbé.

"The part of an honest man, full of courage and real regard. Twenty times he interceded for Edmond. When the emperor returned, he wrote, implored, threatened, and so energetically that on the second restoration he was persecuted as a Bonapartist. Ten times, as I told you, he came to see Dantès' father, and offered to receive him in his own house; and the night or two before his death, as I have already said, he left his purse on the mantelpiece, with which they paid the old man's debts, and buried him decently; and then Edmond's father died, as he had lived, without doing harm to any one. I have the purse still by me—a large one, made of red silk."

"And," asked the abbé, "is M. Morrel still alive?"

"Yes," replied Caderousse.

"In this case," replied the abbé, "he should be a man blessed of God, rich, happy."

Caderousse smiled bitterly. "Yes, happy as myself," said he.

"What! M. Morrel unhappy!" exclaimed the abbé.

"He is reduced almost to the last extremity—nay, he is almost at the point of dishonor."

"How?"

"Yes," continued Caderousse, "and in this way, after five-and-twenty years of labor, after having acquired a most honorable name in the trade of Marseilles, M. Morrel is utterly ruined: he has lost five ships in two years, has suffered by the bankruptcy of three large houses, and his only hope now is in that very *Pharaon* which poor Dantès commanded, and which is expected from the Indies with a cargo of cochineal and indigo. If this ship founders, like the others, he is a ruined man."

"And has the unfortunate man wife or children?" inquired the abbé.

"Yes, he has a wife, who in all this behaved like an angel; he has a daughter who was about to marry the man she loved, but whose family now will not allow him to wed the daughter of a ruined man; he has, besides, a son, a lieutenant in the army; and, as you may suppose, all this, instead of soothing, doubles his grief. If he were alone in the world he would blow out his brains, and there would be an end."

"Horrible!" ejaculated the priest.

"And it is thus Heaven recompenses virtue, sir," added Caderousse. "You see, I, who never did a bad action but that I have told you of, am in destitution; after having seen my poor wife die of a fever, unable to do anything in the world for her, I shall die of hunger, as old Dantès did, whilst Fernand and Danglars are rolling in wealth."

"How is that?"

"Because all their malpractices have turned to luck, while honest men have been reduced to misery."

"What has become of Danglars the instigator, and therefore the most guilty?"

"What has become of him? Why, he left Marseilles, and was taken, on the recommendation of M. Morrel, who did not know his crime, as cashier into a Spanish bank. During the war with Spain he was employed in the commissariat of the French army, and made a fortune; then with that money he speculated in the funds, and trebled or quadrupled his capital; and, having first married his banker's daughter, who left him a widower, he has married a second time, a widow, a Madame de Nargonne, daughter of M. de Salvieux, the king's chamberlain, who is in high favor at court. He is a millionaire, and they have made him a count, and now he is Le Comte Danglars, with an hotel in the Rue de Mont Blanc, with ten horses in his stables, six footmen in his antechamber, and I know not how many hundreds of thousands in his strong-box."

"Ah!" said the abbé, with a peculiar tone, "he is happy."

"Happy! who can answer for that? Happiness or unhappiness is the secret known but to one's self and the walls—walls have ears, but no tongue; but if a large fortune produces happiness, Danglars is happy."

"And Fernand ?"

"Fernand! why, that is another history."

"But how could a poor Catalan fisher-boy, without education or resources, make a fortune? I confess this staggers me."

"And it has staggered everybody. There must have been in his life some strange secret no one knows."

"But, then, by what visible steps has he attained this high fortune or high position ?"

"Both, sir — he has both fortune and position — both."

"This must be impossible !"

"It would seem so; but listen, and you will understand. Some days before the return of the emperor, Fernand was drawn in the conscription. The Bourbons left him quietly enough at the Catalans, but Napoleon returned, an extraordinary muster was determined on, and Fernand was compelled to join. I went too; but as I was older than Fernand, and had just married my poor wife, I was only sent to the coast. Fernand was enrolled in the active army, went to the frontier with his regiment, and was at the battle of Ligny. The night after that battle he was sentry at the door of a general who carried on a secret correspondence with the enemy. That same night the general was to go over to the English. He proposed to Fernand to accompany him; Fernand agreed to do so, deserted his post, and followed the general.

"That which would have brought Fernand to a court-martial if Napoleon remained on the throne served for his recommendation to the Bourbons. He returned to France with the epaulette of sub-lieutenant, and as the protection of the general, who is in the highest favor, was accorded to him, he was a captain in 1823, during the Spanish war; that is to say, at the time when Danglars made his early speculations. Fernand was a Spaniard, and being sent to Spain to ascertain the feeling of his fellow-countrymen, found Danglars there, became on very intimate terms with him, promised to his general to obtain support from the royalists of the capital and the provinces, received promises and made pledges on his own part, guided his regiment by paths known to himself alone in gorges of the mountains kept by the royalists, and, in fact, rendered such services in this brief campaign that, after the taking of the Trocadero, he was made colonel, and received the title of count and the cross of an officer of the Legion of Honor."

"Destiny! destiny !" murmured the abbé.

"Yes, but listen; this was not all. The war with Spain being ended, Fernand's career was checked by the long peace which seemed likely to endure throughout Europe. Greece only had risen against Turkey, and had begun her war of independence; all eyes were turned toward Athens — it was the fashion to pity and support the Greeks. The French Government, without protecting them openly, as you know, tolerated

partial migrations. Fernand sought and obtained leave to go and serve in Greece, still having his name kept, during his sojourn, in the ranks of the army.

"Some time after, it was stated that the Comte de Morcerf (this was the name he bore) had entered the service of Ali Pacha with the rank of instructor-general. Ali Pacha was killed, as you know; but before he died he recompensed the services of Fernand by leaving him a considerable sum, with which he returned to France, when his rank of lieutenant-general was confirmed."

"So that now ——?" inquired the abbé.

"So that now," continued Caderousse, "he possesses a magnificent hotel, No. 27 Rue du Helder, Paris."

The abbé opened his mouth, remained for a moment like a man who hesitates, then, making an effort over himself, he said:

"And Mercédès — they tell me that she has disappeared?"

"Disappeared," said Caderousse, "yes, as the sun disappears, to rise the next day with still more splendor."

"Has she made a fortune also?" inquired the abbé, with an ironical smile.

"Mercédès is at this moment one of the greatest ladies in Paris," replied Caderousse.

"Go on," said the abbé; "it seems as if I were hearing the recital of a dream. But I have seen things so extraordinary, that those you mention to me seem less astonishing."

"Mercédès was at first in the deepest despair at the blow which deprived her of Edmond. I have told you of her attempts to propitiate M. de Villefort, and of her devotion to the father of Dantès. In the midst of her despair, a fresh trouble overtook her. This was the departure of Fernand — of Fernand, whose crime she did not know, and whom she regarded as her brother. Fernand went, and Mercédès remained alone.

"Three months passed and found her all tears, — no news of Edmond, no news of Fernand, nothing before her but an old man who was dying with despair. One evening, after having been seated, as was her custom, all day at the angle of two roads that lead to Marseilles from the Catalans, she returned to her home more depressed than ever; neither her lover nor her friend returned by either of these roads, and she had no intelligence of one or the other. Suddenly she heard a step she knew, turned round anxiously, the door opened, and Fernand, dressed in the uniform of a sub-lieutenant, stood before her.

"It was not the half that she bewailed, but it was a portion of her past life that returned to her.

"Mercédès seized Fernand's hands with a transport which he took for love, but which was only joy at being no longer alone in the world, and seeing at last a friend, after long hours of solitary sorrow. And then, it must be confessed, Fernand had never been hated — he was only not precisely loved. Another possessed all Mercédès' heart; that other was absent, had disappeared, perhaps was dead. At this last idea Mercédès burst into a flood of tears, and wrung her hands in agony; but this idea, which she had always repelled before when it was suggested to her by another, came now in full force upon her mind; and then, too, old Dantès incessantly said to her, 'Our Edmond is dead; if he were not, he would return to us.'

"The old man died, as I have told you; had he lived, Mercédès, perchance, had not become the wife of another, for he would have been there to reproach her infidelity. Fernand saw this, and when he learned the old man's death, he returned. He was now a lieutenant. At his first coming he had not said a word of love to Mercédès; at the second he reminded her that he loved her.

"Mercédès begged for six months more to expect and bewail Edmond."

"So that," said the abbé, with a bitter smile, "that makes eighteen months in all. What more could the most devoted lover desire ?"

Then he murmured the words of the English poet, "Frailty, thy name is woman !"

"Six months afterward," continued Caderousse, "the marriage took place in the Church of Accoules."

"The very church in which she was to have married Edmond," murmured the priest. "There was a change of bridegroom, that was all."

"Well, Mercédès was married," proceeded Caderousse; "but although in the eyes of the world she appeared calm, she nearly fainted as she passed La Réserve, where, eighteen months before, the betrothal had been celebrated with him whom she would have seen that she still loved, had she looked at the bottom of her heart. Fernand, more happy, but not more at his ease—for I saw at this time he was in constant dread of Edmond's return—Fernand was very anxious to get his wife away, and to depart himself. There were too many dangers and recollections associated with the Catalans, and eight days after the wedding they left Marseilles."

"Did you ever see Mercédès again ?" inquired the priest.

"Yes, during the war of Spain, at Perpignan, where Fernand had left her; she was attending to the education of her son."

The abbé started. "Her son ?" said he.

"Yes," replied Caderousse; "little Albert."

"But, then, to be able to instruct her child," continued the abbé, "she must have received an education herself. I understood from Edmond that she was the daughter of a simple fisherman, beautiful but uneducated."

"Oh!" replied Caderousse, "did he know so little of his betrothed ?

Mercédès might have been a queen, sir, if the crown were to be placed on the head of the loveliest and most intelligent. Her fortune had already become great, and she became great with her fortune. She learned drawing, music—everything. Besides, I believe, between our-selves, she did this in order to distract her mind, that she might forget; and she only filled her head thus in order to alleviate the weight on her heart. But now everything must be told," continued Caderousse; "no doubt fortune and honors have comforted her; she is rich, a countess, and yet ——"

Caderousse paused.

"And yet what?" asked the abbé.

"Yet, I am sure she is not happy," said Caderousse.

"What makes you believe this?"

"Why, when I have found myself very wretched, I have thought my old friends would perhaps assist me. So I went to Danglars, who would not even receive me. I called on Fernand, who sent me a hun-dred francs by his valet-de-chambre."

"Then you did not see either of them?"

"No; but Madame de Morcerf saw me."

"How was that?"

"As I went away, a purse fell at my feet—it contained five-and-twenty louis; I raised my head quickly, and saw Mercédès, who shut the blind directly."

"And M. de Villefort?" asked the abbé.

"Oh, he never was a friend of mine; I did not know him, and I had nothing to ask of him."

"Do you not know what became of him, and the share he had in Edmond's misfortunes?"

"No; I only know that some time after having arrested him, he mar-ried Mademoiselle de Saint-Méran, and soon after left Marseilles; no doubt he has been as lucky as the rest; no doubt he is as rich as Dan-glars, as high in station as Fernand. I only, as you see, have remained poor, wretched, and forgotten."

"You are mistaken, my friend," replied the abbé; "God may seem sometimes to forget for a while, whilst his justice reposes, but there always comes a moment when he remembers — and behold! a proof."

As he spoke, the abbé took the diamond from his pocket, and giving it to Caderousse, said:

"Here, my friend, take this diamond; it is yours."

"What, for me only?" cried Caderousse; "ah! sir, do not jest with me!"

"This diamond was to have been shared amongst his friends.

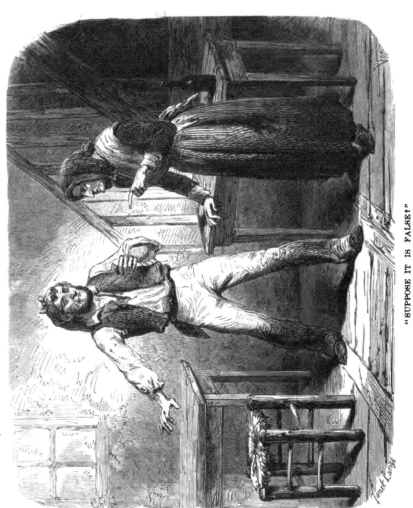

"SUPPOSE IT IS FALSE!"

Edmond had one friend only, and thus it cannot be divided. Take the diamond, then, and sell it: it is worth fifty thousand francs ($10,000), and I repeat my wish that this sum may suffice to release you from your wretchedness."

"Oh, sir," said Caderousse, putting out one hand timidly, and with the other wiping away the perspiration which bedewed his brow,— oh, sir, do not make a jest of the happiness or despair of a man."

"I know what happiness and what despair are, and I never make a jest of such feelings. Take it, then, but in exchange ——"

Caderousse, who touched the diamond, withdrew his hand

The abbé smiled.

"In exchange," he continued, "give me the red silk purse that M. Morrel left on old Dantès' chimney-piece, and which you tell me is still in your hands."

Caderousse, more and more astonished, went toward a large oaken cupboard, opened it, and gave the abbé a long purse of faded red silk, round which were two copper rings that had once been gilt.

The abbé took it, and in return gave Caderousse the diamond.

"Oh! you are a man of God, sir," cried Caderousse; "for no one knew that Edmond had given you this diamond, and you might have kept it."

"Which," said the abbé to himself, "you would have done, it seems."

The abbé rose, took his hat and gloves.

"Well," he said, "all you have told me is perfectly true, then, and I may believe it in every particular."

"See, M. l'Abbé," replied Caderousse, "in this corner is a crucifix in holy wood—here on this shelf is the Gospel of my wife; open this book, and I will swear upon it with my hand on the crucifix. I will swear to you by my soul's salvation, my faith as a Christian, I have told everything to you as it occurred, and as the angel of men will tell it to the ear of God at the day of the last judgment!"

"'Tis well," said the abbé, convinced by his manner and tone that Caderousse spoke the truth. "'Tis well, and may this money profit you! Adieu! I go far from men who thus so bitterly injure each other."

The abbé with difficulty got away from the enthusiastic thanks of Caderousse, opened the door himself, got out and mounted his horse, once more saluted the innkeeper, who kept uttering his loud farewells, and then returned by the road he had traveled in coming.

When Caderousse turned round, he saw behind him La Carconte, paler and trembling more than ever.

"Is, then, all that I have heard really true?" she inquired.

"What! that he has given the diamond to us only?" inquired Caderousse, half bewildered with joy.

"Yes!"

"Nothing more true! See! here it is."

The woman gazed at it a moment, and then said, in a gloomy voice, "Suppose it's false?"

Caderousse started, and turned pale.

"False!" he muttered. "False! why should that man give me a false diamond?"

"To possess your secret without paying for it, you blockhead!"

Caderousse remained for a moment aghast under the weight of such an idea.

"Oh!" he said, taking up his hat, which he placed on the red hand-kerchief tied round his head, "we will soon learn that."

"In what way?"

"Why, it is the fair of Beaucaire; there are always jewelers from Paris there, and I will show it to them. Take care of the house, wife, and I shall be back in two hours."

Caderousse left the house in haste, and ran rapidly in a direction contrary to that which the unknown had taken.

"Fifty thousand francs!" muttered La Carconte, when left alone; "it is a large sum of money, but it is not a fortune."

END OF VOLUME I.

Lightning Source UK Ltd.
Milton Keynes UK
UKHW022305080223
416651UK00001B/346